UP THE CREEK

by Robin Medley

Old Bakehouse Publications

Abertillery

also by the author
Five Days to Live (France 1939-1940)
Cap Badge

First published in June 1999

The right of Robin Medley to be identified
as author of this work has been asserted in
accordance with Section 77 and 78 of the
Copyright, Designs and Patents Act 1988

ISBN 1 874538 47 6

Published in the U.K. by
Old Bakehouse Publications
Church Street
Abertillery
Gwent NP13 1EA
Telephone: 01495 212600 Fax: 01495 216222

Made and Printed in the UK
by J.R. Davies (Printers) Limited

Contents

List of Maps

Foreword

The stories in this book begin in the days following the First World War with tremendous changes taken place in the world politically as well as in advancing technology. The British Empire was at its' peak providing many interesting career prospects for those who sought adventure away from home shores.

The motor car was being mass produced and as a result more families had a car though I remember when the headlights used carbide lamps. The resulting light cast ahead on the road was minimal. This did not matter much as the speeds at which the car was driven were considerably slower than today. Then in the air there was the excitement of seeing a Hawker 'Fury' fighter aircraft in the early thirties climb to one thousand feet vertically from take off in one minute!

The gramophone had to be wound up before the needle was placed on the record and play started, whilst the wireless was still a new innovation.

Films at the cinema were without accompanying sound so the audience followed the story by reading written text shown on the screen. It was 1929 when sound first came to the screen. Television was not available for the public until after World War II.

A De Haviland 'Vampire' fighter with a jet engine gave a demonstration to the staff at General Headquarters Middle East at Fayed in 1947.

In the late fifties and early sixties computers were initially vast complex machines taking up a complete room. Map displays were in their infancy. It was not until the seventies that the micro chip was developed.

Engineering made use of the advantage of reduced weight and space requirements and developed space vehicles. Information technology provided the tools for everyday use of computers.

All these changes have come about since I first went to school. This story is written as a record to give an idea of life in years gone by, to give a feel for its' excitements, its' good times and bad. The joy of long standing friendships, the treasure of family life and the belief that God has a purpose for each individual.

"Flying the Flag"
Office desk at Fort Monroe, Virginia USA in 1966.
Photo of H.M. the Queen Mother with Regimental Officers on wall.

Introduction

I am advised I arrived some six weeks early into this world in 1919 as a squawking babe whom the Doctor rated had only the remotest chances of survival. Apparently I thought otherwise and aided by my Mother put on weight and grew lustily. This was fortuitous as Mother had endured a series of miscarriages and had been advised this was definitely the final attempt to produce an offspring.

My Father was born in March 1884. He was the only child and was brought up and educated at the local Church school where he attained many scholastic prizes. He went on as a pupil to Merchant Taylors and again showed his ability gaining prizes across a wide range of subjects and earning entry to St John's College Oxford as a scholar. He read classics and history obtaining his MA. He obviously enjoyed his time there taking an active interest in rowing and being selected to row in the College 1st Eight. On obtaining his degree he applied and was accepted for the Indian Civil Service.

Grandfather was an accountant with offices in St Brides Street, London. My grandparents keen climbers spent time holidaying in the Swiss Alps. It appears that their exertions at altitude had caused problems with their hearts. The thought of their only son disappearing half way around the world was so upsetting that Grandmother collapsed with the vapours. So Father was persuaded to forego any ideas of departing overseas, a dutiful son he turned his talents to schoolmastering and was appointed to a post at Wakefield Grammar School.

As a small child we visited my grandparents every Sunday both of whom seemed to spend most of their time resting on their beds. I would be ushered into the bedroom and after a short time descended downstairs to be given tea. My earliest recollection is when Grandmother had risen from her couch and I was ushered into her presence. I have a vivid memory of this occasion. Here, to a small child, was a very tall lady dressed in a long flowing grey dress. That is my only memory I cannot recall what was said. The portrait I have of her shows she had very lovely features. Her papers show that she kept detailed records of the Medley family history as well as her family line, the Pellats. She died in 1921 so I was barely two and never really got to know her. I am told that I sang lustily at her memorial service and demanded a repeat of a hymn which captured my fancy causing my parents deep embarrassment. I remember also a few years later being driven in a horse carriage with Grandfather along lanes near Leith Hill.

As I grew older the Sunday visits to Grandfather became a part of my life. He had deep Christian beliefs and was a committed member of his church. He had a memorial window to my Grandmother dedicated in St Stephen's Norbury. He died in May 1936 aged seventy eight.

My maternal Grandfather was born in 1849 and could just remember the Crimean War. I know Grandfather, one of eight brothers, was brought up in his early days in Northern Ireland but little else about his life.

Father was a keen bridge player and I was encouraged to enjoy both bridge and golf from an early age. He loved music and played both the piano and organ, playing the latter at school morning assemblies. He also taught the school choir. After he retired he continued to play the organ as a reserve organist for his church at Bideford and got much pleasure from this voluntary activity. His rendition of 'The Trumpet Voluntary' was played with a panache which I always enjoyed listening to. It is perhaps this love of organ music which reminds me most of the man.

He was a capable railway modeller and spent the winter evenings hand building goods trucks and coaches for his 'O' gauge model railway. He constructed sets based on the London Midland and Scotland Railway (LMS) and each coach was completely fitted out with seats, luggage racks, loo and wash basin etc. The terminus station took up half the garage and the lines on raised supports ran for ninety yards into the garden. In the summer my friends would come for a railway evening and man the stations whilst the trains ran to a strict timetable. In spite of these activities Father also found time to design and create his garden which he cared for with devotion.

Young children listen to their elders and if the comment seems helpful will probably be strongly influenced. I had just started at my preparatory school which set homework and I was feeling the pressure. About that time Father was having a bridge evening and one of his friends was a Mr Gurney the Headmaster of Whitgift School. He had acquired a new motor car and I was taken for a short drive. In the early twenties this was quite an experience. Asked about my new school I explained that I found it hard work. The reply was "Don't worry too much about work there is no need to take things too seriously". That comment became my guiding beacon and from then on I only did enough work to get by. As a result I failed the entrance exam to Whitgift! I suppose I only really settled down to applying myself to proper study when I faced the challenge of having to take the Army entrance exam for Sandhurst.

Chapter One

Early Days

"Five Days to Live" told of experiences in France and Belgium in 1939/40 soon after I had joined my Regiment. I had omitted to tell how I came to join the army or about my early days.

After five years at Homefield preparatory school in Sutton, Surrey it had been intended that I would follow Father to Merchant Taylors where he had been a scholar. After the depression cash was short and Father suffered a ten per cent reduction in salary. I went instead to The City of London School where until I reached the History sixth I never fully applied myself to my studies. I enjoyed games and took part enthusiastically in swimming, athletics and rowing. I took these physical activities seriously and although I trained regularly never achieved much success until my final years. During my 'teens' I outgrew my strength and spent time in hospital for operations for a collapsed gland and for an appendix, quite apart from the usual bouts of the flu and bronchial problems which led to pleurisy. It was only during my last five terms that I enjoyed good health without time away from studies.

Membership of the O.T.C. was compulsory and I found the training to my liking. I took Cert 'A' and was now on the promotion ladder. One holiday was spent at Aldershot doing a PT Course at the Army School of Physical Training which was very well run. The instructors imparted their knowledge with enthusiasm and I came away performing feats I would never have attempted before going on the course and with a closer insight into army routine.

It was about this time that my parents discussed with me my thoughts as to how I was to earn a living. My enthusiasm leaned towards the R.A.F. as I followed the development of the latest aircraft and the breaking of long distance and altitude records with deep interest. This interest took me to the annual displays at Hendon and to open days at RAF Biggin Hill. Father suggested my applying to join the Forestry Commission, an idea received like a lead balloon. No, a career in the R.A.F. was my wish. I wanted to be a pilot but as my maths was somewhat shaky these thoughts were somewhat optimistic. The idea of her only son becoming airborne was too much for my Mother who suggested I apply for the Royal Navy as a forbear had been an Admiral some two hundred years earlier. I had no leanings towards a life afloat and promptly responded "No I'll try for the Army"- a decision I never regretted.

The die was cast and with an aim ahead I finally applied myself to my studies with a view to passing the Army entrance exam. Mr Penn who ran the History sixth was a brilliant teacher. He studied previous exam papers and set me tests on likely questions covering the period nominated for study for the exam. This preparation paid off and I was thoroughly enjoying these studies and history with Latin became my chosen main subjects.

On the physical side I was rowing for the school and had gained my colours. I enjoyed running, was house captain of athletics, and managed to gain second place in the half mile. I also taught life saving and gained the Instructors certificate. In the O.T.C. I had attained the rank of CSM.

The entrance exam dates for the Royal Military College were announced and I went to an interview and was questioned as to why I wished to become an officer. The written exam was in a crowded room in London on two hot days. I struggled with the maths but found the history to my liking. Three of the five questions asked were almost identical to trial papers set me by Mr Penn.

I was on holiday camping in South Wales when the results came through. I had passed and been selected for entry to The Royal Military College Sandhurst as a Gentleman Cadet (GC). I was to join in mid August.

The RMC, as Sandhurst was known, is set in grounds at Camberley in Surrey. It consists of main buildings the 'Old' built at the times of the Napoleonic Wars in 1811, and the 'New' built just before the First World War. The 'Old' buildings with a grand entrance of steps rising between imposing pillars looked out across the parade ground down an approaching drive with mown lawns on either side to a lake backed by trees through which one could see a tall church spire. At the end of this drive, near the shores of the lake, there was an imposing statue of Queen Victoria. The motto of the college was "Serve to Lead".

I found myself posted to No 4 Company under Major Clarke of The Rifle Brigade which with No 5 Company was housed in the Old Buildings. CSM 'Granny' Hobbs of the Grenadier Guards, an imposing man well over six foot six inches in height was our Company Sergeant Major. The RSM was Mr Brand also a Grenadier Guardsman. He was not as tall as CSM Hobbs but was squarely built with a parade word of command respected by generations of RMC Cadets. His nickname was 'The Bosom'.

Shortly after reporting in on Friday August 27th, 1938 as a Gentleman Cadet (GC) I fell in with others who had just joined. We

2

were marched to Blackwoods, the boot shop in Camberley, to be measured up for our boots. Returning to the New Buildings we were measured for Dress shoes. This over we repaired to our rooms to dress for dinner. The whole of the new intake - 'the Junior Division' - dressed in dinner jackets with black tie as formal dress. Mess blues had to be made up by the tailor and would not be ready for nine or ten weeks.

We were summoned to appear in the upper ante-room where we underwent our first roll call and were addressed by Lord Carrington the Senior Under Office of 4 Company, who would later be Foreign Secretary. We next trooped down to the dining hall and were shown our seats. Mine was at the foot of 18 Platoon table. After dinner Major 'Tubby' Martin of The Northumberland Fusiliers welcomed us to his platoon. The next morning was devoted to drawing up kit and books.

I shared room 55 with Brian McGuire who was later commissioned into the Royal Leicesters. He was killed fighting the Japanese in Malaya in December 1941.

Bicycles were a required means of transport and Brian and I negotiated our purchases from the bicycle shop. Each bicycle had a number and recognition stripes, in our case blue, to identify the company to which the owner belonged.

As 'Juniors' we had to earn the right to pass out in free time and until we had earned this privilege were confined to the grounds of the college. Every new cadet was required to set to and polish his chin strap, bayonet scabbard and bayonet to produce a brilliant shine. Brian McGuire and I spent hours on this 'spit and polish' to earn our leave pass so we would be able to visit the shops in Camberley. We knew the Under Officers responsible would not hesitate to turn down the end result should it not measure up to the standards expected. This activity took up our spare time after dinner after completing our studies. The inspection took place some three weeks later and we both passed the test though five of our intake in the company failed and spent another week of polishing before they too passed the inspection.

A normal day started with a roll call and parade before breakfast at 7.15 am known as 'Shaving Parade' which did not last much longer than ten minutes. On this parade cadets were checked to ensure that the face was clean after shaving and all buttons and poppers on pockets were fastened. Failure in any attention to detail of dress resulted in extra early morning parades at reveille under the duty Under Officer. The first parade after breakfast was drill at 8.15 am after which there were three periods of fifty minutes duration covering military subjects as well as history, maths, geography, car maintenance and PT. There was a thirty minute mid morning break which we soon found was needed to allow rapid changes of dress as for example from PT flannels to riding breeches.

All afternoons were free for sports. I had opted for rowing and found myself 'tubbing' on the lake in front of the Old Buildings as part of the initial assessment before joining the bus each afternoon to travel to Caversham to practice on the Thames. 4.30 pm to 7.30 pm was taken up by lectures and dinner was at 8 pm with 'Lights Out' at 10.30 pm.

On Sunday the whole battalion paraded for church with the Roman Catholics at the end of the line. On the order to move off the RCs turned to the left and marched off in the opposite direction, hence the army term 'Left Footers' when describing a member of that faith.

Initially we paraded for drill in denim overalls and performed all executions demanded at 180 paces to the minute. The NCOs address the GCs' as 'Sir' and our response was 'Yes Staff'. At the time formal drill lined up in two ranks which formed into four ranks to move off in column. On the command 'Halt into line Left turn' the second and fourth ranks would resume their places in the front and third rows. It was not long before I reacted incorrectly to a drill order turning to the left instead of turning about with the resultant confusion among the ranks. CSM Hobbs bellowed "Mr Medley Sir, what are you doing? Go and pay your respects to Queen Victoria, Sir". This order meant that I had to double across the square and down the drive to halt before the Statue of Queen Victoria, slope arms and come to 'The Present' . I now shouted out in a loud voice - "GC Medley presents his respects - Maam". The rifle was then returned to the slope and carry and I doubled back to rejoin the squad. It was a salutary lesson and I was not called upon to carry out this task again. During those early days the statue received respects from a number of solitary figures seen doubling to and from their platoons.

We had hardly had time to settle down when our daily routine was changed and we found ourselves digging trenches and shelters throughout daylight hours in response to the 'Munich Crisis'. I believe the Senior Division was all but despatched to join their selected regiments. Fortunately after a week we reverted back to normal and as new boys we marched to and fro between lessons to the appropriate place of instruction.

The life was energetic and challenging. We had good instructors. Officers taught us the book subjects and selected NCOs from The Guards and other Regiments taught us the military skills. Tactics was

4

taken by Captain Tuff of The Buffs. Captain Dalyrymple taught Organisation and Administration. Captain Brodie, who later commanded the 29th Brigade in Korea, taught History aided by Lieutenant Bernard Fergusson who later commanded a Chindit Brigade and was Governor General of New Zealand. Major Phillipo of the DCLI ran the PT and Captain Johnson of The Bedfords taught Car Maintenance, the former was killed in the retreat to Dunkirk and the latter in Tunisia in April 1943.

During those first few weeks we spent a period on drill each day. We knew that if we did not give of our best we would carry on repeating the action until we matched the demand. As future officers we had to excel. This indoctrination taught us to be steady and not to flap and I was to be glad of this emphasis on steadiness some months later. After some eight weeks there was an inter company drill competition for those of us in the Junior Division. CSM Hobbs was determined that he would teach us to work together. His patience paid off and we won the drill competition.

The time came when it was considered we were now ready to learn the intricacies of bicycle drill so as to proceed on wheels between lectures. Lining up, the squad would wheel their bikes in pairs and walk march awaiting the order to mount. On receipt of the order the party would swing into the saddle and peddle on, each rider making sure to keep in line with his partner.

All the Non Commissioned Officer instructors had been selected to represent their regiments and they gave of their best. I recall we were having shooting practice on the ranges. The coaching ensured that the correct procedures were fully understood it was now up to us. Rifles had been zeroed and sights adjusted. We started at two hundred yards - five bulls. Next a move back to three hundred yards and my first round was an inner. "Mr Medley Sir what do you think you are doing. You had five bulls at two hundred Sir you will carry on and get bulls at three hundred, is that clear Sir?" The implication that distance made no difference gave me confidence and steadying myself I carried on firing, took aim and scored four bulls.

All cadets were taught equitation drills by cavalry instructors and we began our riding instruction in the ninth week. These started in indoor riding schools during the second half of our first term and progressed to jumps and tantivys on the open heaths. One morning we were indoors about to take our first fence and must have looked far too apprehensive for our instructor. "Now gentlemen you are looking far too miserable. Cross your stirrups and fold your arms. Now then as you approach your jump I want to hear you show you are happy so you will sing a song". One of our number was on a somewhat restive mount named 'Hitler' which needed firm control. It was evident in the run up towards the fence that the horse had ideas of his own. The wretched cadet started to sing 'Jeepers Creepers', and came to the second word as the horse took off. Losing control the 'Creepers' extended shrilly as the rider fell off. On another occasion when we were out on Borossa Heath a rider lost control of his steed which decided it had had enough and headed for home. No matter what the cadet did it was all to no avail and he disappeared into the trees with our instructor's comments ringing in his ears. History does not relate what words of encouragement passed between the instructor and the cadet when we arrived back at the stables. The instructors were so competent that equitation became a training period I looked forward to and thoroughly enjoyed.

We spent time in the gymnasium and on the obstacle course and on the ranges. Riding and games meant we were becoming fitter and our skills improved. Our final kit arrived after some ten weeks and we now had 'Blues' to wear at dinner in place of our dinner suits. Once each week we sat down to a mess night and learnt the formalities which would ensure we arrived in our regiments with an understanding of the niceties of mess etiquette.

During this first term there was great excitement as a Film Company was putting together a film which was intended to depict the life of a GC. Every now and then a camera would be spotted filming background activities as we drilled on the parade ground and we all strove to do a little better. One day Sally Gray, the leading lady came down and despite orders not to look out of the windows there were those who managed to glimpse the action. In spite of one or two absurdities 'Sword of Honour' was quite a good little film.

Much has been made of 'Streaking' in recent years as though this was something new. I well remember one of our year, who had been promoted to Corporal, had made himself unpopular with his pomposity and it was decided he needed to be taught a lesson. On a hot summer evening he was taken from his room, carried across the square and grass down to the lake where he was stripped and thrown in. The group initiating this act grabbed his clothing and scattered disappearing at a fast rate into the buildings. The unfortunate cadet was left to make his own way back to cover. It should be appreciated that the grounds were open to the public and a drenched body fled across the open greensward seeking cover from their surprised gaze.

It was on the Saturday morning drill parade just before the Easter break some six months later when the teaching of being steady on

6

parade and never to panic paid off. We had lined up under CSM Hobbs and were ordered to fix bayonets. My hand snapped round to reach for the bayonet handle, it was not in its scabbard. I knew I had to follow the orders as though I had a bayonet so I followed all the drill movements of removing my phantom bayonet and fixing it to the rifle. The order was now given to 'unfix bayonets', and again I acted as though I was sheathing my bayonet in its' scabbard. The CSM gave the order again, and once more I repeated all the drills. We must have fixed and unfixed bayonets at least six times before we marched onto the battalion parade. I continued to perform all drills as ordered. As we were marching past the Adjutant, Captain Eddie Gouldburn, Grenadier Guards, before finally dispersing there was a shout "Sergeant Major there is an idle bayonet in the front rank of No 4 company" with the answer "Sir, Mr Smith, in the book". Mr Smith in fixing bayonets had not ensured a connection and his bayonet hung at an angle. The Adjutant then added "Sergeant Major there is another idle bayonet further down the line". The CSM doubled to my front and turning whispered "It fell off during the parade didn't it Sir? See me after the parade". The parade concluded and we marched back to fall out on the company square. On the command "Dismiss" I stood fast and CSM Hobbs towering over me said "Don't you ever do that to me again Sir. Now get off parade". I had not lost my name which I would undoubtedly have done had I become flustered initially on finding the bayonet was not in its scabbard.

I was now rowing in the 2nd Eight and in preparation for the regattas we engaged in a few rowing matches. One I remember vividly. We were to travel to Oxford to row against Worcester College. We lined up and got a cracking start, our crew rowed with verve and led from the start coming in some three lengths ahead of our opponents. My Father had rowed for St John's and I was very touched to spot him on the bank supporting us. He had driven over from Surrey.

The full course of training was eighteen months but during the second term in the late Spring of 1939 we found ourselves abandoning the routine programme for six weeks joint field training with the Senior Division. We took part in night exercises, dug trenches and learnt gas drill and passive air defence drills. At the end we passed out with the seniors in June 1939. This was a few weeks earlier than normal and prevented our rowing crews from taking part in the Marlow and Henley Regattas which was something we had been looking forward to.

The passing out parade followed custom and after the advance in review order on completing the parade both senior and intermediate divisions slow marched off the parade ground up the steps into the main entrance with the band playing 'Auld Lang Syne' whilst the junior division presented arms. The last cadet being followed by the Adjutant riding his horse up the steps and through the main entrance. It is difficult to define the feeling of pride, joy and nostalgia I experienced on passing through the entrance with the sounds of music becoming muted. I was no longer a cadet.

I wished to join a County Regiment. Two of my friends had joined the "Bedfords" and I applied formally to join. The Regiment looked for family links and for sporting achievements. I had been given a half blue for rowing and was accepted.

My life in the Army had now begun in earnest. Sandhurst had been a great experience. I had enjoyed the challenges both physical and mental which had made us all strive to improve our performance. We had been made aware that our first concern if and when we were commissioned was the well being of the soldiers in our trust.

Rowing in the 2nd Eight during the early summer months had been particularly enjoyable, and the advances in riding skills in equitation helped improve self confidence. The application of mathematics to book keeping caught my imagination and accounts were never a problem from then on. I regretted very much that I had had to forego the Senior term as I had not had the grounding in Military Law the Senior Term would have provided. It had been a year of growing up and our instructors had helped us to discover ourselves. The whole design of the course had been to help the individual increase his self confidence. In many respects the approach was not dissimilar to the methods followed after the war by The Outward Bound Trust.

I was gazetted on July 3rd and joined the 2nd Battalion of The Bedfordshire and Hertfordshire Regiment who were under canvas at St Martins Plain, Shorncliffe. In late August we returned to Milton Barracks at Gravesend where we mobilized and received drafts of men and equipment. In September we sailed to France and prepared for war during the 'Sitzkrieg'. A spell in front of the Maginot Line in February 1940 was good for morale and then all out war and the retreat and evacuation from Dunkirk on June 1st.

It had been a very rapid introduction to adult life.

Chapter Two

RCCHI

Those days of July and August in 1940 were indeed momentous and memories of events remain vivid to this day. The 2nd Battalion The Bedfordshire and Hertfordshire Regiment, deployed to defend the coastline at Bognor Regis had received reinforcements to make good casualties after returning to the UK from France and to replace the drafts of soldiers with battle experience sent off from the battalion to the Territorial Battalions. As a result there were many new faces and, beside the urgent preparation of defences, there was the need to train. Emphasis was laid at this stage on training Section Leaders and one hour was spent each evening on return to billets from preparing defences before relaxing. This dual demand meant that there was little spare time and any visit to a local inn was cut short by the evening 'Stand to' which, because of the long Summer days, did not finish much before 2300hrs. Morning 'Stand to' was from about 0330hrs till 0500hrs so there was not much time to sleep before reveille and setting off to our allotted areas along the beaches to carry on digging.

Curiously the news of the defeat of France brought a sense of relief. We now knew we were alone and at our level felt confident we would defeat any attempt at invasion. Whilst those of us on the ground were going about our task of developing defence against an expected invasion, the attention of the media was not unnaturally focussed upon the actions taking place in the skies where the RAF were battling for the survival of the country. Just behind the battalion area lay Tangmere, a Fighter station, and aircraft took off and landed over our heads. Daily we watched the planes twist and weave in battle, saw planes spin and dive into the ground, and pilots float down beneath their parachutes.

After our few brief weeks fighting in France and Belgium many of us now felt superfluous. Three of the Platoon Sergeant Majors who had performed valiantly in France were given immediate commissions as Lieutenants and some eight new 2nd Lieutenants were drafted in to make up our losses. Calls were made for volunteers for the newly forming Army Commandos and Parachute Regiment also for East Africa, where the Italian Army was now invading British Somaliland.

I had itchy feet and encouraged by John Harrison, who was my company commander at the time, submitted an application to be posted to the KING'S AFRICAN RIFLES. Together with Tony Fawssett, who had also put his name forward, I was called for an interview with the Crown Agents in London. Subsequently a posting order arrived detailing us both to report to the Great Central Hotel in London to join Draft RCCHI. This Draft was made up of some two hundred junior officers and four hundred NCO's - all volunteers.

We were provided with a list of the dress and equipment needed for service in the tropics. Armed with an allowance of the princely sum of £30 we sought to equip ourselves appropriately. It was only after arrival in East Africa that we discovered the colour of the khaki drill, which was a rich brown hue, bore no resemblance to any of the uniform worn by the K.A.R. Perhaps the most infamous article was a horrendous item named 'Shorts Long'. This kit had been devised by the British Army to allow soldiers to wear the trousers buttoned up as shorts by day. These could be let down to cover exposed knees after dark providing protection from mosquitos. These shorts when folded up presented an incredible appearance. Their construction was such that no matter how much the wearer tried the last thing possible was to present a tidy soldierly appearance. The other principle items of equipment making up the outfit consisted of a camp bed, canvas bath and wash basin, a collapsible arm chair and a large battery lamp. The camp bed was of such design with a folding frame so constructed it could have supported a twenty stone body. There was a topee and the final article was a voluminous mosquito net all of which was packed into a lead lined trunk. The camping equipment and the steel lined trunk were to be of great use.

I remained with my unit awaiting movement orders and continued to take part in all the routine activities. Our company canteen was manned by young ladies of the WVS whom we got to know. One of these girls was the sister of 'Anton' who drew sketches for 'Punch'. Anton was now at sea with the Royal Navy and his sister had stepped in to provide a weekly drawing. Some of the ideas used in these cartoons arose from incidents noted whilst visiting our company lines. Apart from this I was very favoured as when it became known I was departing for Africa 'Anton' gave me two signed drawings of 1940 flappers as a parting present. A gift greatly treasured which today grace the walls of my work room.

On receipt of orders I duly reported to the Movements staff in The Great Central Hotel. There were a few Regular Officers in the draft one being Pongo Dawson of the Lancashire Fusiliers who had been at the Royal Military College in my year. He had been wounded in the leg at Dunkirk but was now fully fit again. The greater majority were war time officers many of whom were from the Colonies. They had returned to England on the outbreak of war, gained their commissions, and were now returning to their homelands. These individuals knew and spoke the local languages and would teach us Ki-Swahili during the voyage.

In the transit hotel we were accommodated six or more to a room and fed in a large communal mess hall. After morning parade we were free to roam and it was not long before friendships were formed and Tony and I went off to the hostelries around Piccadilly Circus with our new friends, Ken Hayward, Pongo Dawson, Paddy Bligh and Richard Bell. In the evenings after dark the black out was fully enforced. German bombers could be heard in the skies, searchlights sought to illuminate the enemy aircraft and anti-aircraft guns attempted to secure a hit. There was the crash of exploding bombs and the clatter of shrapnel on the streets but we ignored this rudery, as did the rest of the populace, and continued to enjoy our free time.

Ken Hayward, Jasmine Bligh, Robin Medley, Teddy and "Pongo" Dawson aboard the H.T. Khedive Ismael, November 1940.

This life of Reilly went on for some five days then on the sixth morning we were told to be ready to move out after lunch. Carrying our topees we embussed and drove off to Kings Cross station to entrain. Had there been any enemy agent around it was obvious we were bound for warmer climes.

The train lumbered north through the night and boredom was relieved by playing cards. In the dank half light of dawn the train pulled in at Galashields and four large ships could be seen at anchor. Lighters ferried parties to the different ships in the bay and we found ourselves aboard the 'Winchester Castle', a well appointed ship recently taken over for trooping and not as yet re-equipped to increase its carrying capacity. Thus it was that two young Second Lieutenants, Ken Hayward and I, found we had a spacious cabin to ourselves. Embarkation continued throughout the day and had not finished by evening. Next day a few more groups arrived and about midday the ship upanchored and swung her compass.

Boat drill stations were called and we hastened to our appointed position on deck with our life belts. Afterwards we repaired to the dining room for lunch and our group of ten were seated at the same table. The menu had not changed to war rationing and we were to enjoy a first class life style.

The weather brightened and the sun came out then as dusk descended over the loch and with the three other ships we up-anchored and slowly steamed down the channel and out through the boom. The die had been cast and we were heading away from England to distant shores. As Samuel Pepys wrote "And so to bed".

The steward brought us tea and biscuits next morning. I awoke to an unfamiliar sound of creaking joists and an awareness that our ship was riding through rough seas. I awoke happily, less happily I shaved, feeling anything but happy I rushed out on deck hoping fresh air might help to settle a state of equilibrium which felt most unbalanced. Breakfast was not a welcome meal as the many empty seats around the tables showed. Only three seats were occupied at our table. The convoy on leaving the North Channel had run into a medium gale. Breakfast did not really appeal and the bunk seemed a much desired haven of rest. It was not long before Ken also sought similar relief.

It must have been about an hour later when the cabin steward appeared and taking in the situation adopted the correct attitude. "What are you two gentlemen doing lying on your bunks you will not get any better like that. Now get up and out on deck and take some exercise." This shamed us into action though to stand up and walk was the last thing either of us felt like doing. We went up to the deck and saw that four more liners had joined our convoy which was being escorted by a flotilla of destroyers. Such was the sea state that these disappeared completely from sight in the troughs of the waves. The liners were pitching and dipping through the seas first showing thrashing propellers beating vainly against thin air followed by a bow heaving well clear of the water.

A German aircraft appeared overhead and bombed one of the ships which had to go about and return to port with half our destroyer escort. A short time later an RAF Hudson aircraft flew over to be greeted with a hail of fire from all ships. He sensibly flew off. During the morning we passed a convoy of some forty merchant ships heading for the UK. Our destroyer escort turned to join them and we met up with a cruiser which was to be our protector for the remainder of the voyage.

Lunch was still not something which attracted but I felt that I might try an apple. The rolling of the ship matched with the pitching and tossing was still proving more than my system could take and the apple was soon lost overboard. By tea time I felt hungry and eat a good meal, which again proved too much for the system so back to square one. However three of our table turned up for dinner and I enjoyed a hearty meal. Next morning the gale had lessened and eight of the ten seats at our table were occupied. The stewards advice paid off and some, who stayed on their bunks, took as long as three days before they appeared on deck.

Duty rosters and appointments were listed on daily orders. Some officers were in charge of troop decks responsible for the welfare of their soldiers and the cleanliness of the deck space. Each day twelve officers were named for watch duty on the bridge, four on duty for each watch of four hours. This party reported with two each on the port and starboard side with the task of looking out over their quarter for any sign of submarine telescopes or approaching torpedoes.

We were required to do PT, and instead of jumping about on the deck our group found a well equipped gymnasium and obtained permission to work out there. There was also a small swimming bath, which once the weather had calmed down proved very popular. We were also required to attend classes in Ki-Swahili, the lingua franca of Kenya. Ken thought that we should learn morse code as a means of reading messages being passed round the convoy so we practiced flashing messages on our cabin ceiling. By the time we sailed from Cape Town we were able to read the message flashed to us from our old ship the Winchester Castle as it steamed past heading for Durban.

The convoy headed well out into the Atlantic and it was some seven days before we sighted the Azores on the skyline. Now that we were approaching the tropics we saw flying fish for the first time, a Narwhale and other marine life. The convoy followed a pattern of changing direction at frequent intervals in a zig zag. This pattern was nearly disrupted one night when I was on watch. We were just about to hand over at 0200hrs one morning. The watch had passed by uneventfully and whilst waiting for our relief and talking to the Ship's officer of the watch I inadvertently leant back against a protruding knob, which on being pressed sounded the ships klaxon. The blast of sound in the pitch darkness was terrific and it seemed to go on for ever. I was unaware that I was the cause. The Ship's officer rapidly leaped from where he was standing and threw me aside whilst he stopped the klaxon. He knew the Captain would come to the bridge to find out what had caused the alarm. He grabbed me with my companion and shoed us off the bridge just as our relief arrived. As we descended off the bridge I saw the Captain rush out onto the bridge from his cabin. I expected to be called for next morning and given a rocket but I heard nothing. I often wonder what explanation was offered and remain grateful for that Merchant Navy Officer's quick wit and compassion for a young Army officer - lost at sea!

A few days later we put into Lagos for water. Small boats came out and young boys dived for coins. I remember being fascinated by seeing the pink flesh of the soles of their feet as they upended to chase the money. It was roasting hot as we lay at anchor and the iron decks seemed to act as an oven. I think it was the 'Repulse', which was lying in the harbour listing heavily to starboard after being torpedoed. She was being made sea worthy to be taken off to a repair yard.

Some forty eight hours later we set sail again and appreciated the breeze as the ship headed out to sea. The routine was broken when we took part in a 'Crossing the Line' ceremony otherwise day followed day. After some three weeks we came into Table Bay in the morning and saw Table Mountain as a back cloth. A sight of splendour and awe inspiring beauty, which I rate as one of the most beautiful in the world. The convoy steamed slowly into the harbour and tied up.

We learnt that this was where we were to say goodbye to the 'Winchester Castle' and trans ship to the British India line 'Khedive Ismael'. We helped off load all our baggage and had settled in our new home by afternoon. No longer the luxury of a cabin for two but we now shared with eight others and slept on two tiered bunks.

We were told that we could go ashore at 1800hrs to be back on ship by midnight. Ken and I set off down the docks following other groups heading for the dock gates. As we approached the gates we saw a long line of cars, all driven by young ladies. As each party came out of the docks a car pulled up collected that group of two or three individuals and drove off. There was no differentiation between ranks. We found ourselves picked up by a delightful pair of young ladies who said they were our escorts for the evening. Our hostesses first showed us round the city. Apparently we were the first convoy to dock and be granted shore leave for some three months. The last convoy had been sailing in the opposite direction and was taking Australian troops to the UK. On coming ashore at Cape Town we were told the Australians had made 'whoopee' and as a result there had been a ban on shore leave for passing troops. Fortunately it had now been lifted and we were driven round the city and shown the Post Office with steps leading up to an imposing entrance through massive doors. Our guides told us that the 'Aussies' had seen a young blonde in a small car, lifted her in her car shoulder high up the Post Office steps and asked for 'the Parcel' to be mailed to Sydney. Even if there was some poetic licence in the telling it was a good story.

We dined at Del Monica with its starry ceiling and then repaired to a club to dance. Like Cinderella we had to be back aboard ship by midnight. An evening ashore after three weeks on board was something to be relished, to find ourselves accompanied by two lovely young ladies, who acted as guides for the evening was wonderful. We heard that subsequent convoys which had put in at Cape Town and Durban all received the same friendly greeting.

We set sail the next morning at 0600hrs as part of a convoy of smaller ships heading into a heavy swell which proved enough to cause some of our draft to hasten to their bunks. Ken and I felt no qualms and rode this sea happily. Our new ship was slower and we steamed North at a steady nine knots. We found the cabin exceedingly hot and running with cockroaches. I succumbed to prickly heat and endured the creeping itchiness for three days it was all an introduction to a more robust way of living. There was nothing of note about our progress. A week later with land in sight as we headed for Mombasa we heard the sound of an aircraft and looking up spotted a Junkers 52 Bomber. We ducked instinctively. Happily it was not German but belonged to the South African Air Force which had flown out to welcome us.

Our ship was now closing the shore. It was a perfect morning. The mango swamps reached into the sea on the foreshore. In the distance a blue haze showed the rising slopes of the mainland. The harbour at Mombasa is set inland and is approached through a deep channel which twists amid the palm trees and verdant green of the tropical vegetation to the spacious docks. The ship anchored and our baggage was swung ashore. We were paid out in East African currency, ten pence to the shilling. There was still a six pence! We disembarked in the late afternoon straight onto the train which would take us inland.

Chapter Three

Arrival in Africa

There were four of us to a compartment on the train and the back of the seats could be raised to provide four sleeping bunks. This was just as well as the train would not arrive at Nairobi until the next morning. The track soon climbed away from the harbour and entered low bush country. Standing beside the railway line were crowds of African women in colourful dresses with babies slung over their shoulders who stood watching the train roll by. After about an hour the line levelled after the long pull up from the coast and the train stopped at a station to take on water for the engine. More African women stood on the platform offering fruit for sale. The sight of hands of bananas after the shortage at home was too good an opportunity to miss and a purchase was made for as little as a shilling.

Darkness came quickly and from full light at 6 pm it was quite dark by 6.30 pm. The train steamed on stopping at Voi at about 8 pm to take on more water. We were allowed to climb down and stretch our legs. As it was dark we could not see anything of the countryside so we repaired to our bunks early and slept until dawn, which came with sunlight arriving as abruptly as we had experienced darkness fall the evening before. Now we had a view of expansive plains, the engine could be seen puffing energetically rounding bends ahead. Outside were herds of game and zebra grazing nonchalantly not in the least disturbed by our noisy progress. The sight was thrilling and heads were leaning out of the windows. The vastness and magnificence of the backdrop of the rolling plains stretching as far as the eye could see, and the numbers and variety of the grazing herds, was a sight which imprinted itself on memory. This experience was all the more breathtaking as none of us had been prepared for the wonder of these sights which later generations would enjoy by viewing coloured films or television pictures. It was all very new and provided an impression which would never be erased - Africa in all its splendour.

A little over an hour later the train rolled into Nairobi station. We detrained and were ferried with our baggage to the transit Camp at Langata about two miles from the city centre. The permanent camp consisted of corrugated huts raised well above ground level with wide verandas which helped keep the interior rooms cooler. Our draft was accommodated in tents and our group kept together. This was where we found the items of camping equipment, camp bed and mattress, chair, and bath and washing stand were from now on to be an essential part of our life. There were no furnishings or bed side cupboards. We kept our clean clothing in our trunks. Mine had a metal lining which provided protection against termites. The heavy duty torch bought in London though useful was perhaps more designed as an addition to electric light. Electricity as a source was something we would only enjoy when on leave. The main source of lighting was the Hurricane Butty fuelled by paraffin and these lamps were among our first purchases.

We now awaited posting orders to our new units and were directed to take on an African servant. Any African who wished employment had to be registered and to carry a book with his name and references from previous employers. There were many 'boys' eager to be taken on and we read the references they presented to us. All those seeking employment came from the Kikuyu tribe. Now came our first opportunity to test whether the Swahili we had learnt on the ship would serve its purpose. It was sufficiently basic to enable me to formally employ a servant who now set up my camp bed and mosquito net and took my dirty linen away to wash. The servants in the Mess also spoke Swahili so our limited vocabulary which included the words to use when asking for bread, butter and water proved to be of immediate use.

We found that Topees were not the recognised form of head dress but that all KAR Battalions wore the Bush Hat. We also discovered that Khaki Drill jackets and trousers of the appropriate colour and pattern could be purchased from the Indian tailors whose shops abounded in Nairobi.

This invasion on Nairobi of some six hundred pink kneed young officers and NCOs soon earned us the nickname of 'The Imperials' to distinguish us from troops of the 1st South African Division who had come north to help defend Kenya a few months earlier.

Kenya at this time was readying itself to meet a possible invasion by Italian Forces from Abyssinia and Italian Somaliland. British Forces, had been forced to evacuate British Somaliland after a short but fierce battle against vastly superior forces. Italian forces were poised on the frontiers. They had captured Moyale on the border with Abyssinia in the north, and their irregular forces were operating some miles inside Kenya Northern Frontier Territory. British forward outposts were at Wajir and at Garissa and Buna on the Tana River.

Forces available to the Force Commander in Nairobi were the 1st South African Division, two Infantry Brigades of the Royal West African Frontier Force, and the 21st and 22nd East African Brigades of The Kings African Rifles. This force was commanded by General

Alan Cunningham whose Headquarters were in Nairobi. His brother was Commander of the Mediterranean Fleet. The General Staff Officer Grade II Operations was Major Dennis Rossiter, MBE. He had been Adjutant of the 2nd Battalion The Bedfordshire and Hertfordshire Regiment when I joined at Shorncliffe in July 1939 and had attended the Staff College at Camberley after leaving the battalion in December 1939. This was his first staff appointment.

There was not much available air support. Aircraft were biplane Hawker Harts flown by Rhodesians. These could carry four twenty five pound bombs under each wing. There were two Vickers Valencia troop transports capable of flying at some ninety miles an hour flat out. East Africa was at the end of the line for modern equipment we would have to fight our war as best we could.

After a couple of days Tony Fawssett and I received an invitation to go to the Officers Mess in Langata Camp to meet Captain Harris-Rivett. He was a 'Bedford' serving with the Somaliland Camel Corps. He had taken the trouble to find out if any members of 'The Regiment' were on the draft. He entertained us to drinks with one of his officers and wished us well, we gave him such news as we knew of personalities in the Regiment whom he knew before returning to our lines. This gesture of friendship was something I appreciated and tried to follow throughout my service.

After three or four days the papers came through assigning us to our battalions. During this time we had visited Nairobi and the New Stanley Hotel and Torrs Hotel for cooling drinks. Tony Fawssett and I were posted together with four other officers and some dozen European NCO's to the 1st Battalion The Northern Rhodesia Regiment. Bob Tait-Bowie, KOSB whose parents lived in Nyasaland was part of this draft. The 1st Northern Rhodesia Regiment (NRR) had mobilised and moved north from Lusaka at the outbreak of war equipped with all its vehicles which had been funded by the local administration. The battalion was accompanied by a complete Service Corps transport company.

The 1st NRR and the 1/2nd (Nyasaland) Battalion Kings African Rifles had fought against the Italian invading force. After inflicting casualties on a vastly superior enemy they had been evacuated from British Somaliland. We were the replacements for their European battle casualties.

Chapter Four

1st Battalion the Northern Rhodesia Regiment

The battalion was camped at Thika, some thirty five miles outside Nairobi, preparing itself to move forward to front line positions on the Tana River at Garissa. We arrived soon after lunch and I found myself together with Bob Tait-Bowie, KOSB posted to 'C' Company commanded by Captain Pat King of the Suffolks. Lieut Guy Tapson was the second in command and the other platoon commanders were Hobo Burns, Ewen Thompson and Bobbie Boyd. Guy was older than the rest but he had a charming avuncular manner and went out of his way to welcome us. He had married late and his wife had travelled up to Nairobi to be as close to her husband as possible. 'Hobo' had been a regular NCO before the war who had gone bush and lived with an African tribe. He had followed all the initiation ceremonies to become a warrior, which in this instance meant hunting and killing a lion on his own with two spears. His prowess had been acknowledged and he was an accepted tribal elder. On the outbreak of war he had volunteered and had been commissioned. Ewen Thompson had been a District Officer in the Colonial service and had a good knowledge of the language; he was highly regarded by the askari. Bobbie was in the colonial administration. Bob Tait-Bowie had been brought up in Nyasaland, returned to the U.K., obtained a Commission and volunteered to return to East Africa. The lingua franca of this battalion was not Ki-Swahili, it was Cinyanja (the language of the people of the lakes). I was back to square one with another language to master. I still needed Swahili to talk to my 'Boy'.

The key personalities in the battalion were,

Lieut Colonel Lynn-Allen	Commanding Officer
Major Dick Whelan	Second in Command
Captain C Rogers	Adjutant
Captain The Hon Clegg Hill	'A' Company
Captain Willy Spurr	'B' Company
Captain Pat King	'C' Company
Captain Roy Bingley	'D' Company

The organisation of the rifle company at that time consisted of a company headquarters and four rifle platoons. Company headquarters was about sixteen strong and each platoon approximately forty men in total. The company was thus some one hundred and seventy five in strength. The organisation differing from that of the British Army at home which only had three platoons to a rifle company. Each platoon had a European Officer and Sergeant supported by an African Sergeant and three African Section NCOs. Company Headquarters had a commander and 2nd in command and a Company Sergeant Major (CSM) and a Company Quartermaster Sergeant (CQMS). There was also an African CSM.

Pat King introduced me to my European Sergeant, Sergeant Bilson, who came from Rhodesia and I was sent off with him to meet my new command. The platoon was housed in a wooden shack with an open door at each end. The bunks for the men were in a long row on each side of the hut with a narrow passage through the centre. There, smartly standing to attention, wearing bush hats, shorts, boots and short socks were forty black faces. To me they all looked alike. How on earth would I ever be able to distinguish one from another? Their names also were strange to my ears. What had I let myself in for? Sergeant Bilson eased my passage along the line and introduced me to the African Platoon Sergeant. His name was Sergeant Leo - that at any rate was a good beginning I could remember that. Next came the senior section leader. His name was Corporal Enos - saved again I connected him with ENOS Fruit Salts. He was a tall magnificently built man. I learnt he was an Angoni, a warrior tribe resident across Northern Rhodesia and Nyasaland. They were descended from a Zulu Impi which had forayed north after a defeat. The other NCO was Lance Corporal Tauros, and his physique funnily enough was thick necked like a bull. I was told he had distinguished himself in the battle at Tug Argon in British Somaliland and been awarded a High Commissioners Certificate.

I was to learn the three main fighting tribes which made up the strength of the battalion were the Angoni whom I have already mentioned and who came from the Eastern territories overlapping into Nyasaland, the Bwemba whose tribal dances were less ebullient and who were probable more cunning in their attitude to life, and the Baila. The latter were of shorter stature and utterly fearless. Tribal custom required the four front top teeth to be removed and the teeth bordering the gap to be filed to a rounded point. This produced a fearsome sight when the soldier smiled. The reason behind this custom allegedly evolved after the tribe had suffered the ravages of a lock jaw epidemic many years earlier and the gaping gap ensured that nourishment could be fed to the sufferer as necessary. These askari made first class soldiers the sad aspect was that tribal numbers were dwindling. This was in part due to their custom of hospitality and ensuring their wives slept with any guest who came by the village. A refusal on the part of the guest to this offer of friendship would have been the highest insult. The result was a high incidence of VD (I am informed that the tribe has now died out which is very sad as the menfolk made cheerful and first class soldiers). Much later I was to learn that each of these main tribes had sub tribes, tribes which had been beaten at war and were subservient to them. Also there were other clans of an even lower order who performed all the chores and would never be included in any fighting party. This structure meant that it was unwise to recruit from the lower orders for fighting soldiers. In peace time recruiting had been restricted to the main fighting tribes who had no difficulty in providing all the recruits needed. However with the vast expansion of the East African Forces in the war this custom was relaxed and recruits were brought in from any available source including the less warlike sub-tribes. I was to come face to face with the problem this could cause some years later in Burma.

The morning after we joined there was a formal battalion parade when awards and decorations which had been won in the battles in British Somaliland were to be presented. The company fell in and markers were despatched to the battalion parade ground which was out of my sight over a crest. We marched off with my platoon in the lead. Coming over the crest I saw all the markers dispersed around the parade ground but in no way could I distinguish one from another so I pressed on regardless heading towards one of the lone figures. It was obvious to Colonel Lynn-Allen, the commanding officer, I was going to cause an upset and he bellowed "Mr Medley where do you think you are going?". At that moment I really hadn't a clue. Fortunately Pat King sotto voce said "Half left, half left" which allowed me to approach near enough to recognise our marker. The presentation of the awards took precedence and I was saved any further embarrassment.

That night we were repairing to our beds in the company hut when Hobo Burns came in in a very happy state and started to swing from the rafters. Pat told him to quieten down. He replied "I will, but first I am going to tell these 'Imperials' something." He then said a few words which I have never forgotten. He had lived as an African and more perhaps than anyone knew the truth of his words. "You may learn the language in six months and be quite proficient. You may learn it in more detail after twelve months. However adept you become never, never ever think you will know or understand the African". I spent the next four years with this battalion and became well versed in the language getting to know the soldiers I fought alongside very well. Hobo was no fool, his words were not biased but emphasised the different culture and understanding of life of the African. I would over the years begin to understand some of these differences and form a deep respect and

21

affection for the African soldier. An affection shared by any other British Officer or NCO privileged to have these men as his soldiers.

The few days at Thika were spent getting to know my men, seeing how they lived, their fads such as a delight for snuff, and the rations they eat. Bob Tait-Bowie came round with me when we went to inspect the evening meal. The food, posho a form of maize meal, was cooked in a pot and the savoury was provided by a thick gravy which included bits of meat. The section then squatted round the section pot and each individual took a handful of posho. The thumb was used to dig a hole in the posho and the mix was then dipped into the gravy. Sometimes the catch was a piece of meat, at other times it was only juice. The posho and sauce was then eaten. There were jokes about the man who always managed to get the meat. We sat down on our haunches and joined in with a small ration of posho, jammed our thumbs to make a hole and tasted the end product.

Two days later the battalion loaded onto lorries and at a steady 18 miles an hour bumped off down a very corrugated dirt highway. As we progressed the road slowly descended from the highlands around Nairobi, the temperature became noticeably hotter and the scenery varied from open scrub land to closer thorn trees. By 1600hrs we had arrived at a camp site for the night and all the vehicles pulled off into a forest. Camp beds were set up with mosquito nets and a ground sheet above. The cooks prepared a meal after which we all repaired to our beds. I awoke in pitch black darkness to the sound of thunder and a downpour of rain which was more than the ground sheet could cope with. I arose wet through as were all my companions. Fortunately the dawn was not long distant and as quickly as it started the deluge stopped. Not a very fortuitous start to operations but such was the heat once the sun was up we dried out very quickly!

The next day we reached the area of bush where the battalion was to camp some ten miles short of the Tana River at Garissa. 'B' Company was to take position behind barbed wire and mines on the far bank and defend the bridgehead. The frontier with Italian Somaliland was some eighty miles away but Italian guerrilla forces were operating in no mans land between the frontier and the river line. During this stay the only incident was when a young elephant trod on a mine and lost a foot. A tracking party put him out of his misery, all very sad. The African is adept at using nature to help improve his living conditions. Any fool can be uncomfortable but a good unit takes pride in organising its administration well. As a result poles were cut and lashed together to make the structure over which large tarpaulins were fastened to provide cover for the cook houses and the company messes. The battalion was deployed tactically and each company ran its own separate officers and sergeants messes. Our mess cook carried his chickens round from location to location so we had our own supply of fresh eggs.

Camp beds were set up and sticks placed at the corners to hold up the mosquito net. The ground sheet was so placed over the top to ensure any rain drained to one side and did not collect above the bed and eventually collapse onto the body below.

The other important aspect was the 'Chimbuzi' or latrine and much thought went into the siting of the 'thrones' for the Europeans. The problem was flies and everything possible was done to hinder their activities and be as hygienic as possible. There were deep hole latrines, there were also smoke latrines. These latter took account of any prevailing breeze and a trench was dug to funnel the air towards a brushwood fire lit close beside the thunder box. The smoke generated was intended to deter the active fly population though a fly in search of muck takes a lot of deterring. As may be imagined there were times when over enthusiasm in tending the fire resulted in a 'hot seat' for the individual using this facility. It would be interesting to have recorded figures to show the effectiveness of this method in discouraging the fly population.

There was always a demand on the 'chimbuzi' in the morning as time was at a premium. One of our number, who shall be nameless, required an inordinate time to meet his needs and there was a rush to reach the seat first. To make matters worse he had the infuriating habit of taking the latest copy of a newspaper to read. This action added insult to injury!

One day I was sent out on a patrol across the River Tana with my platoon to link up some fifty miles out in the bush with a patrol from the East African Armoured Car Regiment which was overdue. Sergeant Bilson was adept at reading the bush and after some five hours drive we found the place where we turned off the main track and headed into thick scrub. The trees were thorny and about thirty feet high and a path had to be cut to allow the vehicles to move forward. Progress was slow and after about four hours we had not gone much more than five miles off the main track when we heard distinct sounds of activity ahead. We halted and dispersed, standing ready to engage an enemy. It was our friends so we decided to camp where we were for the night as it was too far to return to our lines before dark. We returned next day without encountering any enemy. Back in camp training continued we were given coaching in the language and I was tested on my vocabulary each evening by Guy Tapson. Before dark some of us took a stroll into the bush and I had the joy of seeing a dik dik, a miniature deer not much bigger than a large hare. It was accompanied by its young. In spite of its size it was surprising how agile and fast it was in its movements. On the patrol I had seen a small herd of Gerinouk. These are deer which have an elongated upright neck not unlike a giraffe and were brown in colour. I had also seen a pack of five wild dogs.

After two weeks we returned to Thika and 'C' Company was sent to Langata Camp to carry out field firing exercises. There were other things to discover. Wooden boxes which had contained petrol tins were used as bedside tables. Wood is attractive to termites who thrive on it. I found a book in my box had been added to their menu and chunks of some of the pages were missing. The other scourge was the jigger flea. This insect lived in the dirt and waited to find a welcome piece of flesh between the toes. It would then bore in under the skin and establish its home to nest and produce its young. It is also small that initially its entry remains unobserved by the host. A few days later as the insect twisted and turned biting its way to enlarge the home for the expectant colony an itch would make itself felt. Inspection would then indicate a minute black head, the insect, and a round white sack full of young just showing under the skin.

It was advisable to ask an African to relieve one of this pest. The extrication was skilfully done. First using a needle the area of skin round the sack was slowly broken. The flap of skin was then prised up to allow the needle to spike the insect itself and draw it out without breaking the sack. I experienced this action a number of times and wonder at the gentleness of the African in performing this act. I had one flea extracted by a European medical orderly and it was agony. These problems became a bore and Bob Tait Bowie suggested we wipe our feet with paraffin oil after our evening bath. This we did and never had any further problem with jiggers.

Each morning Pat King had the whole company on parade in shorts for physical exercise. Usually we finished up on a football pitch playing 'Karamoja' - a form of rugger with a soccer ball. With sixty bodies on each side there was not much room to manoeuvre to try and get the ball across the opposing line. A second draft of volunteers had arrived from the UK and Charlie Grieve, DWR a former Scottish Rugby international full back was posted to the company. It was quite a sight to see this rotund figure weave his way through a surprised pack of Africans. Gillies Shields, R Leicesters was posted to 'D' Company. Subsequent drafts from England were not volunteers but pressed men.

British Forces in Egypt had advanced and captured thousands of prisoners. Training in learning the language continued and we now described the battle actions in the Western Desert to an askari and responded to his questions.

Apart from shooting on the ranges we would set out at dawn in transport onto the Athi Plains to organise field firing exercises. Our mess cook would come out and a break was taken while we enjoyed breakfast in the bush.

At week ends we would repair into the town and gather in The New Stanley to quaff cold beer. There were various means of deciding who would pay for the round such as doling out three matches to all concerned. Each individual then determined how many matches he would retain. Everyone placed their clenched hand on the table and in turn stated what they thought was the total of matches held. The individual nearest to the correct figure dropped out and the guessing game continued until the last man left in footed the bill. Another means of selection was by playing 'Cardinal Puff'.

Christmas came and I found it strange to be eating turkey and Christmas pudding with the temperature in the nineties. In the evening we repaired to Tors Hotel for dinner and joined a party organised by Pat King. Our time on detachment came to an end but not before the startling news which rebounded round Nairobi of the murder of Earl Errol.

One evening before we returned to the battalion fold at Thika camp Pat King authorised a beer and dance evening for the askari. The beer was brewed up during the afternoon from maize meal and gave the appearance of a thick porridge. The officers were invited to watch the dancing and seats were placed in a row at the edge of the area where the dances would take place. The dances were performed to the rhythmic beating of the drums and the chanting of the participants who had discarded their military dress for their tribal finery. Armed with spears they followed the traditional war dances handed down from generation to generation. It was a fascinating introduction to African folklore. As raw officers from England we were initiated into the spectacle of a howling group of spear thrusting Africans charging straight towards us at a fast run. The group were all but in our laps when they skidded to a halt sideways on kicking up the dust as they slid to a halt. This was their way of determining whether any member of the audience would move or bat an eyelid. If one had flinched face would have been lost. Another facet of the learning process was behind us and through the months ahead we would marvel at the ingenuity of the askari in their preparations for these evenings. At the same time our vocabulary was improving and the African was accepting his new 'Bwanas'.

Chapter Five

The Advance to the Border

Shortly after the company rejoined the battalion we set off in transport heading towards the Northern Frontier District. Instead of crossing the River Tana at Garissa we headed towards the coast. We ferried across the river at Buna some fifty miles downstream from Garissa where we set up camp on the river bank. There was still plenty of water flowing. The chance to bath was not to be missed but as crocodiles were spotted no one ventured far into the water. Armed sentries were posted ready to fire should a crocodile be sighted heading towards the beaches where the soldiers were enjoying a good soak. There were no mishaps.

The company set out the next morning and camped a few miles short of the frontier at a place named Garba Giri staying there a few days before moving to join the battalion dug in in an area of open scrubland on the frontier at Kolbio. There were no signs of habitation. A battalion perimeter defensive position was taken up and individual trenches completed. The whole battalion then set to, cleared the shrub and levelled off the ground to create a forward landing strip. Two days later an uneven area had been cleared of obstruction and a Hawker Hind landed watched by the whole battalion. It refuelled and bombed up before heading off over enemy territory.

These planes belonged to a squadron manned by Rhodesians. Bob Tait Bowie had got to know some of them when he visited the airfield behind Garissa. They were an amusing crowd with a great esprit de corps. One or two of their observers were older men who found flying at height caused bladder problems. This matter was resolved by carrying empty beer bottles with them when on an operational flight. This provided the necessary receptacle when a pee was required. The side of this story which amused us was to be told that once the bombs were dropped on a target a second run followed when the filled bottle(s) would be thrown overboard. These would tumble with a whistling sound and it was hoped add extra terror at the receiving end.

Each night a platoon size fighting patrol was sent a mile forward of the perimeter with the task of intercepting any enemy patrol attempting to reach our lines. The area was alive with armies of ants which wound in long columns across the terrain and which would set upon anyone who inadvertently obstructed their line of march. The inevitable happened. The patrol was resting before its next foray when all of a sudden an askari leapt to his feet slapping his legs and body.

This did not relieve his situation and he started to strip off. He had sat down on an ant trail and was now trying to divest himself of tens of viciously biting insects. The episode would have been very funny in other circumstances, it would however have been awkward in the extreme had an enemy patrol intervened at that moment. The patrol returned at dawn without any further incident.

The days were spent in training. Off duty we messed in company locations and disturbed the peace by playing an old gramophone. There was inevitably repetition as some records were more popular than others. Books were in demand and chess was played with an enthusiastic competitiveness. The 'Weekly Times' was sought as soon as the mail arrived. The chess article was studied avidly before anyone else had a chance to read it so a new opening gambit could be used against an unsuspecting opponent. It became obvious after a while who had first acquired the latest edition and it helped sharpen the competitive spirit. We were now on hard tack. Rations consisted of bully beef and rice and we lived on this issue for the next month. It was amazing how our cooks managed to disguise the dishes. Even so this menu in the heat of the tropics became tedious to say the least.

One morning the Armoured Car Regiment passed through to reconnoitre the route ahead. They found the enemy dug in some twelve miles over the border and one armoured car was blown up on an anti tank mine but the position was taken.

The day selected for the big advance into Italian Somaliland was fast approaching and 'C' Company set forth in transport to pass through our forward company at last light. Our task was to advance on foot at speed through the hours of darkness and clear as many miles as possible of the main Divisional route of mines for the column to pass through at first light. The main route was a dirt track of one vehicle width. Not long after we had started this task we unearthed two box mines. The rest of the night's work was a tiring slog with no further discoveries. We halted for a rest at dawn when the head of the Divisional column arrived to pass through. We had covered some eighteen miles.

In the lead of the divisional column were a group of volunteer officers astride motor cycles which had a drag hook attached behind the rear wheel. The idea was for the cyclist to drive down the track, his weight was sufficient to ensure the hook performed its task of scouring the track. It was hoped this system would drag out the mines and clear the route for the convoy which followed. We watched this party set off followed after a small gap by the leading elements of the column, which passed through for the rest of the morning. One of these dragsters was Felix Sheerman, Essex Regiment who later was posted to the battalion. He modestly stated their drive ahead of the column raised dust but was otherwise without incident.

Our 'A' Company was with this column and we chatted to them as they passed by. We were not to know we would not see them again for five months. They carried on with the thrust to Addis Ababa as an independent company and rejoined the battalion after the Abyssinian Campaign was over. The greatest enveloping move by a battalion in military annals! It should be recorded in 'The Guinness Book of Records'.

'C' Company had reached a place named Obe, indistinguishable on the map except for two water holes approximately two miles apart on each side of the track. Here we dug in, erected wire and were directed to prevent man and beast from taking water from natures resources. As this was the end of the dry season this was an order all but impossible to fulfil as game was concentrating on this source of water from miles around. Our only opposition was considered to be Italian irregulars.

My platoon was despatched to one of these water holes where we took up a defensive position. There was no sign of life by day but after dark all kinds of game including elephant came to drink and no amount of noise or shooting stopped their need for water. The platoon cooked on site but I returned to the company location for my meals. A company of Somali Irregulars were camped in the bush between the road and the water hole. Their transport consisted of some thirty or so camels. They seemed a well disciplined unit.

The other platoon of the company were treed by elephants one night after one of the herd had been shot and killed at the water hole. This proved to be a magnificent beast with a fine pair of tusks. Permission was obtained to keep these and they were later sent back to the Officers mess in Lusaka. A young elephant had been killed in my area. The Askari, after the spate of bully beef, were delighted at this free issue of fresh meat. They hacked their way into the dead beast. An askari disappeared inside the belly of the animal to cut out the liver and heart and emerged covered from head to toe in blood. After these labours the Askari gorged themselves silly. I now decided to ignore the order to shoot wild life. This decision was backed by Pat King.

Sergeant Bilson walking around the perimeter of the water spotted a green mamba slithering through the foliage of the acacia trees above our heads and fired at it. In all he fired six shots before it was killed and I never spotted it throughout this time as it was so well camouflaged.

The tusks - Pte. Ptulo, Pte. Mukaka, L. Cpl Manupala & Pte. Mwanaka.

There was a little excitement one day when three Italian guerilla fighters were captured but apart from that our stay at Obe was uneventful and we endured the daily ration of rice and bully.

The advance into Italian Somaliland was going well and Kismayo and Modagishu had been captured. The thrust on this front was rolling the enemy back. At the time we did not appreciate we were to pull back and cross the width of the frontier to relieve the South African Division in the Moyale - Mega area to allow them to follow the advancing forces into Abyssinia as the main reserve.

The battalion was ordered to pull back to Buna. In the short few weeks we had been away the River Tana had dried up to little more than a stream. Once again the whole battalion took to the water, which was little more than waist high, and revelled in the joy of frolicking in the river after being rationed for the previous four weeks.

The battalion now found itself moving across the width of the frontier from Bura through Garissa and Modugashi across a vast sandy desert area of the Northern Frontier District. Our trucks got stuck in the sand and had to be dug out. On to Wajir where we rested for a week (Map 1). There was a small 'Beau Geste' type fort at Wajir which is sited in the middle of a desert and scrub area. It is renowned for 'The Royal Wajir Yacht Club' in spite of the fact

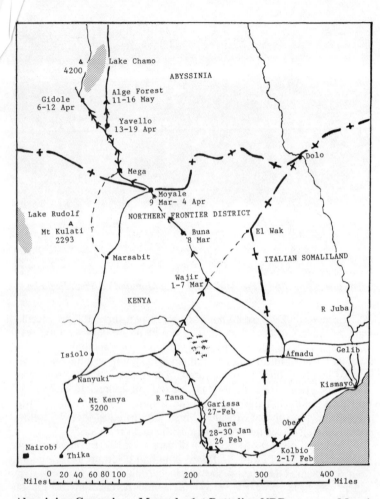

Abyssinian Campaign - Moves by 1st Battalion NRR   **Map 1**

there is little more than a pool of water in the area. Water for the nomadic tribes was drawn from deep wells dug down into the dry surrounds.

The Askari's of the 1st Northern Rhodesia Regiment - River Tana, Feb 1941.

Prior to setting off for this location we had heard stories of a troublesome complaint suffered by South African Soldiers who had been stationed there. The soldiers had had awful problems with their waterworks and the act of passing water was painful in the extreme. The complaint was quickly named 'Wajir clap'. Jenks our company second in command sized the situation up and filled up our water tanks with fresh water before we set forth from Garissa and this kind act saved us from personal torture.

The move then passed through Buna to Moyale, the latter being perched atop an escarpment some two thousand feet above the plains of the Northern Frontier District (NFD). We spent the night at Buna and camped alongside a South African Anti Tank Battery which was travelling in the opposite direction. This was manned by wealthy businessmen from around Cape Town and nicknamed 'The Millionaires Battery'.

Moyale was on the frontier with Abyssinia and a deep valley separated British Moyale from its Italian counterpart. The contrast between these two frontier villages was vivid. In British Moyale there was a small church, the District Officers House and a small building for the company of the Kings African Rifles stationed there. This outpost had been captured by the Italians and had been retaken by a South African Force. Across the valley the Italians had built a number of houses, a hospital, a school, and a fort in solid stone work. A small town was being developed which made British Moyale seem somewhat pathetic. 'B' Company was left in British Moyale whilst 'C' Company moved into the Italian Fort. Over the next four weeks we patrolled the surrounding frontier district with the police and guarded a small holding camp for prisoners of war. It was at Moyale where I sweated through my first bout of malaria. It is interesting to recall that whilst at Moyale both companies used to parade formally for the last post and lowering of the flag each evening.

In the evenings in the mess, when not playing chess or bridge, I made notes which subsequently were used for writing 'Five Days to Live' the story of life in France in 1939/40.

After three weeks I moved from the fort on detachment in Italian Moyale with my platoon guarding a small POW Camp with some fourteen prisoners. One morning a runner arrived from company headquarters with a message. I was to hand over my prisoners to another unit, obtain a signature and return to the fort ready to move.

Later we were to learn that these moves from one flank of the thrust to the other were all part of the deception plan. A mock Division had been created in the North alongside the 1st South African Division to give the impression the main thrust would be along the shortest route to Addis Ababa.

In early April we motored to rejoin the battalion at Yavello a small town sheltering in a valley surrounded by mountains. An Italian Fort perched above the town its entrance marked by two ornate wooden 'fasces'. It was in a dominant position overlooking the town and surrounding countryside. Yavello itself nestled in the valley with houses astride the central road. There were probably not more than one hundred houses in the town.

The battalion was camped about half a mile outside the town and we found we could purchase extra vegetables locally to supplement our rations. There was also a fine brew of local honey beer.

Chapter Six

Giarso

We spent about a week at Yavello getting to know the rest of the battalion, seeing a 3" mortar shoot and taking part in an inter platoon drill competition. After about a week we moved out heading some forty miles up a route leading towards a town named Gidole. Our task was to act as a diversionary force to the remainder of the Brigade which was thrusting up a parallel route through Soroppa. After a days drive the battalion took up a defensive position in thick scrub and camouflaged all vehicles. This was just as well as not long after this an Italian bomber aircraft flew overhead heading down the valley.

The next day a Hawker Fury flew up the valley showing us we had air support. A recce force had set off with Sapper support and headed up the valley to determine where the Italian positions were. They made good progress and that evening I was summoned by Pat King and told to take my platoon as escort the next day to provide cover for the Sappers who were checking the route for mines.

We set out early in the morning after stand down. The road climbed steadily, twisting and turning as we drove up the valley. As we progressed the mountains closed in on our flanks rising some thousand feet above us. We had set off in fine weather but now the clouds were closing in and it began to rain. This was just as well as a three engine Italian bomber came heading down the valley towards us just below the clouds which were dusting the mountain crests. We debussed rapidly and took cover. The aircraft flew overhead and dropped his bombs some eight hundred yards down the valley fortunately missing the Sappers and their transport. This act of aggression was sufficient to satisfy the aircrew and they returned whence they had come.

We embussed and continued to head on up the valley. After a mile the ground rose sharply up an escarpment with high peaks on either side. We debussed at the foot of the sharp rise in cover and I advised Lieut Williams who was commanding the Sappers that I would picket the high peak on our right. By this time the clouds had come down and it was pouring with rain. We climbed through thick mist scrambling up over terracing and reached the top of the peak to find it unoccupied. We could not see anything.

About four hours later the clouds lifted a little. Ahead was a valley with high ground to our left flank and the ground to our front rose to the same level some two thousand yards ahead curving around on our left flank. To the right were a series of high features and centrally where the track ran up the hill a rounded hillock rising from the valley. What was so amazing was the sight of a series of some dozen smoke trails caused by fires rising from enemy positions sited along the ridges. I sat down and drew a panoramic picture to define the layout of these enemy positions.

At that time which must have been about 1500hrs Williams appeared on my hill and said he had cleared the road forward as far as possible. He saw my sketch and asked if there was any way we could have a go at the Itis. I remarked the range was outside the limits of the Brens but the .5in Boyes Anti Tank Rifle should just about reach the nearest positions. He asked to fire the Boyes while I sighted the shoot. The first shot was high and there was no reaction. The next shot hit some 'Iti' earth works and caused consternation. I could see figures scurrying all over the place. This shot brought a response in the form of rapid fire from all small arms weapons in the position lasting some ten minutes. All this enemy fire falling well short of our positions.

Just about that time I received an order from Major Whelan, the battalion second in command, who had come to the base of my hill, to pull out and withdraw back to the battalion lines. We came down off our hill, embussed and returned to our positions. The weather was clearing up and the sun broke through. I had not eaten all day and feeling hungry finished off a whole tin of bully beef.

I reported my findings to the Commanding Officer, who unfortunately thought I had a vivid imagination and declined to accept the detail of my report. The next day the Commanding Officer went forward with company commanders and determined the objective for our assault. In the evening Pat King called us together for orders and told us "C" Company was to attack the prominent feature on the right of the road. His plan was a night approach march to attack the enemy position from the right flank at dawn. We were to have artillery support during the final approach up the steep incline towards the enemy position (Map 2).

The next afternoon we set out and debussed below the escarpment. As I had been forward before I was given the task of sending sections to picket the peaks and protect the company assembly area. Pat King called an 'Orders' Group and pointed out the the enemy position and the ground. We were told there was no wire. 14 Platoon (Ewen Thompson) on the right, and 15 Platoon (Charlie Grieve) left, were to lead the assault with 16 Platoon (Bob Tait-Bowie) in reserve. Once the company set out I was to gather in my platoon and follow along the approach route to join up and hopefully to take part in exploitation.

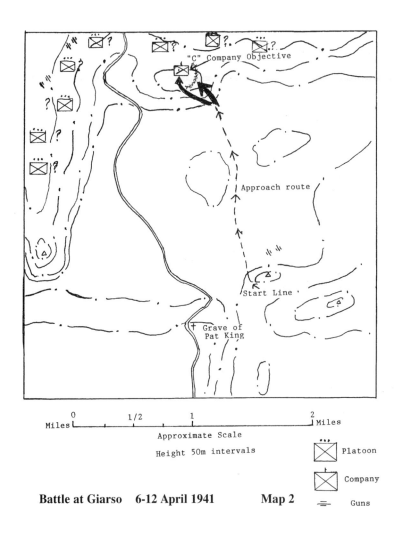

"C" Company Objective

Approach route

Start Line

✝ Grave of
Pat King

0   1/2   1   2
Miles └──┴──┴──┴──┴──┴──┴──┴──┘ Miles

Approximate Scale

Height 50m intervals

⊠ Platoon

⊠ Company

Guns

Battle at Giarso   6-12 April 1941   Map 2

After these orders Pat King asked me to stay behind and to point out to him the positions where I had seen the smoke from the fires two days earlier. Three of these sites were to the rear behind the feature we were to attack. Pat King thanked me and said he accepted my report as being accurate. I never spoke to him again as he was killed the next morning during the battle.

The guns were driven up the escarpment after dark and their tractors made a hell of a row alerting the enemy to our preparations. At 0330hrs the company were issued with hot cocoa. Unfortunately the cooks had used salt instead of sugar and the taste was quite horrible. After this mishap the company set off but not before we were told we would not now receive any artillery support. Apparently it was felt the gun positions were deemed to be too vulnerable as they were over-looked by the enemy. This piece of news did not cheer us one little bit.

I collected up my platoon following the main party some thirty minutes later. We made good progress and I had reached the bottom slopes of the objective and was leading the platoon up the hill side when the battle erupted ahead of me. There was the sound of heavy rifle and automatic firing and after a few moments a sound of rushing bodies as some askari hurtled down the hill towards me. I called to them to stop and some of them did so and rallied. Proceeding forward I found Bob with his platoon moving forward to take up firing positions. He told me that when Pat King launched the attack they ran into barbed wire where the enemy were waiting for them and fought with bayonets over the wire. The enemy then withdrew and our troops came under heavy rifle and automatic fire from strong entrenched positions. It was evident our attack was anticipated and the enemy were waiting for us. The initiative was lost and as he could make no immediate impact and seeing a number of askari had been wounded Pat ordered a withdrawal. He used a word in Cinyanja, 'Choka', which being interpreted strictly means 'Get out of here fast'. Initially there was a mad scramble away from this killing field but after the first feeling of panic the askari rallied to their officers. Ewen pulled back and tried to work his way round the right flank to the rear of the enemy. As he was making this movement he came under heavy machine gun fire from enemy positions further back. These were the positions I had previously identified. He was pinned down and only extricated himself with difficulty suffering a number of casualties.

Charlie Grieve in the meantime had moved round to try and find an approach from the left. Meanwhile Bob moved forward towards the right and I filled in in the centre coming into position on the right flank of 15 platoon.

As I came over the crest with my men we came under heavy machine gun fire from positions behind wire fifty yards ahead. We took up firing positions using available cover with heavy fire preventing any immediate movement. The automatic fire was particularly vicious and a long burst parted the leaves of the bushes we were lying under. The Askari alongside me firing his rifle had the bolt of his rifle hit taking off his thumb cleanly at the joint. He turned a pale grey colour and asked to pull back. Fearing a general exodus if he ran back I ordered him to stay put and apply a first aid dressing saying he would be attended to by stretcher bearers later. Meantime the battle was now hotting up and besides Medium Machine Guns there was now the TAC-TAC-TAC of a Heavy Machine Gun to add to our problems. We did not know what had happened to Tommy and 14 Platoon. 15 Platoon and Charlie Grieve was somewhere away on the Left and I was in the gap between him and Bob Tait Bowie.

Our grenade discharger cups had been withdrawn some weeks earlier so we had no means of using our grenades as the distance was beyond throwing range. The enemy were directing effective fire against us from strong positions behind wire and held the initiative. Continuous bursts of fire were kicking up the dirt all around us and I felt one burst pass close by my head. It was only after the battle I discovered a bullet had passed through my bush hat from front to rear. I moved to try and find if I could work my way round to a better position to launch an assault. All this activity seemed to drag on and in fact the minutes were passing by and the action had been going on for well over an hour.

As the battle had stabilised into an exchange of fire I gave permission to the askari who had lost his thumb to go back to the battalion First Aid Post for attention. He set off at a steady trot and ran the two miles back to Headquarters. He was transferred to the Field Ambulance where it was discovered that he had taken a burst of five rounds through his right chest! This gives an insight into the stoical bravery of the askari when wounded in battle.

Some forty minutes must have passed when I heard a rumour Pat King had been hit and moving to my left verified this report was true. He had been hit in the head and was unconscious. A few askari were carrying him towards the rear as it was hoped to treat his wound.

It was not long after this Charlie Grieve, who was now in command had received an order from Battalion Headquarters to pull back and he relayed this instruction to Bob and me, giving us the task of providing covering fire with one bren gun each whilst the remainder made good their withdrawal.

With our bren teams we stayed engaging the enemy while the main body slipped away down the slope along the route they had used in their approach march. We then withdrew back directly from the Italian positions moving in bounds covering one another and firing at the enemy who had come out of their defensive positions and who were trying to close with us. The initial withdrawal was through a wooded area which sloped gradually away for some four hundred yards before falling sharply down towards the valley below. We closed together at the top of the crest and after making sure we had pinned our pursuers down belted down the steep slope and raced as fast as we could so as to put sufficient space between ourselves and the enemy before they could bring effective fire onto us. As we ran along the valley bed we came under machine gun fire from the reserve enemy positions. Bob and I were about thirty yards apart and I headed one side of a small house whilst Bob charged down the other side. It seemed to me that my route provided better cover so I called to Bob to head in my direction. His reply was "You bloody well go your way and I will go mine". Fortunately none of our party was hit. Our delaying tactics had allowed the rest of the company to get away unscathed. For reasons of their choosing the Italians did not make any attempt to follow us.

A few moments later a Hawker Hart bomber flew over and proceeded to dive bomb the enemy position which had caused us so much trouble. The sight of the plane diving, bombing and machine-gunning our tormentors helped raise our morale after our failure.

After a mile I noticed a group of our askari ahead of me making their way under cover down a dried up river bed. On catching up with them I found they were carrying Pat King, who was dead by this time. They were determined that his body would be brought back to our lines and would not be left for the Italians to bury.

Tommy Tompson came in later having had a worrying time avoiding enemy fire from all the reserve positions and being totally cut off from the rest of the company.

We buried Pat later that day at the foot of the sharp rise to the valley which was the scene of the debacle. Pat was twenty eight and a fine company commander. He was adored by the askari and expected his officers to emulate his enthusiasm. He was a natural leader and set high standards. In the few weeks I had served with him I grew to respect him and was shocked at his death. After the short burial service we pulled back to our battalion area down the valley. The next day the battalion vacated its positions and returned to Yavello having lost a first class company commander and with some eighteen askari wounded.

It is surprising the company got off so lightly as every possible warning had been given of the intention to attack. Not only had a Sapper party been forward clearing the approach route of mines but the move forward to the Assembly area and deployment was in daylight in full view of the enemy. Further warning was provided by the noise in the middle of the night of the revving of engines as the gunner tractors dragged their guns up the final escarpment prior to deploying to their firing positions. The planned artillery support of 240 rounds we had expected was cancelled and finally the enemy position was well wired on the flank which was our main approach. Our task had been to act as a diversionary force and draw attention from the main thrust north from Yavello. As a junior officer I was not privy to the orders given to the colonel and we may well have met the overall tactical requirement.

Jenks, who had been a regular soldier in the Gloucesters, was now in charge of the company which set up camp below the Italian Fort. I was sent off to dig in beyond this fort some three hundred feet above the company lines.

Jenks devised a means of ensuring we were fully occupied and did not have time to brood over events of the proceeding days. Each morning the officers were despatched at the double to head for one of the surrounding peaks which was to be climbed. This party had a ten minute start before the askari were set off in pursuit. Our task was to reach the mountain top before being caught by our soldiers and to check them all through. Only after all his men were checked in could the officer set off on the return run. Officers were expected to arrive back before the majority of their men. This activity certainly made us very fit and bonded us closer with our men. One morning Jenks really excelled himself standing in front of the mess he pointed across the valley and said "You will climb that peak this morning". We set off at 0630hrs, it was 1030hrs before the last askari trotted back into our lines.

A leave roster was in operation and after a week at Yavello I set off for a spell of leave in Nairobi some three hundred and fifty miles away. Pat Garstin, RUR who was later killed on the Bruneval raid was also in this party. Leave parties travelled with the convoys which had brought forward supplies and were returning for further issues. The journey through Mega, Marsabit and Nanyuki to Nairobi took four days.

It was four months since we had been in a major town with civilian men and women. We stayed at the Torrs Hotel and enjoyed good meals and social company of the East African FANY's.

Whilst on leave Pat discovered that we had been gazetted Lieutenants on the 3rd January, it was now late April, news took time to reach us as traffic came via the Cape. Pat had heard that lists of promotions were at Headquarters and went to the appropriate staff officer and asked to see the list. This news gave us good reason to celebrate our new rank.

On returning to the battalion three and a half weeks later we found they had advanced north of Soroppa and were now competing with the rains in Alghe forest at a height of over 7000 feet.

Chapter Seven

The End of the Abyssinian Campaign - Frontier Duties

On rejoining the battalion in Alghe forest we found that the 1st/2nd Battalion of The Kings African Rifles (KAR) of the 21st East African Brigade, to which we belonged, were the lead battalion. They were held up by a strong enemy position atop a high peak. The rains had come with a vengeance and the road through the forest up which all supplies came was churned into an impassable mud morass. The Italians had felled huge trees across the route to further delay progress.

This meant that the 1st NRR and the 1st/4th KAR had the task of ensuring ammunition and supplies reached the forward battalion. The only way to enable trucks to go forward was to build corrugated tracks by laying timber across the water filled rutted road, pinning these lengths down to hold them in place, and providing a dry surface. The askari spent the whole day cutting timber and laying it down along hundreds of yards through the forest. This was a time consuming activity but our efforts meant that vehicles laden with supplies could use the road and the 1st/2nd were provided with the resources they required.

It was now mid May and the Abyssinian campaign came to a close. By a quirk of fate the weather changed and we saw the sun again. In the Middle East German forces under Rommel had counter attacked and driven the British Forces back towards Egypt. However a defensive perimeter around Tobruk was held which the Germans failed to over run.

Whilst the battalion was still in the Alghe forest area an incident during a routine rifle inspection of my platoon is worth recording. An askari, who up till then had never put a foot wrong, showed a dirty rifle. The remaining rifles in the platoon were spotlessly clean as was the usual practice. I instructed the African platoon sergeant to bring the soldier concerned to me with his rifle cleaned thirty minutes later. On his return the rifle was still dirty. It was customary at this time for a platoon officer to have powers of summary punishment for minor offences up to a permissible six strokes on ass. I sensed my powers of command were being tested so I ordered the soldier to be given two strokes for ass and to bring his rifle clean for inspection thirty minutes later. The platoon sergeant and askari disappeared back to the lines.

Half an hour later the sergeant and askari returned, his rifle was spotless. When complimented and chided for the time taken to sort things out and not to repeat the offence he grinned widely, saluted and said "No Bwana". I am satisfied this incident was set up. I also am sure that no punishment was enacted. My askari now knew how I intended to enforce discipline. I do not remember any further problems throughout my four years with the battalion.

The order came for the company to move back to Mega and to set up a prisoner of war transit camp. A site was selected on the flat lands at the foot of the escarpment below the town. We set up a perimeter with a single barbed wire fence and went to collect our inmates who were in cramped conditions. Italians and Eritrean askari were housed in the walled fort which dominated the town. It was there I was accosted by an Italian soldier who proceeded to unbutton his flies and showing me his penis asked for help. It was a very fine example of venereal disease. This was something I was totally unprepared for and there was little I could do as we had no medical support with us.

Civil Government was being set up and Jenks arranged for a beer hall for our askari. That evening those soldiers given a pass set off hoping to enjoy a good brew and the company of the local girls. Next morning their faces were somewhat glum and it was only later we heard from the District Officer that the ladies in question had turned their noses down at our soldiers as they had been expecting to entertain Europeans. Subsequently we learned that some of the Italian Officers stationed at Mega had set up house with these not unattractive ladies whose facial features were aquiline akin to pictures of ancient Egyptian women.

Meanwhile we had to do something about providing shelter for our prisoners as at some three thousand feet it became very cold at night. Jenks lined them up and dividing them into parties of about fifty under their own Eritrean NCOs directed that they construct their own huts. This was accomplished by felling trees to provide the main support, fetching brush to line the walls and finally puddling mud to daub onto the walls. The end product was completed in rapid time and all our prisoners were housed by evening. After a few days transport arrived and they were sent on their way to more permanent accommodation in Kenya.

Our stay also was soon to end as the battalion was to set out on another long journey which took us through the Houri hills south of Mega, across a lava desert before climbing to the elevated oasis of Marsibit for a night stop. On the next day dropping down to cross further bush country before climbing through Isiolo to Nanyuki where

42

we rested for a few days. The move then continued via Thompsons Falls to Nakuru, Eldoret and Kitale. Kitale was a hill station at a rail head with a hotel and a main shopping street - something we had not seen in months as our camp at Nanyuki had been some miles outside the town (Map 3).

We heard we were to head north into the NFD and before we set out the colonel decreed there would be a 'pombe' (beer) evening for the askari with more tribal dancing. During the afternoon the askari prepared for the evening. All the preparations were away from our view as their work was jealously guarded tribal lore. They created shapes representing animals as they had been taught in their tribes and the end result was remarkable and most entertaining. Apart from the more energetic dances there were those who performed their gyrations on stilts which they had manufactured for the occasion. There were dances which showed the African sense of humour.

The Baila dance depicted a somewhat stupid old man searching for honey. The actor brilliantly portrayed the problem of trying to extract honey from a honeycomb without disturbing the bees and getting stung. Whilst engrossed with this task he suddenly found he was being stalked by a lion. The askari acting as the lion had a splendid tail attached to his stern which was swung from side to side in a life like manner. The lion is foiled as the honey seeker manages to escape into a tree. Some time later a party of young warriors come along, fight and kill the lion and rescue the old man. The whole party return to the village where a dance and celebration take place.

I watched this dance performed many times and never grew tired as those participating put their whole energy into enjoying acting their parts. It was fascinating to see how different askari interpreted the actions of the lion twitching its tail. These evenings gave an insight into the simple pleasures of our soldiers.

The next morning we embussed and set forth from Kitale dropping down a steep escarpment to the scrub lands some two thousand feet below. It was noticeable that the temperature after our time in the highlands was much hotter. The tail end truck was manned by our sergeant fitter a dour Rhodesian. After some four hours the convoy had halted and he was feeling drowsy in the heat after a good night on the beer. Tipping his hat back he lay back in his seat and sought relief in a short nap. It was not to be two local tribesman full of curiosity appeared from the bush. They were carrying spears, wore short loin cloths and were adorned with necklaces of coloured beads. They also had decorative headdress and baubles attached to resilient wire hanging below their mouths. They approached and gazed into the

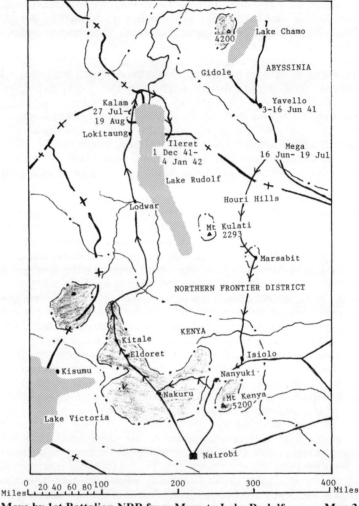

Move by 1st Battalion NRR from Mega to Lake Rudolf   **Map 3**

44

cab. The sergeant not wishing his snooze to be interrupted decided to frighten his observers away. Removing his false teeth he gave a toothless grimace. This caught the interest of one of the tribesman, who putting a finger in his mouth removed the bauble dangling on a wire protruding from a hole in his lower lip and proceeded to waggle his tongue through the hole in the lower lip. There was no doubt as to who gained marks for originality. The sergeant gave up any further attempt to enjoy a nap during that halt.

Continuing the move after the break the route dropped down a further fifteen hundred feet onto an open sandy plain. Palm trees to a flank indicated the line of a river and after two hours the battalion came to Lodwar and camped alongside the river. With its supply of water this was a natural gathering place and habitation. Apart from the vicinity of the river bed the whole area was dry with no vegetation. The local tribesmen wore little more than a jock strap and the women graced a small beaded leather flap. They also wore quite a few heavy bangles round their ankles as well as around their arms and these clanked noisily wherever they went. No chance of going out for a quiet gossip with a friend.

The drive the next day to Lokitaung was over arid country to a line of barren hills through which the battalion passed to reach the northern most shores of Lake Rudolf. Companies were dispersed North across the border into Southern Sudan along the Omo river. Our task was to guard the frontier to protect the local tribes from raiding parties crossing from Abyssinia. The company camp at Kalam in the southern Sudan was in the hottest location we had been in. To try and keep cool Tommy Thompson devised a system of digging down into the ground and setting up camp beds below ground level. This system did in fact provide a measure of relief from the heat.

As platoon commanders it was our task to prepare a weekly training programme for our platoons and the days were taken up on honing the different military skills. Officer and askari alike were separated from home and family and there seemed no likely end to the war in months or even years. This acted as a spur to us all to improve our capability. It might be thought that this routine became boring but the opposite was true as new ideas to increase combat techniques were discussed and tried out. Games were included as it was important to keep fit. There was little need of cash and officer and soldier saved his earnings. Every few months the askari would ask to have money sent home to his village to buy a cow and this entailed a lot of paper work. After dark officers wore long trousers and sleeves rolled down even then mosquitoes still found flesh to settle on and seek blood. The evenings were taken up with writing letters, reading, playing chess and cards before early retirement. I drafted notes on the campaign in France in 1940 as a means of keeping myself gainfully occupied.

The Omo river, which fed into Lake Rudolf flowed by some five hundred yards from our camp site. It was some one hundred feet wide and abounding with crocodiles. We tried to sneak up on them as they were basking on the far shore but they moved like a flash into the water as soon as they sensed the slightest movement. Their agility was awesome as they were huge creatures at least fifteen feet long. We were amazed at the courage of the local tribesmen who fished from precarious dug out canoes in these infested waters

The local tribe were the Turkana and a number of the tribesmen had been recruited as irregulars. They were fine warriors who wore ostrich feather plumes stuck into a mud pack head covering. We were to learn that the mud pack was sacrosanct to these men as it was made up from the ashes of their ancestors mixed with cow dung and hardened by the sun. Normally these young men wore no clothing but for the sake of propriety these soldiers now wore a brilliant red kilt. These tall Africans standing in line with their red kilts, shining black torsos and ostrich feather head dress drilling with their Lee Enfield rifles were a most impressive sight. Their kilts were rapidly torn off in a rain storm and placed over their heads to ensure the ashes were not damaged in any way.

I was now sent off for an engineering and explosives course at the training centre at Gilgil about sixty miles outside Nairobi in the Rift Valley.

Chapter Eight

Courses and Escort Duties

I went down to Nairobi with the ration convoy and reported to Langata Depot where I found myself detailed to act as guard to some five officers awaiting Court Martial. This duty and acting as Prisoners Escort was a fairly frequent chore for any officer passing through Nairobi at that time. Expecting a nominal casualty rate for the Abyssinian Campaign the staff had calculated the numbers of officers they estimated would be required to make good casualties suffered in the battles ahead. Accordingly a draft of some two hundred pressed war time officers had arrived from England in February to meet such a contingency. The total casualties in the short Abyssinian campaign were minimal and these young officers sat around awaiting posting to units. The weeks passed by and they had no real task to get their teeth into. Time hung heavy and with nothing to do they let loose in The New Stanley, the Norfolk and Tors Hotels with problems arising from boredom and too much drink. I can not vouch as to how many of them were charged with unbecoming conduct but the numbers were sufficient for them to be known as 'The Court Martial Draft'. I must have been involved in escort duties with these officers on some four or five occasions.

The last incident I remember vividly. I had been having a drink in 'The Norfolk' with a friend and we joined another group which included two newcomers. Returning to the Depot I found I was on escort duty the following day. Entering the room where the officers awaiting trial were housed I saw this officer I had had a drink with the day before. After his lunch time drinks he had decided to go up to the Depot to commiserate with a friend awaiting Court Martial. Walking somewhat unsteadily he tripped and fell down outside an office just as the adjutant was coming out. Picking himself up and saluting a little unsteadily he asked permission to visit his friend. The adjutant obliged by placing him under arrest.

This was a sorry episode which more than anything emphasises idle hands are likely to get into mischief. Although the young officers themselves were guilty the staff might have been more understanding and thought of ways of keeping these active minds and bodies fully occupied.

The short engineering course taught how to use explosives and recognition of enemy mines and bombs which was helpful. I was interested in getting onto the next company commanders course and was given a vacancy. The course had about twenty students and ran alongside a commanding officers course of twelve. Instruction was orientated to the tactics in use in the Western Desert. Demonstrations dealt with the problems of coping with an airborne assault in a rear area.

At the end of this course we intended to celebrate in a local hotel but were told there was no room as the senior course had already booked. Not unnaturally this made us somewhat cheesed off and three of us on our course decided to come up with some means of ragging the seniors. Whilst those of us on the junior course shared billets members of the senior course each had a room to themselves. We decided to move all their beds to a dormitory in another vacant hut. This all depended on our being able to get into one of their rooms. Luckily one of their number had not locked his door so the beds were carried to a selected dormitory hut and neatly set out. Each bed had a bedside table with the individuals name on it. Pyjamas were neatly laid out ready for wear. Beside the bed was a bottle with a request for a urine sample at dawn for taking to the Aid Post. On the door of each senior students bedroom was pinned a notice which read to this effect; 'Owing to the incidence of a highly contagious disease among the batmen of the Senior Course it has been found necessary to isolate you. You will find your bed and belongings in Hut 43'. All this planning and move of kit took quite a while but was completed long before the seniors returned from their end of course celebrations.

Having set the scene we repaired to bed and about an hour later heard the noise and turmoil as the seniors found what had happened. One of their number tried to start up a tractor and ram the huts we were sleeping in but in his happy state he was unable to master the gears. The beds were then retrieved apart from one individual who decided to sleep in his isolation hut. The next morning the Commandant addressed both courses and summed up the plus and minus of all our efforts. At the end of his address he said "Finally gentlemen I wish to compliment those members of the junior course who planned and executed the emergency orders yesterday evening. It shows that the teaching given over the last few weeks has been taken in. (Raising a bottle and the sheet with the request for urine from below his lectern) I would ask gentlemen of the senior course to comply with orders before they depart". The whole room burst into gusts of hearty laughter.

I now returned to Nairobi to await transport to return to the battalion. Imagine my shock when I was summoned to see a staff officer at Headquarters who said I was to be posted to the staff of a

Prisoner of War Camp. I protested that as a Regular this was in no way what I wished to do and would not be helpful for my career after the war. I was told very firmly it was an order. I knew there were other officers in the depot and suspected at least one of them would jump at the idea of such a cushy job. I accordingly said "If I can find someone else to replace me will you release me to return to my battalion"? The reply was in the affirmative I knew what had to be done. Returning to the depot I found a willing volunteer and took him down to the Headquarters office. Satisfied that the appointment could be filled I was released from this posting and returned to the battalion but not before I had taken some fifty askari to Mombasa to collect and escort Italian prisoners of war from the Desert by rail to Jinja.

This episode was comical as the askari were nearly all young Swahili speaking recruits. Having collected the prisoners and seen them aboard the cattle trucks an askari, armed with rifle was placed in the truck alongside the prisoners. The train took two days on the journey and stops were needed for supplying drinking water and to allow the men off the train to relieve themselves. At these stops the askari climbed down with his rifle and took up a position with the others to ensure no attempt was made by the prisoners to escape into the bush. The driver would blast on the horn to signal the time to get aboard and watching from the rear I could not help but be thankful that my charge were so kind in helping their askari escort back onto the train. The effort to get aboard was such that the askari needed to hand up his rifle to a prisoner whilst others of his charges helped pull him into the truck. I was glad to hand over a full complement of prisoners at Jinja. After a couple of days I returned to Nairobi and journeyed back to the battalion.

On arriving back I found the company ready to move across the Omo river and drive round to the North East side of Lake Rudolf to a place named Ileret though there was little to define the place on the ground. The journey took a full days driving. Ileret was some ten miles inside Kenya. Arriving there we found a building which before the war with the Italians had been used as the office of the local Italian District Officer!

This shore of the lake was far more lush with pasture and vegetation and our camp was wired in to prevent the hosts of wild game from rampaging through the lines. No one was allowed to shoot within two miles of the camp and the flat lands around were milling with all species of wild game. We had a wonderful view of these lovely animals feeding within yards of the perimeter fence. This was probably the loveliest location we enjoyed during our stay in Africa.

The difference between Ileret and Kalam on the other side of the Omo river was amazing.

One week end whilst we were at Ileret a tribesman ran into the camp and asked for our help. Through an interpreter we learnt his group of families had been attacked by marauding Boran raiders and our assistance was needed. A platoon was assembled and went off in trucks guided by our friendly tribesman to where his family had camped. The camp was surrounded by a thick thorn fence, a 'Zariba', but there was no sign of cattle or life. We did find two shallow trenches and hyenas had partially uncovered and attacked the body of a youth. The raiders had killed some of the men and the youths and made off with the cattle. Our guide now directed us some ten miles through the bush where we came upon the survivors of this raid an old man and five or six women, some with small children. Four of the women had deep spear wounds around their thighs and breasts. Those striking them had thrust for the genitalia. In spite of their wounds they were resting and accepting their fate without a murmur. The African is remarkable in facing up to anything he can see and understand and stoically reacts to wounds. On the other hand if he is struck down with dysentery or some major internal disorder which he cannot see and does not understand his will to fight to live is non existent and he visibly fades away.

There was a disease prevalent in this region which was akin to malaria but did not respond to any medicine prescribed and twenty six askari of the unit we relieved had died from this disease. One of our askari suffered from this complaint and we saw him deteriorating week by week. Some five months later by the time we had moved to Ceylon he was admitted to an Indian Army hospital where the disease was identified as Kalahaza if I remember correctly. This disease was known in India, the treatment was known and he returned cured.

Border raiding and cattle thieving was the way of life of the nomadic border tribes and control in peace was the responsibility of the Kenya Police. Cattle at this time were a key commodity in African life style. A tribesman was judged by the number of cattle and goats he owned. A young man paid his dowry for his bride to his father in law in cattle. This is understandable as cattle provided milk. The Masai tribe of Kenya bled their cattle and drank a mixture of blood and milk. Thus our askari saved up money from their pay and every so often sent cash home for the express purpose of buying a cow. The administrative task required a detailed form to be filled in giving full details of the mans village and the nearest District Office. The District Officer then saw that the request was fulfilled. I spent many hours completing these forms for my askari.

It was while we were at Ileret that the news came through of the Japanese attack on Pearl Harbour, the invasion of Hong Kong and Malaya. We celebrated Christmas by firing three 3' mortar bombs into the lake and apart from that nonsense enjoyed a marvellous meal prepared by our cook. He excelled himself by enclosing a chicken inside a duck itself inside a turkey.

Not long after Christmas the battalion was recalled to Thika camp to join the 1/2nd and 1/4th KAR battalions of 21st East African Brigade to mobilise for movement overseas.

Since joining the 1st NRR most of our time had been spent many miles away from civilisation. We had become used to our monastic form of life in the bush and not seeing a European girl in months and only seeing African women as we journeyed in convoy from location to location. Even on those few times when we visited Nairobi there were very few young ladies available to join a party. There was a local FIRST AID NURSING YEOMANRY (FANY) unit, which provided support for the Force Headquarters, and there were a few daughters of the local settlers. There was a very distinct shortage of members of the opposite sex and the girls were usually acting as hostess to more than one beau. This aspect of life was peculiar to those overseas areas of operations outside the European theatre. Feminine company was as a result a rare change from our daily routine.

We continued to make our own amusements and managed to occupy our spare time without surrendering to boredom. Living continued to revolve around the company officers and sergeants messes. It was more practical than attempting to organise a central mess on battalion lines as companies were more often than not located many miles away from battalion headquarters. At times when the battalion was camped together the company system prevailed and this gave individuals the chance to pay visits to other companies and to receive visitors in turn. As liquor was rationed it was customary to take ones bottle with one so as not to scrounge off a friend. This may seem strange but the ration was restricted to one bottle of spirits a month. In other words a drink was exceedingly precious as the bottle owner tried to spread this liquid gold over the thirty days until the next ration lorry. It will be seen that there was little danger of there being a drunken orgy. It also meant that the hotel bars did a roaring trade to those on leave.

Another aspect of this way of life was that every officer and sergeant in a company soon became aware of individual foibles. It taught each of us to respect one another and over the years created a very close bond of friendship.

Chapter Nine

Ceylon March to July 1942

The situation in the Western Desert saw the start of an offensive by Rommel in January which rolled the Eight Army back beyond Benghazi with the loss of large quantities of stores. The front line then stabilised while each side rested and built up strength. In the far East Hong Kong had surrendered to the Japanese on December 25th and Japanese forces were advancing down the Malay Peninsula. In the Phillipines the Japanese had driven the Americans from Luzon. In Russia German forces had penetrated into the Crimea and driven the Russian Army back along the whole front and were not far from Moscow. Thus the overall picture was not a very happy one for the Allies even though the Americans were now actively in the war.

The battalion having journeyed down from the Northern Frontier District joined the remaining battalions of the 21st East African Brigade at Yatta Camp on 18th January and immediately started preparations for a move overseas. Reinforcements made companies up to full strength and equipment was packed ready. A series of exercises were run and I was tested in command of a company. The end result was promotion to Captain and a posting to Headquarters Company as second in command to Frank Johnson. The other officers in the company were Scottie Kinghorn - Mortar Platoon, Davidson, Hugh Willard - Pioneer Platoon, Tony Fawssett and Roger Hawkins. The latter in later years was to be the Minister for War in the Smith Government in Rhodesia after UDI. Other changes in key battalion appointments had taken place:

Battalion Second in Command	Major Pat Glass (Foresters)
'A' Company	Capt Leonard Bagshaw
'B' Company	Capt Charlie Grieve
'C' Company	Capt Wilkinson (Wilkie)
'D' Company	Capt Roy Bingley

Battalion exercises saw us practising moves in transport in columns spread out across the open plains based on Western Desert concepts. We anticipated that when we moved it would be North to the Western Desert.

A new GOC, General Platt, had arrived in Kenya to replace General Cunningham who had been sent to the Western Desert. The new GOC came from commanding an Indian Division at Keren and he had new ideas about man management of African soldiers based on his knowledge and experience with Indian troops. There would be a saving in the number of European Officers needed and selected Africans would attend a six week course and on completion be given command of a platoon. This was an ambitious approach as courses for training officers for the British Army in the UK took nearly three times as long! This change in structure did not affect the Royal West African Frontier Force (RWAFF). We discovered that their infantry battalions in action in Burma not only retained British platoon commanders but also had two British NCOs in each platoon, double our compliment of Europeans.

HQ Company 1st NRR - March 1942.
Back row: Lieuts. Davison, Fawssett, Willard, Rogers.
Front row: Lieut. Kinghorn, Capt. Johnson, Capt. Medley, Doc Wellstood.

Another order stated that an interpreter would in future be used in all Courts Martial cases. I attended such a trial as the senior member soon after this order had been implemented. The need to have every definition, question and answer interpreted increased the length of time for the trial considerably. In addition it was not long before it became very obvious that the interpreter was not translating either the questions or the answers accurately. Certainly the President and I understood the language far better than the interpreter. Eventually the President became so angry at the very biassed interpretation of questions and answers that he decided to carry on without the interpreter and told him to keep quiet.

My vocabulary and understanding of Cinyanja had progressed considerably as I was in constant daily contact with my askari and only spoke English off duty. Learning was made easier as an askari was not allowed to try and speak to his officer in English. In 1942 the number of askari with a working knowledge of English in the battalion was very few, mostly confined to those in the Signal Platoon. Knowledge of Cinyanja was invaluable and was to provide security of information in later operations.

There was one incident whilst the battalion was at Yatta which might have been very serious. A disagreement occurred between Kikuyu and Nandi tribesmen of the 1/4th KAR and Angoni of the 1/2nd KAR and fighting between the tribes started when one party crossed the boundary road between the battalion lines. The fighting flared up and it was not long before Angoni from the 1st NRR started to join in. Luckily the noise of this fracas was such that duty officers alerted other officers from all the battalions who placing themselves between the participants, managed to separate the dissenting parties and order them back to their own lines to cool off before any serious injury had been inflicted. The order to disengage was obeyed immediately. This is an example of the respect the askari had for their British Officers and NCOs.

Our time at Yatta drew to a close and the battalion entrained for Mombasa to embark on HT Polaski. This ship had been on the immigrant run from Poland to the USA between the wars and was not designed to operate shut down at night in the tropics. It became extremely unpleasant when all port holes were fastened at night to ensure no lights were shown.

The ship had two 4" guns mounted alongside one another on a platform at the stern. Volunteers were called for to man these guns from our European element as there were no members of the maritime artillery aboard. The gun crews would be required to man the gun deck from dawn to dusk and be ready to go to action stations in an emergency. I decided this task was preferable to acting as an officer of the watch and with eleven others was trained in the procedures of manning, loading and firing the gun. Once trained and at sea we were allowed to fire the guns at a target of refuse dumped overboard so as to gain confidence should we have to fire in anger. There was one important requirement. We were to ensure that in action the guns fired in rotation as it was feared that if the two guns fired together the recoil action of both guns would cause the stern of the ship to fall apart. Fortunately for all concerned we did not have to fire the guns in anger.

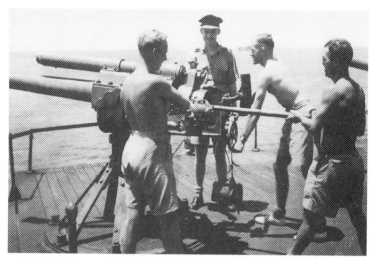

No.2 Gun Crew. H.T. Erinpura Indian Ocean March 1942. Ken Scott on the gun.

Many of our askari had never been onboard a ship before let alone out of sight of land. Although the sea was as calm as a mill pond many were violently sea sick. There were also some interesting theories as to the means of propulsion for the ship. Perhaps the most amusing being the idea that a series of legs akin to those of a centipede attached below the ship ran along the sea bottom. The ship kept its position in the convoy and we headed out into the Indian Ocean. The sea was calm and the voyage was uneventful though the news of the Japanese advances into Burma made depressing listening of the news broadcasts from the BBC. After some ten days at sea in the half light at dawn the outline of a coast line was seen ahead. Drawing closer it was possible to read a huge hoarding which read 'Ceylon for good tea', this identification sign was soon to be dismantled.

The convoy drew into Colombo harbour which was chock a bloc with shipping so much so there was little room to manoeuvre. Our ship tied up behind other ships in the middle of the harbour, there seemed to be ships everywhere. Staff officers came aboard but no orders came to disembark. We remained tied up like this for two days and then we heard we were to land and entrain for Anuradhapura. We were to learn that our arrival had not been foreplanned as originally we had been destined for Rangoon. The Japanese had beaten us and arrived there whilst we were at sea so our convoy had been diverted. Also in Colombo harbour were ships carrying the 6th Australian Division from the Middle East to Australia and the 16th British Infantry Brigade. Apart from this influx there was shipping which had got out of Singapore and Sumatra. One Australian Brigade was released to sail to Australia all the remaining troops were to disembark to prepare for the defence of Ceylon against a possible Japanese attack.

The two days sitting in the harbour were very hot. The atmosphere was very humid and quite different from the dry heat we had become used to in East Africa. We disembarked and marched to the railway station where we sat and waited for at least an hour for a train to arrive. Eventually our train came in and set off through wet paddy fields interspersed with palms. There were attap huts and natives working in the fields. Alongside the railway line were good metalled roads. After a while the scenery changed and we passed through rubber plantations before entering dense jungle.

Anuradhapura, where the 21st East African Brigade was to deploy initially, was the ancient capital of Ceylon. There were numbers of magnificent Buddhist temples with highly decorated spires. There was also the ruins of the ancient city much of which had been overgrown by the encroaching jungle. This city which had been resplendent in Roman times was set out in meticulous design with avenues one hundred yards wide. The system of water irrigation which had been used was far in advance of any concept in the West before the 18th century. It had been a very advanced civilisation which had succumbed to internecine strife and the scourge of malaria. The modern town consisted of well built houses, hotels and a hospital and a shopping street. There was an ancient Boabab Tree of great religious meaning. All the principle roads were metalled and our impression was that the infra structure of Ceylon was far in advance of that of Kenya.

The battalion, fortunately for us so it happened, was to camp in park land surrounding one of the large tanks or reservoirs which abound throughout the island. These tanks had been built to hold water brought down in canals from the highlands which were then used to irrigate the farmers fields. The canals some of which were twenty or so feet wide and over eight feet deep were all constructed with stone. The more we saw the more fascinated we were at the engineering capability of this ancient civilisation about which few of us had any previous knowledge.

Now I was in headquarters company I was to be in close touch with any medical problems as Doc Wellstood lived in our company mess. My medical education on constipation and other simple ailments was greatly extended. Doc had no other qualified medics to natter to so we heard tell of many fascinating case histories. On our second day Doc told us that Ken Scott had suffered from acute heat exhaustion towards the end of a morning route march. He now advised the colonel that water should be drunk at each halt to prevent this and avoid any fatality. This was very different from our under-standing of water discipline and strict control which we practiced in Africa. It was obvious that the humidity combined with the heat was something which had to be respected.

Next Doc told us that askari from the battalions camped in the brigade lines were falling ill and some forty had been admitted to the Field Ambulance. Next day we heard cholera had been diagnosed and over one hundred askari were in hospital and over twenty had died. There was an immediate check on all water supplies and all water was boiled before use. The source of the epidemic was traced to the brigade water well which had been inspected and declared safe by the medical services already in Ceylon. A dead body of a local, murdered in a fight, had been dumped in the well after the initial inspection had taken place and this was the cause of the cholera infection. The senior medical officer responsible for declaring the water safe to drink was sacked. As our source was different from that of the brigade we were not affected by this outbreak however every man had now to be inoculated every three months against cholera.

We stayed at Anuradhapura from the 24th of March to the 9th of April when the battalion moved to a new site on the outskirts of Horowupotana, which was half way to Trincomalee, camping in the jungle. (Map 4)

Our task was to send foot patrols out to learn to live in the jungle and to get to know our whole area of possible operations should the Japanese land. Ken Scott was deep in the jungle on such a patrol when the askari leading the patrol came rushing back agitatedly shouting 'Njoka, njoka' indicating he had seen a snake. Ken wondered why the askari had been so excited but rounding the bush obstructing his view saw three massive pythons the smallest being at least twenty plus feet

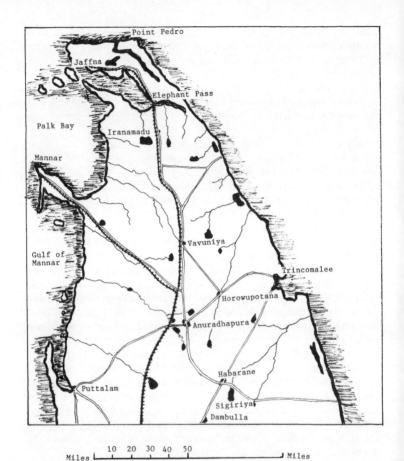

```
            10  20  30  40  50
Miles └─────────────────────────────┘ Miles
```

Ceylon - Area of Operational Training 1942-1943   **Map 4**

long. Over the next few months we were to see kraits, pythons, cobra and rat snakes by the score whereas in eighteen months in East Africa I had only seen four snakes. A possible explanation was that the civil population in Ceylon were predominantly Buddhist and killing of creatures was forbidden.

Communications to Brigade were yet to be established over military lines and in the meantime our headquarters was tapped into the civil line. Brigade could call us but we could not use the line ourselves. So a duty officer sat in the battalion office truck with head phones on to await any orders. The duty officer also recorded any interesting conversations coming along the line from civilian operators. It was by this means we heard that the Japanese navy had sunk two Royal Navy cruisers in the Bay of Bengal and that five Swordfish aircraft had been shot down. These conversations were reported and intelligence followed up to check out on any fifth columnist or possible enemy agent. The Japanese fleet launched air attacks against Colombo and Trincomalee. The attack on Colombo was repulsed as Hurricane fighters had been assembled in secret and these aircraft shot down some thirty five of the Japanese air fleet. Unfortunately our anti aircraft gunners failed to identify our Hurricanes as friendly and one plane was shot down. The gunner officer whose battery had fired on our aircraft was admitted to hospital suffering from malaria. He found himself in the bed next to the downed pilot. He was removed to another ward for his own protection.

After the bombing of Trincomalee the battalion was ordered to set up a road block and to check all persons and vehicles evacuating from that town. After some fifteen hours a steady stream of men of all ages came trudging down the road carrying personal baggage. Some twelve hours later they were followed by their womenfolk.

The Japanese fleet departed and the battalion settled down to active training. Ceylon Command under General Pownall ran regular four day exercises every three or four weeks and the battalion became used to operating deep into the jungle. One of the lessons from Malaya was the need to ensure that transport was not isolated close to the fighting and unable to reverse. Many of the roads were narrow and raised and possible turning places were few and far between. As second in command of Headquarters Company I was appointed Battalion Motor Cycle Officer. My task was to proceed down the designated route for the battalion with the leading troops and to identify vehicle turning points. I carried out this task on a number of major exercises.

As the days passed we found that supplies took an inordinate time to reach us as everything had to come round The Cape. There was a shortage of quinine as our source in the East Indies was now not available. To add insult to injury any one suffering from malaria was deemed responsible for not having taken full precautions and all recuperative leave was forbidden. Doc Wellstood could not get new needles to use for inoculations which were now coming round at quarterly cycles. He explained he would have to make do with his small supply. He found these needles were becoming blunt and we watched him sharpen them with emery paper in the mess in the evenings. In spite of his efforts there were times when a needle broke off during an inoculation. It was indeed the low ebb of the war. None of us could envisage an end to the war but in spite of this we all were quite sure the Allies would triumph in the end.

I was now to leave Headquarters Company and to go to "C" Company as second in command to Tommy Tompson. We had worked together in Abyssinia and I had great respect for him. Tommy had been a District Officer in Northern Rhodesia before the war, he spoke the language fluently, was a fine leader and was highly regarded by the askari. We now had the episode of seeing which company could train all its askari to ride a bicycle as bicycles troops had been used to good effect by the Japanese in their rapid advance down the Malay Peninsula. The company which reached efficiency in riding bicycles first would become the battalion mobile company.

Each company at this time had two old heavy army general purpose bikes. There were no more than three of four askari in the company who had any idea of balancing and riding a bike so the task of encouraging our askari to entrust themselves to this piece of metal required all our energy and imagination. A bicycle was something which any African wished to own but few had the means to purchase one. One of our marching songs was all about a man whose bicycle fell into the river by accident.

'Njinga wa Njinga, Njinga nyapita m'mardse. Pelekene ku Boma, pelekene ku Boma. Njinga, Njinga nyapita m'Mardse'.

"The bicycle. The bicycle has fallen into the river. Take it to the village, take it to the village. The bicycle has fallen into the river."

There was a dirt road alongside our company lines which dipped down a slope of some two hundred yards to a hump bridge over a culvert before rising on the far side. This was chosen as the training ground. The askari was placed in the saddle at the top of the slope and told to pedal hard and holding the handle bars firmly to point his bike straight ahead. Patience was in great demand as the unwilling askari was launched on this frightening piece of iron-mongery. Initially the man fell off almost before starting but with coaxing and encouragement he found his balance and pedalled away enthusiastically. There still remained the need for coordination between the actions demanded of the legs to ensure forward movement and the arms to ensure the bike headed down the road instead of into the ditch.

Training was persevered with and it was not long before there was a nucleus of askari who had mastered this new technique. This helped in the teaching of the others as they now demonstrated that the officers were not demanding an impossible task of them. There were inevitably the problem squad who whatever was tried would wobble down the slope failing either to use their legs on the pedals or to point the front wheel ahead. These few had been reduced to four wretches and upon their mastering this art fell the honour of the company. They were cajoled and encouraged by officers and NCOs. They crashed into the ditch, they crashed into the culvert, they fell off more times than one could count but eventually they found the knack and proved they could ride confidently.

The adjutant came to observe each askari ride and stop and start. Satisfied he went off and we awaited to hear whether we would become mobile. A week later we took part in a major exercise and went off mounted on bicycles. This was a great achievement and proved to be a most interesting exercise. We found that we could pedal for three hours before dismounting and that we were fresh for ground action. After that initial exercise the use of bicycles was discarded probably because of the extra transport required to carry the bicycles when the users had taken to the bush on foot.

We were gaining confidence in using the jungle to help us to get round enemy defensive positions and Scottie Kinghorn had experimented with firing his mortars from a base plate position against a target selected off the map but not sighted by an observer. This was something quite innovative at this time.

Tommy also felt that we were far too visible in jungle surroundings in our khaki drill. He therefore purchased some green dye and our tunics and shorts were boiled up in this evil brew. The end result was a rich green hue which was far less conspicuous than the khaki and the company wore this attire on the next major exercise. What had not been appreciated was that the products in the dye would cause major problems in the weeks ahead. The climate was extremely hot and humid and we were setting off on five day exercises wearing our kit throughout this time without taking anything off or washing. Minute organisms from the dye entered the skin around the area of the crutch resulting in a very uncomfortable form of crutch rot exacerbated by the humidity. The treatment was painful consisting of a ready application of strong iodine to burn off the affected skin continuing until three or four layers of skin had been removed. Although this remedy had a short term effect the problem reappeared and in some cases required the patient to be admitted to hospital. I suffered a mild dose of this rot but fortunately for me Doc Wellstood had by this time come up with his own remedy and gave me a bottle of liquid containing a mercury solution. This proved to be most effective and I had no further problems on this score.

A reorganisation of the structure of the battalion took place and we were to be equipped with armoured carriers and anti-tank guns. We were at this time part of 34 Indian Division which consisted of two new Indian Brigades, each of which had one British Infantry Battalion and the 16th British Infantry Brigade which had come from the Middle East. We had acquired a reputation of knowing how to make ourselves comfortable in the jungle and of knowing how to move and operate in jungle conditions. On the other hand we had little or no knowledge of the use of these new equipments. It was therefore decided that we would provide training for members of the British Brigade in those aspects of training which we were good at whilst the British would reciprocate and teach our askari how to drive and maintain carriers and the anti tank weapons.

The Queens Regiment had a reputation in the British Army at that time of always being particularly well dressed and turned out. A delegation from their battalion consisting of the commanding officer and two other officers came down to meet our commanding officer and to arrange this exchange training. It was a typically very hot afternoon and the adjutant Eric Langevarde was sitting in the Officers Mess tent dressed in shorts and short socks rolled down to his boots reading a newspaper. Eric was an Australian engineer who had graduated at McGee University in Canada and then obtained work on the Copper Belt in Northern Rhodesia. He was a delightful character and in the terminology of today very laid back. The Queens party immaculately dressed in tunics, shorts, puttees and boots with highly polished sam browne belts climbed out of their staff car. The commanding officer seeing Eric thought he was a clerk and asked to see the Colonel. Eric rose and called for Colonel Lynn Allen who appeared in similar dress to his adjutant but equipped with a splendid fly whisk. The Colonel had the solid physique of a large second row forward - bare chested and sporting a black mandarin type of moustache - he presented a splendid figure of a man. He welcomed the visitors who appeared somewhat taken aback. After introductions they settled down to discussing how each battalion could help the other. Eventually the visitors rose to go and climbed into their vehicle. The Commanding officer of the Queens was heard to comment as they drove off "Dressy mess, what".

Another high light during this period was a visit to the battalion by The Duke of Gloucester. Rehearsals took place for the big day and askari and officers practiced their formal drill. The parade itself went off without a hitch and The Duke was entertained in the Officers Mess in a large tent beside the parade ground before he departed.

The author at the Parade for the Duke of Gloucester in Ceylon, May 1942.

C.S.M. Jamavingkeya, "Jam" at the Parade for the Duke of Gloucester in Ceylon, May 1942.

Major exercises continued and there was the time when the battalion acting as enemy were ambushed by a company of Gurkhas. The Gurkhas had never seen the African before and could not believe their eyes. The fighting stopped and the Gurkhas stood up shaking with laughter and pointing at the askari. The askari too had not seen a Gurkha before and the sight of these short statured men of different facial features also struck them as funny and they too stood and laughed at the Gurkhas. The umpires could only call a halt and separate the two groups and allow things to settle before starting up the exercise once more.

I went down with malaria and spent a few days in hospital. Once my temperature had settled I was discharged to the battalion which was setting off on a three day exercise. Although I went with the company I was not given any active work to do which was just as well as I felt very weak. It was at this time that we were visited by Fred Sladen (Bedfords) who had been at RMC Sandhurst with me. He had been with the 5th Bedfords in Singapore and had escaped to India under orders. He was now touring round all units and lecturing on the Japanese tactics. It was great to see him again and to reminisce. He returned to India and took part in a special force activity in Sumatra and was not heard of again.

It was during this exercise that the commanding officer headed off down the road in a carrier ahead of his forward troops. The inevitable happened and he ran into an enemy ambush. He was somewhat put out when the umpire, an Australian Officer, commented "Colonel, you and your Sambos are in the bag".

We had been fascinated when we first arrived in Ceylon to see the waiters in the hotels dressed in sarongs, their tops covered in white jackets. These waiters all wore long hair which was held in place by ornate combs. On being called to take an order the waiter would shuffle forward with each hand held close to the body at a right angle commenting "Coming Master". The local volunteer force was the Ceylon Light Infantry and some of their officers were descended from early Portugese settlers and of a very dark hue. They were also somewhat conscious of their status. On one occasion two Australian soldiers coming out of the cinema failed to salute a major of the Ceylon Light Infantry. This officer drawing himself up the his full height of 5' 3" called out - "Hey you fellows can you not see I am an officer". Pointing meanwhile to the crown on his shoulder. The Australians taken aback for an instance quickly regained their composure and adopting the posture with hands at their sides waddled forward and saluted.

The battalion now moved to a purpose built camp at Iranamadu in the North a few miles south of Elephant Pass. The camp consisted of concrete hard standing on which attap huts were built spread out in a cleared area among trees. Officers had a room to themselves and each company had its own officers mess. After living under tentage for some four months this was a great improvement and good for morale.

Chapter Ten

Ceylon August to December 1942

The battalion settled into its new surroundings and continued with an active training programme. A broadcasting unit had been established in Colombo and it was decided that a programme would include a story about African Askari. A representative party went down from the battalion who took part in a live broadcast singing tribal songs and with individuals answering questions. Tommy Tompson described what was to happen and our askari were gathered outside our mess to listen to this broadcast. The effect was fascinating as hearing and recognising the voices of their friends the askari could not accept that they were over one hundred miles away in Colombo. They stood up and started to search in and around the hut to find their friends. Not finding any sign of the originators of the songs and dialogue they deemed the result magic. Much discussion took place when the broadcasting party returned to try and fathom this wonder.

The location of our camp site was very bad for malaria. Doc Wellstood instituted a system of circumnavigating the camp with a team of askari who sprayed every pool and puddle of water with diesel fuel. The fuel lay atop the water and prevented any mosquito larvae from breathing. This task was performed diligently and all possible breeding places were attacked including small pockets of water trapped in hollows in tree trunks. There were still cases of malaria but not sufficient to cause major concern.

On the 18th July 'C' Company was sent on detachment to Elephant Pass. This was where a long road and rail bridge crossed over a lagoon which all but separated the Jaffna Peninsula from the rest of the Island. The Company took up a perimeter position on the Jaffna side of the lagoon and set about preparing defences, laying wire and a minefield.

I had a healthy respect for anti-tank mines after my experience in France when an instructor had jumped onto an armed mine and blown up half our young officers course in December 1939. Tommy therefore decided that we would first lay the mines for the whole mine field round the company perimeter. Arming of the mines would be carried out later by officers and NCOs trained on how to perform this task. Arming would also be carried out in the first hour after sunrise to avoid working in extreme heat which might possibly set off a sensitive primer. This work started and on the first day the allotted number of mines had been armed. On the second day a loud explosion was heard. An askari Corporal had caused the arming mechanism to fire. He and his companion were flung many feet and we had the miserable task of picking up the pieces. Inevitably there was a 'Court of Inquiry' to try to determine the cause but the answer was speculative as there was no one alive who had been close enough to see where the arming drill had gone wrong. The result was that Tommy decided that he and I alone would complete the arming task. We set out each morning at dawn and were both a great deal happier once the task had been finally completed.

There were some brick built houses alongside the lagoon and these were taken over for office, stores and mess and living accommodation. The buildings were well built and the breeze off the lagoon helped ensure a cooler nights rest than we had enjoyed for many weeks. Some two hundred yards away was a 'Rest House'. These Rest Houses were sited around the island and provided good clean accommodation for anyone needing a bed and good food. Because most non indigenous families had been evacuated from Ceylon after the fall of Singapore there were now few demands for these facilities.

It was not long before Tommy decided that we might sample a curry. Accordingly one Saturday lunch we all trooped over to try a local authentic curry. It was very hot but quite delicious. Tommy commented upon the heat and we were all somewhat taken aback when the Rest House Keeper told us that it was only 35% strength. He said "A hot curry would be more than any of you could stomach. You need to eat curry regularly and gradually increase the strength to adapt to the heat. In this way you will appreciate the finer tastes and enjoy your meal more".

This was a challenge and it was arranged that we would attend each week when the curry would be raised in temperature by 5%. These Saturday curry sessions were a happy break from routine and we had graduated to a strength of 65% by the time we moved on. These lunches also helped the Rest House keeper from becoming utterly bored through lack of trade. I often wonder whether we would, even with this approach of gentle strength increase, have managed and really enjoyed a 100% curry?

Whilst at Elephant Pass we also took part in football matches against the Europeans of 'D' Company and afterwards drove to a beach some eight miles away for a swim in the sea. The place chosen was a small fishing village and the boats were tied up close in shore. These swimming parties were interrupted from the start by individuals being set upon by some creature which seemed to bite the foot and which caused excruciating pain. Anyone affected writhed in agony and there were those who had to be sent to hospital. One evening as I was swimming I felt as though my big toe had been gripped tightly by a vice like claw and thrashing my feet above water I swam for shore. Whatever had attacked me was not in sight but the pain in my foot and leg was so severe I had difficulty in placing any weight on that foot. On inspection I noticed two holes in the ball of the big toe. The pain continued and the glands in my groin swelled up. I sat and rested for some thirty minutes before I was able to walk and the pain began to decrease. Others continued to suffer from similar attacks. We eventually discovered that the local fishermen who cleaned out their boats threw offal and scraps overboard which was then scavenged by small sting rays. The puncture in my big toe was where the sting had penetrated the skin and fortunately broken out so I did not receive the full strength of the venom. I had been lucky and from then on we bathed along the beach well away from the boats and never suffered any further problems.

This phase of the war was interesting as the Allies had suffered so many defeats there was no sign of any end to the struggle. In Ceylon we were at the end of a long supply line which journeyed round the Cape. It took six weeks for mail to reach us from home which made exchanges of information somewhat outdated by the time an answer was sent in reply to a question. As yet the welfare support was negligible so it was up to us to occupy what spare time there was and make our own amusements. As we were scattered in company groups bridge and chess were popular. The liquor ration was still one bottle of spirits a month. Mess rules forbad offering a drink to anyone other than a visitor from another unit. A single drink after dinner was something to savour and enjoy. It was later in 1943 that cinemas were built in the larger airforce camps and we travelled many miles to see the Bob Hope and Dorothy Lamour films. Life was indeed simple and uncomplicated and we continued our monastic form of life.

We had one great advantage the battalion had been together over a period of months. Isolated as we were from civilisation and living cheek by jowl with our soldiers our vocabulary and knowledge of the language had progressed considerably. Officers and askari had melded together into a confident team

It was now eighteen months since I had taken any leave. Our time in Ceylon had all been spent in the hot, humid lowlands and it was felt a spell up the highlands would be beneficial health wise as well as a pleasant change. Three of us set out for Nuwara Eliya, a hill station some 6000 feet above sea level. The housing nestled in a hollow surrounded by high peaks covered in trees. There was a fire in the hotel lounge in the evenings all very different from our camps at sea level. There was a golf club close by and it was not long before we were out on the golf course playing thirty six holes a day. Roy Bingley had brought his batman with him who was to prove invaluable. The Sinhalese caddies were adept at concealing any ball which had gone off the fairway into the rough. Finding a ball which had gone into the rough they would secrete it between their toes and move it to a hiding place a few feet away from which it would be retrieved later. Subsequently these same balls would be offered for sale to other players. Finding we were loosing far too many balls Roy placed his batman down the fairway with instructions to move rapidly to the area where a stray ball had drifted. This action did reduce the losses we sustained from then on. Initially our game was erratic to say the least but the daily game saw great improvement and provided a great deal of satisfaction.

Whilst in Nuwara Eliya we were very hospitably entertained by some of the local tea planters. We also climbed up the local peak, Mount Pedro, which rose above 7,500 feet. In all the break was very welcome and we returned back to the battalion feeling much refreshed.

The company moved to a camp on the Jaffna Peninsula on the coast about six miles from Jaffa town with responsibility of patrolling to prevent any illicit landings from India. The local police and District Officer were aware that the army was to carry out these patrols.

There was a fishing village named Point Pedro on the north coast with a sheltered harbour and quite large fishing vessels tied up there. It was suspected this was where any smuggling would take place. The company set about active patrolling with about fifteen men going out on bicycles during the afternoon. It was important that the selected patrol ambush location be kept secure so not even the police were informed. At dusk the patrol having visibly shown themselves would make camp, cook a meal and give the impression to any observer they had settled down for the night. The patrol would get up at about midnight, pedal furiously to the predetermined ambush site near a landing beach, and await developments. One evening such a patrol astride the headlands on the approaches to Point Pedro caught a boat coming ashore and apprehended those aboard. The local police and District Officer were called in to take over responsibility for the catch. These patrols were popular with the askari and a change from training and exercises.

After two successful patrols we received orders to cease these activities. Rumour had it that these boats were bringing in goods from

India which were providing a profit for the embargo runners who were local government officials. Agreement resulted at a high level when a promise was given that no person would be shipped into Ceylon illegally.

The location of our camp was somewhat isolated from the rest of the battalion and the company commander was given powers of a detachment commander. We inherited a motor boat and eight boats. These were to be used to evacuate the company by sea should the Japanese invade and cut the land link to Elephant Pass. It was important that the motor boat was used regularly to keep the engine in good running order thus we enjoyed using it to go swimming in deep water once every week.

I found myself in charge of the company with Eric Sharman as second in command. The askari enjoys playing and gambling with cards and we suspected a gambling school was operating clandestinely. This was something which had to be discouraged as it could cross rank barriers and be bad for discipline and morale. The losers would be beholden to the winners and there was a danger some askari would get badly into debt. Eric and I decided that we would use the next pay day to set the scene for a simple plan. The pay parade was managed in the usual way with the askari lining up and signing for their pay. Unbeknown to them Eric had listed down all the bank note numbers against the askari to whom the money was handed. Even before the end of the pay out three or four men including two corporals had lined up at the end of the queue. Once the pay parade was over Eric asked them what they wanted. "Please Bwana will you please give me change". The askari handed over a twenty rupee note and was taken aback when Eric told him that this was not the note which he had given to him. The response initially was to bluster but the amazement on the soldiers face showed plainly when Eric told him that note had been paid to Pte So and So. When this procedure had been repeated with other askari seeking change the soldiers were dumbfounded. This was magic indeed. It was possible to sense the feeling of wonder and awe coming from the lines.

We now waited until after dark and lights out before pursuing the next phase of the plan. At about 11.30 pm the orderly sergeant was called for and a full inspection was made of the askari lines. All mosquito nets were down but in each hut there were one or two beds which were unoccupied. All bedding and kit of the absentees, about twelve in number, was impounded in the guard room. Eric and I now set out into the surrounding bush with a patrol to see if we could find the missing askari. Some two hundred yards into the bush we could

70

hear the sounds which as we crept closer we took to be the slamming down of playing cards by a triumphant winner. The players were so intent on their game we were almost upon them before they realised what was happening. Their reaction was very fast and they dispersed in a rush into the bush and we knew there was no way we would catch them and that they would be back in the lines long before us.

On returning to their huts they all found that they had no bed or kit and knew the game was up. They spent the night in a guarded compound and came before me the next day. The catch showed who were the gamblers and we were able to keep a closer eye on their activities from then on. They also received a spell of field punishment for their pains.

The battalion continued to take part in major exercises and became more and more adept at operating deep in the jungle both by day and by night. Feet were hardened with route marches which were livened by the singing of the askari who sang lustily and in harmony. Their songs were repetitive but could be compared to folklore in our country. Many songs were based on experiences earlier in the war. Those who had fought in British Somaliland in August 1940 had wondered at the paucity of air support. One marching song portrayed this;

> 'Opandeke, opandeke.
> Opandeke, opandeke,
> Onse akala pambuyo kwa Azungu

A rough translation being;

> No aircraft, no aircraft,
> No aircraft, no aircraft,
> They are all in the rear areas with the Europeans.

The refrain would be repeated time and again with the lines of askari marching along singing and keeping in step with the lilt of the tune. There were many of these marching songs. A soloist would give the lead and the rest of the platoon would pick up the refrain and sing the chorus. It might be thought that such repetition would become tedious but the harmony more than compensated and the rhythm made the marching that much easier. It was a joy to join in and become part of the chorus. I for one was captivated by the rhythm and beauty of the singing. Anyone fortunate enough to serve with African askari I have met since those days has confirmed this impression. Their sense of timing with their drums and hand made instruments was something which showed an exuberance for life which seemed to get into the blood. I still remember the words of seven or eight of the songs which helped us to march many miles in Ceylon and Burma.

The battalion spent Christmas at Iranamadu and all Europeans sat down together for the turkey. Afterwards a three legged football match was played between the Officers and Sergeants Mess. I teamed up with Doc Wellstood and we each wore a wellington boot on the inside leg. The boots were firmly bound together and we were able to chase after the ball faster than many other pairs and even scored a goal. We were by now quite used to the rationing of spirits but still managed to enjoy the holiday.

Training exercises took the battalion to many differing areas which allowed us to gain a better understanding of the history and culture of the peoples. The Island was split roughly North South with Bhuddism primarily in the South and Hinduism in the Tamil North. The Bhuddist temples were particularly inspiring around Anaradapura with their colourful domes. The Hindu temples we saw on the Jaffna peninsula were resplendent the whole frame of the structure adorned with statues of men, women and animals posing in descriptive sexual posture.

It is a practice of the Hindu religion to burn the body of the deceased on a funeral pyre. The body being placed on the top of logs and wood rising some three feet above ground level and tidily fastened in place. Driving past a village one day I witnessed the deceased being placed on such a pyre. The torch set the wood alight and the flames took hold the heat causing the deceased to partially sit up. In a country where decomposition is hastened by the climate this method of saying farewell seemed so logical.

Another impression was the total subservience of the women. I remember writing home in one letter describing the sight of a man walking across a paddy bund at the head of a group of some eight women and children all of whom were carrying loads. The man carried nothing other than the stick he used to assist his progress!

There was plenty of evidence of early Portugese settlement and many of the locals enjoyed such family names as De Silva. These settlers had brought the Christian religion and churches were evident in the main towns.

We continued periodically to arrange a beer drinking evening for the askari when they could relax and unwind. It was possible to make up a fearsome brew from fresh coconut juice which fermented rapidly. Our soldiers much enjoyed the resulting beverage.

Chapter Eleven

1943 - Ceylon and East Africa

In early January 'C' Company moved to camp near Dambulla to carry out jungle training in an area which was new to us. A few miles away an airfield had been constructed and Liberator bombers were based there. The camp was well set up with a cinema and on Sunday evenings we went in the back of an open truck to see the films. This was quite something as up until then our chances to visit a cinema were only possible when we visited Colombo - hardly ever. One of the first films shown was 'The Wicked Lady' which was one of the best films made in that era.

Also not far away was Sigiriya, the Lion Rock, so called as the shape of this feature was akin to a sitting lion. This rock rose abruptly some three hundred feet out of the surrounding jungle and had been used as the palace and fortification of one of the earlier rulers centuries ago. There were only two possible means of reaching the top of the rock where the palace together with a large pool had been built. One route was a ladder hanging down over an overhang which passed close by wild bee nests which could be aroused to sting any unwelcome visitor. The other climb up the rock face was guarded by a sentry post and guard room hacked out of the side of the rock. What was so fascinating about this were the beautiful painted drawings of maidens in colourful saris which remain to this day on the guard room walls. This was yet another example of the advanced civilisation of this country.

One evening whilst we were in this area a Liberator got into difficulties after take off and failed to return to the runway. It crashed into the jungle with the loss of all crew members. We helped find the wreckage and cut a track to enable recovery of key items. A very sad episode.

Trincomalee was a natural naval harbour and although the Royal Navy was not using it had to be denied to the Japanese. A Brigade of the Army in Ceylon was tasked to be the garrison to defend the port from any assault by land. A defensive perimeter with wire and obstacles had been constructed for this purpose. 21st East African Brigade took on this role from January to April. 1st NRR was in a static camp with attap huts but with numbers of locals living close by. It was difficult enough as it was for us to try and prevent fly borne disease but now our task was all but impossible and we suffered from dysentery. I awoke one night with a stomach pain and although I rushed to the latrine there was no relief. The journey from my room to the latrine became very familiar and Doc despatched me to the local military hospital.

On discharge I was sent to recuperate in the highlands at Diyatawalla. I had only been there two days when my benign malaria bug struck and the cycle of fever laid me low for the next week. I was to endure this fever roughly once every eight months from now on.

Returning to the battalion I found Tommy, who was a black belt Judo expert, had decided that we should learn the art to help us should we come face to face with a Japanese. We spent a number of evenings before dinner practising this art until one evening an officer delivering a kick broke his ankle against a correct defence posture. The commanding officer was not amused and decreed that Judo would no longer be part of our training!

In spite of living in a highly populated area a cobra was discovered in one of our trenches. Fortunately no one was hurt.

We held an exercise to test our defensive tactics. This was linked to simulated air attacks with the light and heavy anti aircraft guns sited locally putting up a barrage in the skies overhead. After three months we returned to our old camp at Iranamadu just south of Elephant Pass. Life continued with daily training and with the battalion taking part in a number of major exercises. We were learning to use the jungle to our advantage. Acting as enemy on one scheme it became obvious that a platoon outpost was too isolated and could easily be over run and that the company was the essential fighting brick. Having delayed the opposing force throughout the day the commanding officer decided to entice the enemy force into a battalion ambush. After dark each company left the road and moved some eight hundred yards into the jungle so that over a mile of road had been evacuated before the next defensive position. The signal platoon then laid a line through the jungle to each of the rifle companies. That evening it poured with rain however the jungle was so dense we were able to light fires to keep ourselves warm without any danger of being seen from the road.

The next morning the Border Regiment, who were leading the advance, came along the road passing all our companies lying hidden in the jungle. On the order over the telephone line our companies all deployed and assaulted the attacking force from the flank. This debacle caused the exercise director to call an end to this battle.

In June I was posted to relieve an officer in charge of a new African transit camp in Colombo. This camp had been set up to receive drafts coming from East Africa. It had been decided that the

11th East African Division would form in Ceylon round 21st East African Brigade. This division would train for jungle operations and eventually go to Burma.

The camp was on the coast between Colombo and Mount Lavinia and huts had been built for the askari. Two large houses had been requisitioned for use as accommodation for officers and sergeants. A larger reinforcement camp was inland at Kurunegala commanded by a Lieut Colonel who was my commanding officer.

The whole establishment was still being agreed and I spent time visiting Army Headquarters in Colombo seeking equipment, stores and vehicles. The staff sergeant who was my senior NCO managed to pull a fast one on me by overdrawing his pay to a large amount. After about four weeks when he came in to ask for pay I looked at his book and remembering that he had drawn a sum a few days before checked and saw this sum was not entered in the pay book. I paid out the cash noting the date and sum paid for the last three entries. Later I enquired of the paymaster and on checking pay sheets and entries it was found that there were discrepancies. Further investigation proved that he had been making use of three separate pay books. He had been doing this for many months long before I became involved. My memory had served me well and he was prevented from continuing this fraud. There were other incidents where crooks came up with different ideas to defraud the system. Perhaps one of the most imaginative which I heard of was the individual who formed his own unit and drew pay for some thirty fictional characters for a period of time before he was caught.

Apart from this minor problem the transit camp ran smoothly though there was the odd interesting incident when an askari got hold of ammunition for his rifle from one of the guard and threatened to shoot anyone who tried to disarm him. I gathered a team of European Officers and NCOs and we deployed all round the askari making use of the little cover provided by palm trees. As we closed in towards him he pointed his rifle and reloaded, ejecting a live round in the process. He continued to load and reload saying "I have no argument with you Bwanas. I want to go back to Africa". I counted the rounds and as soon as the magazine had been expended I gave the order for us all to rush and seize him which we did. He was placed in the guard room and sent off to hospital for checking. Visiting him there I found he had tried to attack an orderly with a knife and was now being treated as a mental case to be repatriated home. I was to travel back to Africa on the same ship and I am convinced that askari was as sane as anyone else. As we headed back across the seas his whole behaviour changed and he became more settled and normal. I believe that young man had managed to bluff all those who dealt with him.

The 1st NRR even after four years still had a high percentage of prewar regulars and their influence on reinforcements was reflected in the high standards of turnout and behaviour. The same regrettably did not apply to some of the drafts who arrived at the transit camp who had to be shown how to use the bucket latrines. In spite of demonstrations by NCOs simple hygiene was ignored. Instead of making use of the seats these were stood on whilst the askari squatted thereby fouling the seat. Others left the lids open so the sight and smell in the heat of morning inspection was utterly foul with flies breeding like mad.

Finding the latrines in this mess the askari were lined up facing this hygienic horror and lectured again on the correct usage whilst finding out for themselves how disgusting the smell was. They then scrubbed the whole place clean before being dismissed and advised not to misuse their latrine facilities in like manner ever again. This salutary approach paid off as there were no such further incidents.

There were also batches of officers passing through on their way to join their units. We had an excellent cook who managed to produce some first class meals and good use was made of the giant jumbo shrimps. It was here that I first came across the sight of one of these characters cross dressing and trying on a long ladies evening dress. My education was such I had never heard of transvestites and I assumed he was merely preparing for a part in a stage show.

Whilst new units were being ferried across the seas from East Africa a decision was made to grant leave back to their home villages to the askari of 21 East African Brigade. These men had been away from their villages in some cases for nearly four years and many had served The King for some years before the war. It was felt that they should enjoy leave at home before they were sent to fight the Japanese. Some two thousand askari were affected. They were to be escorted by their own officers. I was lucky enough to be included in this party.

This return to East Africa was strange as in October 1941 after attending a course at GilGil I had spent a couple of days in Nairobi where I had met Mary Steele the wife of Gerry Steele of The Bedfords. She had invited me to go to tea with a friend to meet a Mrs McCarthy whose husband had also served in The Bedfords. Having drunk our tea this lady suggested reading the tea leaves. Picking up my cup after a pause she said "You are going to go away and sail across the seas to a far land and you are going to return here again". I did not feel at the time that this forecast meant much as once I left Africa I expected to be on my way home. However two years later this forecast was coming about. Make of it what you like but how did this lady single out this totally unforeseen movement. I do not believe in the superstitious but this prediction was uncanny.

Our leave party sailed from Colombo aboard the 'Nieuw Holland' without any other troop ships. There was a cruiser and a destroyer acting as escort. We felt very secure. Landfall some ten days later was at Dar es Salaam an attractive land locked harbour. The water was deep enough for our ship to drop anchor a few yards off shore whilst men were ferried ashore. Having dropped off the troops who were going to travel south to Northern Rhodesia and Nyasaland the ship sailed for Mombasa with soldiers for Kenya and Uganda.

A troop train took our party to Nairobi where the askari were sent off to their villages. We had been advised to go to the Voluntary Service and the ladies in the office found a tea plantation at Kericho in the highlands which offered to have Felix Sheerman and me to stay for three weeks. The plantation was owned and run by a Colonel Braine a retired Indian Army Doctor. We hired a car and drove the one hundred and sixty odd miles to the estate.

We could not have been treated more hospitably the colonel and his lady were quite charming and made us feel very much part of the family. We were shown round the tea estate and the factory and the colonel explained the whole process of producing the finished packages from the selected leaves plucked from the fields. He even suggested that we might be interested in joining him working the estate after the war. The estate was some six thousand feet above sea level. During the day the temperature was pleasantly hot with little humidity all very different from Ceylon. At night the temperature dropped rapidly and there were log fires in the dining and sitting rooms. We also needed ample blankets to keep warm in our beds. The leave passed all too quickly and we bade a sad farewell to our kind host and hostess and set off back to Nairobi. On the last few miles Felix drove past a long convoy of vehicles which were throwing up clouds of thick red dust which got up my nostrils and affected my breathing. This was to have an affect a few days later when I was in hospital for an operation.

Our askari had yet to return from their leave in their villages so as I was having trouble with an ossifying ganglion on a wrist I reported sick. After inspection the surgeon decided I needed to have an operation so I found myself in hospital in Nairobi. The ward was filled mostly with officers undergoing minor operations for such problems as infected tonsils. Pentathol was a new drug which was in use and individuals coming round from their operations behaved as though they were highly inebriated. This caused much amusement to the other occupants who looked forward to this entertainment whenever another inmate returned from the operating theatre.

The time for my departure arrived and I was sent off with a great cheer and wheeled off to the operating theatre. The anesthetist seeing that I was having difficulty with my breathing ruled out the use of a general anesthetic. Instead I was to be immobilised down the left side of my body. I was now able to watch what was going on. A massive syringe, which might well have been used on a horse, was thrust into me near my left shoulder down into the upper body injecting the numbing fluid. The surgeon then set about opening up the skin along the side of my arm - it sounded just like ripping a sheet apart. He then proceeded to chisel away at the offending growth. Meantime a doctor seated to my right was timing and writing down every action as it took place. The operating theatre was hot and time passed by and I must have appeared a little restless, in fact I had been lying there for over two hours. I was asked if I had any problem to which I replied that I was very thirsty. The surgeon apologised and rested whilst I was given a sip of water.

The operation complete I was wheeled back to the ward where all my friends were alerted by my return and sat up to enjoy my return to consciousness. They felt very cheated when it was evident I was not under the influence of the drug. The surgeon had done a great job and after a few days I was posted to a recuperative hostel on the outskirts of Nairobi.

The daily routine was very relaxed and I was allowed to go into town to meet up with Felix Sheerman at Torrs for drinks with other friends. We had got in touch with the friends we had made in the FANYs during our earlier stay in Kenya and managed to enjoy a few lunch and evening parties and were introduced to new female friends. This led to invitations to parties at their homes. This break from our solitary monastic form of living was a most welcome change. We also enjoyed meeting some of the nursing sisters who were waiting to come over to Ceylon with an East African Hospital. We arranged to get in touch with them when they arrived in Ceylon.

After two weeks I was declared fit for duty and was ordered to go to Mombasa to board a freight ship with Felix and ten other officers as apparently our services were needed back in Ceylon. Not before we had celebrated Christmas with some of the FANYs.

The ship was collecting freight from coastal ports in East Africa to transport to Ceylon and India. We sailed from Mombasa and cruised down the coast to Tanga where we tied up for four days and took more freight on board before setting out on our own without any escort across the Indian Ocean. To say the journey was eventful is no exaggeration as the ship could not make much more than eight knots. It also had the habit of breaking down every so often. The sound of clanging metal whilst the engineers hammered some piece of ironmongery into place with the ship wallowing on the tide and a very large shark circling around by the stern did not cheer us up much. This repair activity recurred three times during the course of this voyage and the noise after dark seemed even louder.

The Captain was full of enthusiasm and was more than delighted to show off all the latest gear to be used against enemy ship or aircraft. One afternoon we had a full brocks benefit with all systems and guns firing.

The breakdowns had delayed our time of arrival at Colombo and we arrived after the boom had been closed for the night. The ship was ordered to return to sea and cruise up and down off the coast until dawn. We were in our bunks sleeping when the alarm bells sounded. The gun crews rushed to their stations and we donned lifebelts and stood by the rails. Our ship was manoeuvring to allow the guns at the stern to engage a submarine which we could see on the surface. This submarine had signalled our ship to "Heave to, and not to send out any radio messages". The response of our splendidly 'Gung Ho' Captain was to take on this threat. Fortunately for all concerned before any shots were fired by either party it was discovered that the submarine was friendly. It was returning from patrol late and had run out of the correct challenging codes.

We followed the submarine through the boom next morning after daylight thankful that neither our Captain nor the Captain of the submarine had opened fire.

Felix returned to 1st NRR but I was posted to a training company with the Divisional Reinforcement Battalion. Approximately two weeks later a convoy from Mombasa with divisional reinforcements arrived. Something had happened on the voyage and all we knew was that the convoy had been attacked. A blackout was imposed on discussing what had happened but it was obviously serious. Johnnie Johnson, who had been Headquarters Company Commander at Horowupotana, was on board one of the ships and was now running the Divisional Transit Camp in Colombo. Some time later I heard that the 'Khedive Ismael', one of the larger ships in the convoy had been hit amidships by two torpedoes in the early afternoon. The ship broke in two and sank rapidly before many of the passengers or crew could get off. Among the passengers were the nurses of the hospital, and a party of WRENs and FANYs. The only ship with women aboard. Also aboard was 301 East African Artillery Regiment who were due to become the regiment in support of 21st East African Brigade.

There were I believe only six girls rescued. One WREN was in her cabin when the torpedoes struck. The ship sank so quickly there was no chance of trying to get to the deck so she struggled to scramble out through the port hole. This was no easy task and she found herself going down below the water with the ship. A Lascar sailor seeing what was happening dived down underwater and grasping her hands managed to heave her out through the port hole. They both made the surface and were picked up. Only one of the East African FANYs was rescued and only four of the complement of nursing sisters survived. Among the FANYs who were drowned was Kay Le Poer Trench who had invited us to her parents home when we were on leave.

The destroyer escort sank the very large Japanese submarine which had made this successful attack on the convoy. (Nearly fifty years later I met a lady who had been married to a British Gunner Sergeant who had been drowned in this action. I have the notification papers she was sent informing her husband was missing and later that he was drowned at sea).

Although this incident was highly sensitive at the time so many individuals were involved that scraps of news got around. As an example the surviving WREN was coming to CEYLON where her husband was with the KAR which is how the story of her escape became known. Johnnie Johnston had been on one of the other ships in the convoy and confirmed the suddenness of the attack and rapid break up of the ship. No mention was made of the units involved or estimates of fatal casualties nor were these aspects ever talked about.

It was a shattering piece of news as it affected so many in our Division. We had more personal reasons to have a go at the 'Japs'.

Chapter Twelve

1944 - Ceylon and move to India

Arriving back in Ceylon we were treated as first line reinforcements and posted to the 11th East African Division Reinforcement Battalion. I found myself with a Cinyanja speaking company which was on jungle training near Puttalam. After two weeks we marched back to the battalion location at Kurunegala awaiting posting instructions. New orders had been issued which decreed that temporary rank would be forfeited on posting. Orders came through for my return to 1st NRR together with four other officers and a party of askari. We set out having removed our extra pips from our shoulder lapels. This was something which the askari did not understand as they were sure we had committed some serious offence! Even worse was the battalion second in command inspected us before departure to ensure compliance with the rules. On arrival with the battalion I was promptly ordered to dress properly and put on my third pip!

Shortly after rejoining the battalion was visited by Lord Louis Mountbatten who had been appointed 'Supremo' in the Far East. He told us that we had been selected to continue the fight in Burma during the monsoon rains as he felt we were fully capable of taking on this task. Previously both the Japanese and British forces had eased up on operations during this time of year. He had all the charisma which marks a natural leader and his address was well received.

The emphasis was on further training to improve the techniques we had been practising over the years since arriving in Ceylon in 1942 and there were numerous battalion and higher formation exercises. Shooting skills were honed and African NCOs armed with the Thompson Sub Machine Gun acquired the skill to fire single aimed shots with the safety catch set on automatic. We were not to know that our Thompsons would all be withdrawn for use in the European Theatre of Operations and that we would receive the Sten gun in lieu. This exchange took place after we had arrived in India and our views of Higher Command were unprintable.

Commanding a company on a major exercise I felt unwell after two days in the field and feared the oncome of a bout of malaria. I reported to the M.O. who sent me to the Field Ambulance who in turn sent me further back to a Casualty Clearing Station. This was a Belgian unit and I was fascinated to hear all the askari orderlies speaking French. In turn I was sent back to a hospital in Kandy where although my temperature was rising it was not following the usual pattern for malarial fever. The temperature rose and stayed at a set height for a while before rising another degree. There was no rise of temperature to a peak followed by a rapid drop and further surges until a normal rate was reached. Approximately every forty eight hours my temperature would rise by a degree and stay at that level until the next increase. After a week my temperature was well over 103% and I felt exceedingly cold and incapable of moving my limbs. The nurses wrapped me up in vast numbers of blankets and dosed me with aspirin which caused me to sweat profusely and by morning my temperature was normal. It was assumed I had suffered a mild attack of Tick Typhus as the battalion had been exercising in an area where cattle roamed and I had had an infected bite on the leg. Whatever it was it was not something I would wish to experience again.

The 81st West African Division was operating in Burma and the battalion was invited to send an officer on attachment to learn at close hand about operations against the Japs. It was also decreed that all seconds in command of infantry battalions would be regular soldiers. A Major Birkbeck arrived to take over from Leonard Bagshaw who returned to command "A" Company. Birkbeck left us after a month or so to take command of 11 K.A.R and Major Beresford came in his place.

We were told that we would have to back pack our necessities once we were committed. This meant a reappraisal of what we needed to have with us in the way of clothing and ammunition and personal necessities. The small pack was discarded in favour of the large pack. This was quite an increase in the weight to be carried and we would need to adjust to get used to the new load. On the initial route marches everyone found the new load a strain but gradually we adjusted and it became a normal part of life. This adaptation was taking place in high humidity which did not aid things.

Further exercises followed with our artillery firing live rounds over our heads. The sound of artillery shells crashing into the jungle a few yards ahead was frightening as it was difficult to determine the line of fall of shot through the foliage. Very different from artillery support in open terrain.

A new Brigade arrived in Ceylon from East Africa. We handed over our vehicles so that the locals would not realise we had moved to another camp miles away. Everything was being done to confuse the enemy. The battalion sailed from Colombo aboard 'HMT Etna' on June 30th. Once we had embarked we were told to wear our hats in the same way as the West Africans with the side flap down. On the voyage officers were taught to distinguish the Japanese hieroglyphics for Armour, Artillery, Engineers and Infantry. We were taught to read numerals so as to be able to understand and interpret the markings on the identity disc of a Japanese soldier. In first aid we were taught how to use phials containing morphine and the frequency of use for a wounded man. All this training was invaluable once we were in contact with the enemy.

Our convoy disembarked at Chittagong on the 9th of July and the company was left to check and off load all the battalion heavy baggage. This was then left in store and was the last we saw of it until after we came out of the line. This task took two days when we entrained for Fenua and a ten mile march to the battalion concentration area. It poured with rain and we all got soaked. The askari were singing their marching songs. Our route passed through an Indian village and a local Indian rushed out recognising the language and began talking to the askari. This incident was reported as it was important to prevent the disclosure of the arrival of the East African Division. We were told the wretched Indian was interned until this news was no longer classified.

Arriving at the battalion location we set up camp and started a rigorous training programme prior to deployment. We worked through the day and into the night every day of the week. Sunday afternoon was time to deal with administration principally filling in forms to send back to Africa for askari to purchase another cow. It was a time of feverish activity. As second in command to Tommy Tompson in 'D' Company my task was to train section leaders in patrolling and battle drills.

One evening an undercurrent of despondency affected the whole battalion and this sense of foreboding continued through the next twenty four hours. It was an uncanny atmosphere and one could almost smell a feeling of grave concern. Tommy tried by talking to the NCOs to find an explanation but there was a veil of silence. It was as though the bonds between the Officers and askari no longer existed. All efforts to break down this communication barrier were of no avail and the atmosphere was heavy. It was obvious something was afoot but no explanation was forthcoming.

We were as usual feeding in company messes which were somewhat cramped into a one hundred and eighty pound tent. On the second evening after this strange feeling of being cut off in full communication with our askari a shot rang out in 'C' Company Officers mess. The Kenyan servant of Major Wilkinson had taken a violent dislike to Duncan Haines one of the officers. He stole his officers shot gun and bursting into the tent after dark fired into the group sitting tightly around a central table. The gun was knocked out of his hands before he could fire the second barrel but his first shot critically wounded Duncan who died from his injuries. The servant was arrested and sent away for trial but as we had moved on we never heard the end result. Now that the incident was over the whole atmosphere in the battalion reverted to normality. It was obvious the Africans were aware something was being planned but not sufficiently aware to be sure enough to justifiably lay an accusation.

This was the first incident of this kind in the four years I had been with the battalion. The culprit was not one of our askari but a civilian servant of a different tribe who had followed his employee to war. He had already left his homeland and spent months in Ceylon. He now found himself transported further by sea to another strange land. All this undoubtedly preyed on his mind and the discipline required to accept rebuke was more than his temperament could stand. He had no members of his own tribe to confide in. He must have felt horribly alone. The askari were not only from other tribes but they all spoke different languages. This issue raises the wisdom of allowing a civilian of a different ethic group to follow his peace time employer as a civilian batman.

After three weeks the battalion moved to rail head at Fenua at the start of a long journey via rail, river boat and road to relieve the 26th Indian Division on the Chindwin Front in Central Burma. We spent twenty four hours at the station and relaxed by taking part in an inter company swimming competition in a large water tank. It was here we heard of the capture of Rome. The next morning we entrained and set out on our journey to the front.

Chapter Thirteen

Move to the Burmese Frontier

The battalion now set off on yet another long journey by rail, ferry and boat which was to spread over a week before arriving near Imphal (Map 5).

The whole of the first day was spent travelling North by train passing Comilla and eventually detraining in the evening at a Ferry alongside a vast expanse of open water. The ferry took about two hours to take us to a quay where we were met by Movements Staff and hustled to a transit camp for the rest of the night. Next morning with another company beside ourselves we boarded a river steamer and set off up the Bramaputra. This journey was slow but steady and very restful as the boat glided through the water and the scenery passed by. There were cattle and villagers tending their fields and the landscape was well watered and lush. We travelled in reasonable comfort and the officers all had a cabin to themselves so we just relaxed and enjoyed the break after our hectic three weeks of training. It was two days and nights before we arrived at Gauhati to spend another night in a very makeshift transit camp before entraining for Dimapur.

This rail journey was memorable for the incredibly beautiful views enjoyed of the snow capped foothills of the Himalaya range. The height of these mountains was breathtaking and the sight of the snow glistening in the bright sunlight quite wonderful. It was all the more memorable as this was not a sight to be seen as a single vision as this picture of loveliness extended over many miles of the journey. It was awe inspiring. All such delights pass and after dark we came to Dimapur and detrained to go to yet another transit camp.

Dimapur was a base area and we were able to go to see a film at the cinema that evening. There were numerous staff officers and those responsible for managing the logistic tail. There were also a few ATS and Nurses the last females we would see for the next five months, we were about to revert to our monastic life once more. The next day part of the battalion set off in transport but we had to await until more vehicles were available to lift us. That day it poured with rain in the only way it can rain in the tropics and our camp was awash with water. Such was the state of things I managed to walk into an unmarked sump pit which was immersed below the water line and indistinguishable. Luckily I scrambled out before sinking below knee level and without too much garbage on my clothing!

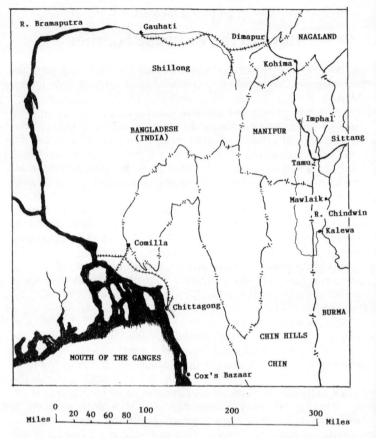

Burma - The Central Front 1944

Map 5

The next day transport arrived for the company and off we set up the road from Dimapur to Kohima the mountain station where the Japanese thrust towards India had been held and defeated. The road climbed steeply winding its way up a narrow valley but we could not really appreciate the surrounding scenery as the cloud base was below the mountain tops. Some two hours later we reached a crest where the landscape resembled a scene from Flanders in the First World War. The ground had been churned up by shell fire with innumerable craters and jagged and torn trees. There were trenches along the ridges with but a few yards separating friend from foe. A scene of total devastation which made us wonder at the feats of endurance of those who had fought in this battle.

Our road wound its way through this battle ground precariously hugging the side of the mountains which rose precipitously above our heads and as precipitously fell away on the other flank to a valley many hundreds of feet below. The mist and low cloud persisted and at times we were caught in a damp form of drizzle. As we progressed on our way we passed groups of vehicles with Indian troops parked alongside the road to let our small convoy pass. These were members of 26 Indian Division which our Division was relieving in the line. Our route was beginning to descend slowly from the heights around Kohima and in the late afternoon we pulled into an open area to camp for the night. This area had earlier been a Japanese position and next morning we studied the layout taking care that we did not accidentally set off any booby trap. We had to wait until the afternoon before moving off again to allow transport returning from Imphal to Dimapur use of the road which could only carry a single line of traffic at any one time.

This last phase into Imphal saw the road breaking out of the mountain ranges into the more open territory of the Imphal Plain. This was an area of flat lands surrounded by a series of hill features which had been used by the defending forces to hold the Japanese attacks aimed at Imphal. We passed a number of infantry and tank units camped alongside the road before setting up camp about three miles from Palel on the road to Tamu on the frontier.

We remained in this camp from 11th to the 20th August continuing our training. We had received 'Sten Guns' to replace the 'Thompson Sub Machine Gun' and were bitterly disappointed as the Sten was very different in construction and did not pack the same punch. Our company looked towards the RAF airfield at Palel and we watched the Hurricanes taking off on their operational missions with as many as twenty four aircraft in a sortie.

Tommy Tompson was taken ill and evacuated so I found myself temporally in command of 'D' Company when we received orders to move. Next morning transport arrived but some of the transport which should have come to me had been purloined. As a result I set off having to leave half the company behind. Passing the airfield at Palel the route climbed steeply for over one thousand feet and wound through a series of crests at a place named Tegnoupal. There was little to determine whether or not there had been any habitation there as each of the peaks were scoured with trenches ringed with lines and lines of barbed wire defences. These were the outer perimeter defences during the battle for Imphal and again there was ample evidence that heavy fighting had taken place there.

Brigade Headquarters were moved forward on foot and we heard that a Staff captain had collapsed from heat exhaustion climbing this ascent.

Arriving at Battalion Headquarters I reported in and was given permission to return in my jeep with orders to get more transport for the remaining troops.

Arriving back in Imphal about 2100hrs I found Divisional Headquarters and bearded the Staff officer responsible for managing unit moves in his office. "We provided sufficient transport for your battalion you should not need any more". I explained that the only transport which had arrived at my company camp was four vehicles short and I needed four trucks to take these soldiers to rejoin the battalion. Eventually I was given a note to take to a Transport company. It took time to find the company office in the dark and more time to encourage the officer to let me have the four trucks I needed. Having acquired my transport I led the trucks to the company lines to find that everyone was abed and asleep so they had to be roused. With a great deal of muttering everyone was loaded with all their kit and the convoy set off behind my jeep arriving back at the battalion location at about 0100hrs.

Reporting to Tony Fawssett the adjutant I heard the battalion was to set off on foot at 0300hrs. He gave permission for my party to lie in until 0600 hrs and follow the marching party in the transport. Awaking at 0245hrs I dressed and fell in with the other half of 'D' Company. We were due to march to a staging area some eighteen miles further down the road and by setting off in the dark we would cover more than half the distance before the sun became stinkingly hot. The battalion had also selected a long halt site to coincide with the end of a four hour stint of marching. A tarpaulin was erected there and filled with drinking water so that everyone could refill water bottles. Water drill was such that lips could be wet after one hour and a drink could be taken at subsequent hourly halts. It was up to everyone to keep sufficient reserve to replenish water loss during the march until a final quaffing of thirst before refilling water bottles. Everyone was required to take a salt tablet daily in addition to the anti malarial mepocrine. We made good progress as initially our march was down hill to cross a bridge over a stream at the bottom of the valley before climbing a further range of mountains on the far side.

The long halt was reached and besides a replenishment of water we eat a cooked breakfast before relaxing whilst the road was used by transport columns heading back towards Imphal. It was evident that the Division was reliant on this narrow track for all its supplies and that management and timing of the use of the route was a key factor in our future operations. The road was free to us again at about 1100hrs and we marched uphill through the heat to the next staging post where I found Lieutenant Ferraby camped with the remainder of the company.

That afternoon I was called to see Pat Glass the commanding officer and given orders to set out at 0300hrs with the company. My task was to march forward through Tamu on the frontier some thirteen miles down the road to a ferry site on the Ye Yu river on the Sittang road at Hessin and protect the ferry. I returned to the company and gave out orders to the platoon commanders for the next morning.

We arose in darkness and set off in a light rain which became a downpour as we marched so we all got very wet. As quickly as it had started the rain ceased and with the rising of the sun we dried out very quickly. Passing through Tamu we could see the signs of battle and a number of scattered Japanese corpses beside the road and alongside some of the local houses. These dead were burnt using flame throwers soon after to prevent the outbreak of disease.

Our route was now on the level passing through close jungle at times. Our General 'Fluffy Fowkes' had acquired a reputation as a firebrand during the Abyssinian campaign and we all knew that he would jump down the throat of any officer who was not alert and on the ball. The advice was never to let the General have the first word. Should he appear and ask a question the rest of his visit would be a disaster for the unit involved.

The company was having a routine break beside the road at the end of the hour when I heard a Jeep coming and saw the flag on its' bonnet denoting it was the General. I stood to attention as the jeep came to a halt and saluted. I then immediately gave my name and unit and where I had come from, where I was going and what my orders were. The General stayed in his seat, answered my salute and saying "Well done" motored off. Another of our companies at another location a few miles further along the route to Sittang did not notice the General appear. He asked an askari where his officer was and once that unfortunate man arrived demanded a full tour of the position. There was little that pleased the General and the officer caught the full blast of his wrath.

After the break we set off once more and reached the Ye Yu river after a further forty minutes. The river was about eighty feet wide and fast flowing. The ferry had been constructed to carry vehicles across when the water was too deep at the ford. The company position was on the enemy side of the river and had been a Japanese defended post with numerous tunnels and trenches. Our forward troops were fighting some twenty miles ahead and had passed through this area some ten days earlier. One of the extraordinary aspects of this phase of operations was that we kept finding dead Japanese soldiers all around in the jungle where the individual had retreated when feeling ill when his unit was withdrawing. The Japanese soldier feeling unwell had sat leaning against a tree and too weak to move died where he sat down to rest. His officers were not concerned about trying to care for the wounded or ill soldier. Many hundreds died in this manner during the retreat of the Japanese forces from Kohima and Imphal. Perhaps the strangest case was finding a dead Japanese soldier within the boundaries of our position at the ferry site.

This line of communication task was not very exciting. To keep on our toes I sent our patrols to beat the bush in all directions around our position to visit any local village and to seek information on the enemy. There was some compensation in that senior staff officers passed through to visit the forward brigade and would join us in our small mess for a cup of tea whilst waiting in the queue to cross the ferry. We would then hear in general terms what our role would be in the weeks ahead.

A week or so later I was ordered to detach a patrol to guard a position on another route leading into Tamu. Visiting this platoon one afternoon with the African CSM I arrived as an askari came rushing in from his sentry post foaming at the mouth, divesting himself of his equipment and throwing down his rifle. I was informed that the soldier was under the spell of a witch doctor and that he would die. Further enquiries showed that the askari had in fact received a long letter from his wife in Northern Rhodesia that afternoon. The CSM said the letter was couched in sweet terms but that the wife wished to get rid of her husband. She had therefore used a witch doctor who had created a spell which was incorporated in the ink used. As the letter took time to read the reader would be worse affected the longer the letter. Although the askari was in Burma thousands of miles from his village in Africa it was evident the man who was foaming at the mouth and immobile was completely under the influence of the witch doctors spell. I got on the line to our Regimental Medical Officer, Doc Wellstood, and asked his advice as I did not want to loose a good soldier in this odd way. He told me he had had a few similar cases referred to him but that there was no medicine he could prescribe which would have any effect. He suggested I got hold of the senior NCO of the same tribe to sort out this problem. As the CSM was of the same tribe I told him that I was not prepared to have a soldier of Kingi George on active service incapacitated in this way and he was to sort things out.

The CSM promptly issued a series of orders and askari rushed into the bush returning with a variety of leaves and roots. These were mashed up into a pulp to which was added the ashes of the offending letter which had been burnt. The whole foul concoction was then forcibly fed to the recumbent soldier who seemed to shudder and then fall into a deep sleep. I left the platoon having been assured that when the soldier woke up he would be quite normal and would have no recollection of any of these happenings. This is in fact what happened. The soldier woke up next morning smiling and fit for duty.

This tale is told as it is so strange and unless I had experienced the event at first hand I would have thought such curses unbelievable. It is amazing that the spell was not weakened by the vast distance between the witch doctor and the recipient. It is an event which I still remember vividly.

Whilst visiting this detached platoon I was taken round a number of huts in the jungle close by which had been part of the Japanese support base during their invasion of India earlier in the year. There was evidence of their comfort units and discarded feminine attire together with reams of papers. They had withdrawn at such a pace they had not had time to destroy documents.

It was not long after this that the company was ordered to move to a camp at Milestone 3 on the Kabaw Valley road a few miles South from Tamu. The area alongside the road where we camped was primarily teak forests which had become overgrown by encroaching jungle in many places. There were some clearer areas. It was here that we saw a teak tree some twenty feet high shaped as a phallic symbol close by where the local inhabitants had set up their wood cutting tools. We were to see other such carvings as we progressed down the valley.

The rains were such that the road was becoming impassable for traffic. Once again we found ourselves cutting down trees to lay corrugated tracks on the road way. This task was boring though essential. It was relieved as close by was the grass strip airfield where a 'Spitfire' had crash landed after being shot down by the American bombers it had been sent to escort. It was possible to sit in the cockpit and get a feel of the restricted space for the pilot. We also found weapons both friendly and enemy which had been discarded in the battles which had see sawed up and down this valley since 1942.

Gillies Shields arrived back from hospital and took over command of the company so I reverted to second in command. The battalion was now gathering along the road and with the rest of 21st (East African) Infantry Brigade, commanded by Brigadier McNab, was in reserve.

Lieut Colonel H.P.L. Glass (Sherwood Foresters) was in command and he had been with the battalion for eighteen months. Major Peter Beresford was Second in Command. There had been minimal change in those commanding rifle companies all of whom had seen service from the outbreak of the war.

'A' Major Leonard Bagshaw   .
'B' Major Charles Grieve
'C' Major Wilkinson
'D' Captain Gillies Shields

Of the remaining officers some had been commissioned before the war, others in the initial output from OCTU, and the most junior had at least three years commissioned service with the battalion. The battalion had lived and trained and fought over many months. Changes in personalities had been minimal and all ranks were at a high state of training. The askari knew their officers and had their nick names for them. There was no problem of communication due to language. We were part of a pre war regular brigade to be strengthened by a fourth regular battalion when the 1/5th KAR was brought under command. We looked forward to the challenge ahead.

Chapter Fourteen

Burma - Initial Moves

We had been working on road improvements for about a week when orders came through for an advance party to set out the next day led by Major Beresford the battalion second in command. Early next morning I joined this party with my batman. We marched for some four hours and arrived at Brigade Headquarters at Milestone 16. They were packing up to move on and we were to take over their site.

Our progress down the valley had crossed four or five streams in deep chaungs and there were further streams ahead. The day had started fresh and dry but quickly turned to a regular downpour. We were glad that the structures for our camp had already been built which meant our ground sheets could be set to protect our blanket and mosquito net. This rain continued for another day by which time we were isolated and cut off from the battalion by the raging torrents flowing down the chaungs.

As soon as the weather improved we set off early one morning and doubled back some nine miles along the track with Major Beresford leading us to collect rations. A wire rope had been erected across the water obstacle which separated us from the battalion and our rations were drawn over. Having collected the rations we then ran back to our camp. This was all part of our improving standards of fitness.

As the weather cleared we felled trees to make a bridge over the chaung some four hundred yards down the track. On the far side was an open space with tents of a Field Ambulance on the jungle edge. This open area was used over the next few days as a dropping zone for 'Dakota' aircraft dropping our supplies from the air. These RAF pilots were remarkable as they flew over the mountains during the monsoon weather through turbulent conditions and ensured we received our munitions and rations.

As the heavy rain subsided the water in the chaung became clear and fresh so we used to walk down and strip off for a bath. As I was cleaning up one day a Dakota appeared overhead and circling came in for a drop. Imagine my consternation when I saw the plane was flying straight towards me with heavy sacks being pushed out of the side doors. I could see and hear the thud of the sacks hitting the ground as the string of flying sacks headed towards me. There was little I could do but move as fast as possible to one side whilst a sack splashed into the water a few feet away.

These days with the advance party enabled each of us from different companies to get to know each other better. Major Beresford was a born leader with a wry sense of humour. He was affectionately known as 'Uncle Drunkle' as his earlier drinking exploits had preceded his arrival with the battalion. He carried a small pocket chess set with him so this was used after dark. We were also able to play cards though we usually turned in by 2100hrs at the latest as we rose at 0545hrs.

It has been said that warfare is ninety per cent boredom and one per cent sheer terror. Actions in contact are certainly frightening and any man who denies fear has not been in action. We had so many interesting activities to fill our time when we were not in the line that there was never a dull moment. One afternoon we set off to see where our small stream running down the chaung near us went to. Naturally we carried our arms and moved in a loose formation. After walking a couple of miles we came to a Burmese village with the occupants living as though there were no outside activities affecting their living. We tried to show we wished them all well and they must have wondered whether our armies would yet again withdraw back up the valley before the Japanese forces.

The village was perched on the banks of a fast flowing river and we all dived in for a refreshing swim. Returning along another pathway to our main track we came across another dead Jap soldier sitting alongside the track.

On another morning I was asked to walk forward to Brigade Headquarters some nine miles away to gather the latest information as to what was happening at the front. It took about two hours to reach Headquarters where I visited the Brigade Major and the Intelligence Officer and was briefed on the latest actions. I returned home and was back before mid-day.

Eventually after about ten days on our own the road had dried out sufficiently for the battalion to move up to its next position at Milestone 23 and I rejoined 'D' Company. We were still in reserve and kept ourselves occupied by training and by sending out deep patrols into the jungle around us. I took such a patrol out and spent most of the first day cutting a path through the jungle to link up with a track indicated on the map. We spent the night camped on a dry river bed. During the patrol we had noticed some deep pools in this river with plenty of fish. We decided to return and fish with the odd grenade. It was as well we did. Arming a couple of grenades we dropped them into the pools and waited for the detonation and a hoped for collection of dazed fish. There was no explosion after the five seconds delay so we threw in two more, again no result. Not one of this batch of twelve grenades exploded when armed so we reported the batch of detonators as being useless. The batch was withdrawn and we received a further issue which worked. So our fishing experience was opportune as otherwise we could well have used these fuses against the enemy with very negative results.

It was while we were at this site I met up with Colonel Dennis Rossiter of the Bedfords who had been my Adjutant in France in 1939. He was now in charge of welfare for the East African Forces and had been visiting the forward troops. We gossiped before he went on his way.

The battalion now received orders to join up with the rest of our brigade which had struck off through a range of mountains with the task of capturing Mawlaik on the Chindwin. The 1st 4th K.A.R. were leading the advance and having cleared the heights were pushing the enemy back. Warfare in Burma was a matter of fighting from peak to peak and the ground and jungle helped the enemy to fight where he chose.

The march forward was no more than nine miles and the whole battalion camped beside a broad river. The Pioneer Platoon Sergeant set off an anti tank mine upstream and not only did the catch provide a mass of food for the battalion it also fed the local village. Next day crossing the river we faced a very steep haul for two hours up the side of the range. Halting after three hours we were given a cooked meal by 'A' Company which was camped in an open area half way up the mountain. We set off after this break and I led the company advance party setting off about ten minutes ahead of the remainder. The track climbed steadily winding its way up and up twisting and turning with the folds of the terrain. The going was heavy as the track was churned up into a mud bath by boots and mules. The mud rose above one's ankles with every pace taken. This effort was very tiring and needed bloody mindedness to press on and not slow down. After some two hours climbing the pass at the top of this range was reached and the descent began. This was a happy relief after the agony of the climb.

Our camp site for the night was an old company position so we did not have to dig trenches or prepare sleeping areas. This was fortunate as the company followed in a few minutes after us. There was just time to cook an evening meal before dark and close down for the night. The practice was to mount sentries, everyone else stayed in a shallow protective trench next to their trench. Each trench was dug for two men and there was no movement outside the trenches at all after dark.

Our march continued next morning and it was not long before we came to an area alongside the path which had been cleared of trees. This was the brigade dropping zone and Brigade Headquarters and the Field Ambulance were round its perimeter. Our battalion position was just across the valley in the jungle and we now dug a company perimeter defensive position. The 1st 2nd K.A.R. were a short distance further down the valley with the 1st 4th preparing for an attack on the Japanese at Leik Hill. Although we were some two thousand yards behind the forward troops we still experienced the Japanese nuisance patrols. These patrols would roam round inside our positions after dark rattling tins, calling out 'Tommy where are you, and Tommy come here' in an effort to draw fire and so pin point our positions. They often carried a torch and one could watch this light moving around between the trees. We sat still ready with a bayonet should the enemy come within striking distance. These patrols prevented any relaxation and were a clever form of harassment. Our enemy was well practised at the art.

We were now receiving British Army compo rations and it was amusing to see our askari mix tinned peaches with potatoes and bully beef in their mess tin. They thought this new type of food was great.

The attack on Leik Hill by 1st 4th K.A.R. was supported by the 3" mortars of all the battalions as well as the Indian Mountain Battery which was with our brigade. This battery had been provided to replace the East African Artillery Regiment which had been lost at sea coming from Africa to Ceylon. After a fierce fight with individuals clambering up almost vertical slopes the feature was captured. The 3" mortars of all the battalions were providing fire support. Ken Mortlock the 1st NRR Mortar Officer was wounded in the attack on Leik Hill whilst taking part in the attack. The 1st 2nd K.A.R. now took over the lead and progressed forward to the next ridge where they found the Japanese well dug in in a strong position. Preliminary skirmishes showed the position was well developed and a night attack was decided upon. At the same time 1st N.R.R. was to make a wide encircling move round the right flank to come in on another range of hills astride the track some five miles further on.

We had been in our reserve position three days and watched the 'Dakota' aircraft fly down the valley and throw out the sacks of sugar and rice and drop their parachutes on the Dropping Zone (DZ). The sacks would hit the ground with a thud and bounce heavily before coming to a halt. It was essential the DZ was cleared of troops before the drop began.

The Field Ambulance was set up at the end of this DZ so should an aircraft start its drop a little late the Field Ambulance tents were in the line of strike. The inevitable happened and a sack landed on the operating table killing the wretched patient and one of the team of doctors. Another quirk of war.

Chapter Fifteen

The Battle for Mawlaik

Brigadier McNab who commanded 21st Infantry Brigade now planned a wide encircling movement to cut in behind the Japanese positions on the massive bulk of the Sadwin cliffs which were holding up the 1st 2nd K.A.R. 1st N.R.R. were to carry out this manoeuvre with the aim of cutting the Japanese lines of communication at a village named Kun.

The next morning the battalion set off moving off the track into the bush. No matter how careful one is a whole battalion moving in single file is bound to leave quite a foot print. However the rule of picking up any litter was rigidly followed. We were marching light carrying two American 'K' ration packs each. This pack provided the soldier with three meals for the day. However so as to carry extra ammunition we were to make the rations last for six days by which time it was planned we would have completed the task and secured a safe dropping zone for further supplies. Accordingly we teamed up in parties of three and made do with a third of a ration for each meal.

The march took most of the first day as at times the jungle was so thick a path had to be hacked out to allow forward progress. The route was across country with precipitous slopes to be negotiated. By evening we had come to within two miles of our objective which we were to attack the following morning. We settled down in a river bed for the night. Our defences were not tested and our presence remained unknown to the enemy.

Our objective was a ridge which the track to Mawlaik cut through some three miles away from another ridge where the 1st 2nd K.A.R. were fighting. Two companies were to seize the ridge with another in support whilst 'D' Company was to cut the track between the ridge and the 1st 2nd K.A.R. (Map 6).

We dumped our large back packs in a secure area so we could move unencumbered into our assault and set off into the low scrub bush at the time decreed. For a while all was quiet then sounds of firing came from our flank where the remainder of the battalion were. We continued our advance and cut the track but found no enemy.

The ridge had been seized after a small skirmish with a few Japanese who managed to kill Leonard Bagshaw the company commander of 'A' Company. The only other casualty was Pat Glass who had been injured by a grenade and had to be evacuated. Major Beresford now assumed command and Eric Sharman took over 'A'

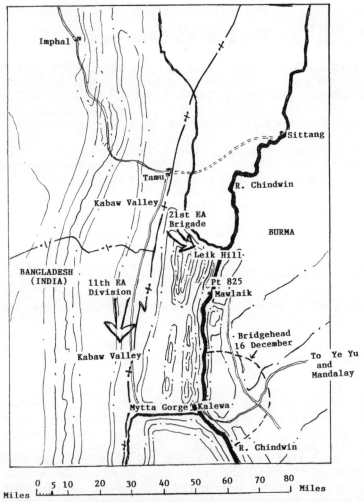

11th East African Division - Kabaw Valley and Chindwin   **Map 6**
August - December 1944

Company. The battalion now took up a perimeter defence with 'D' Company at the foot of the slope protecting the rear.

The ridge astride the track to Mawlaik overlooked a valley. On the far side some twelve hundred yards away stood another craggy ridge between our present position and the River Chindwin with a peak at each end, Point 752 at the northern end and about three quarters of a mile at the southern end nearest Mawlaik was Point 825. The face towards the battalion was steep and precipitous. A series of patrols were sent out all of which suffered casualties from Japanese posts dominating the ridge. Sgt Van Plaster was killed on one of these reconnaissance patrols.

One patrol which went out at night decided to adopt the Japanese tactics of inhibiting sleep by shouting, banging tins and throwing grenades close below a known enemy position. This tactic paid off as after less than an hour the enemy shouted 'Tommy go away' and eventually before the party ended they were howling and screaming with fright. After this incident we were not troubled any further by Japanese night patrols.

One of the regulations in force meant that all Europeans were required to 'black out' for all operations. There was no camouflage paint available to us so we used rifle oil and charcoal. This mess was smeared over our skin, round the eyes and eyelids and into the ears as well as the front of the hands. It was messy and most uncomfortable as it inhibited perspiration and was itchy. Any effort to scratch would remove the camouflage so we suffered in silence. Thus whenever a battalion perimeter defence position was taken up we would do our best to wash the mess off our faces by sitting in a trickle of water in a stream and scrubbing our faces with sand. This was a tedious requirement but sensible as most engagements were at short range and with the few white leaders in the companies there was no point in advertising to the enemy where the leaders were. This was very necessary as there were only four officers in each rifle company and the third platoon had an African commander.

The commanding officer now decided that an assault should be made on Point 825 at the far end of the ridge and gave this task to 'D' Company. The company would set off after dark and attack the feature at dawn.

No reconnaissance had been made of the ground ahead and the company set off down the road before heading off into the jungle. After two hours a cliff face blocked the way forward and as no way round could be found Gillies Shields decided to wait for daylight before proceeding further. The company deployed and took up a perimeter defensive position and waited for dawn. No one slept.

Daylight showed that a sheer cliff blocked our progress. There was one spot where a tree had rooted itself close alongside the face of the cliff. This seemed to provide a means of ascent and an askari scrambled up with his back against the tree using his legs to lever himself upwards. Having reached the top he was followed by the rest of the company one by one. This took many minutes and it seemed ages before loaded with my large pack and aided by 575 Private Mutale my batman I struggled to master the seventy foot ascent and report the whole company in.

Coming over the crest was a frightening experience as a fire fight was taking place and bullets were flying all over the place. To make matters worse the company had gone to ground so initially I felt very isolated. It took but a brief moment, which seemed a life time, before I was able to read the situation and make my way forward to company headquarters. Our arrival on the ridge had been spotted by a Japanese outpost which was making a fighting withdrawal back to Point 825 with our forward platoons deployed and in pursuit. There was rolling wooded ground to our front with yet another ridge some four hundred yards ahead rising about one hundred feet above us and this feature lay at the foot of Point 825 which rose abruptly to a rugged peak.

The next incident was a straffing attack by a squadron of Hurricanes and although most of them did fire on the enemy peak one pilot straffed our forward platoons. Fortunately there was only one casualty. It indicates the remarkable skills of the pilots when those of us two hundred yards away could see a blue turban on the head of a pilot as he skimmed the tree tops below us. Having recovered from this minor set back the advance continued until it was halted at the foot of Point 825.

As the leading sections moved up the steep slopes they were met with a shower of grenades and light machine gun fire giving the impression the position was strongly held. The peak itself was covered in thick scrub and trees affording good cover to the enemy and it was difficult to pinpoint all his positions. Attempts were made to encircle the peak and come in from a flank all to no avail. We had not appreciated that the Japanese hand grenade, which was smaller than the British 36 hand grenade, was armed by striking it hard to set its fuse and that a single soldier could when desperate bang four of these grenades together before throwing them. This was what our foe was up to with the steep slope of the hill in his favour so the bombardment of sixteen grenades really indicated four positions as against sixteen! Further attempts were made to locate the enemy posts accurately but they had the advantage of height and cover and our casualties were mounting. There was little space to manoeuvre and only one platoon could be launched into the attack at a time. Four separate attempts were made by Lieut Ferraby who carried back his wounded batman and had his sten gun shot out of his hand. Other attempts to move round to the other flank were also pinned down. Time was passing and Gillies decided to pull back and dig in some three hundred yards below the peak. We buried our dead and I read a short funeral service.

Next morning after stand to I felt an urgent call of nature and crawling out behind my trench squatted in a very recumbent position. Just as I was finishing this chore all hell broke loose. A hail of fire was directed against our lines from a crest two hundred yards to our front from at least three machine guns supported by light mortars indicating a counter attack. The company responded bringing down fire onto the suspected enemy posts and raking the ridge. I hastily scrambled back into my trench which I shared with 575 Private Mutale my batman. At that moment in the thick of this fire fight àn askari leapt from his trench and started to run to the rear. I got out of my trench and intercepted him calling him every name under the sun and ordered him back to his trench. As I had my revolver aimed at his stomach he felt it more prudent to take his chances with the rest of us.

This askari was a member of one of the minor subservient tribes and not from a recognised fighting tribe. In peacetime this man would never have been considered suitable as a soldier let alone enlisted. His forebears had been beaten in tribal battles and were the lackeys and servants of their conquerors. He had no instinctive fighting spirit and he and his kind should not have been asked to face the rigours of the infantry. There were a few askari like him in the battalion at this stage of the war and it was important that the officers were aware of their characteristics and able to help compensate for any likely problem by ensuring these men were teamed up with men of fighting tribes who would take them under their wing.

The decision was now made to call for air support before a further attack was launched. A platoon from 'B' Company under Peter Bomford was attached to the company to help replace our casualties. The air strike was scheduled for 1400hrs and we would mark the enemy position with smoke. We had however to withdraw back some five hundred yards so as to be out of the danger zone while the aircraft made their bombing run. Precisely on time twenty four aircraft arrived overhead, each aircraft carrying two two hundred and fifty pound bombs slung below their wings. Led in by their leader the aircraft dived in pairs with their machine guns and cannon firing. We were glad we were not at the receiving end. The bombs had a short delayed action fuse to allow the aircraft to avoid the blast as they flew within feet of the crest of the hill.

The air attack was an inspiring sight and the accuracy of bombing something to marvel at. As soon as the last two planes had made their attack Peter Bomford rushed into the attack killing two Japanese with his sten gun and seizing the peak. As I was moving up to reinforce him and consolidate I heard the sound of aircraft in the sky and spotted a further twelve Hurricanes circling overhead. An urgent message ordered me to get back into cover and with Peter and our two platoons we raced to trenches two hundred yards back. Only just in time as the straffing and bombing began again. The noise of the cannon and machine gun fire was horrific. Chunks of dirt and debris from the fall of shot fell on Mutale and me in our trench with bullets kicking up the earth just above our heads. It was not a happy state.

I knew that unwashed as I was I could only be obnoxiously smelly with ghastly body odour. It is strange how in times of stress the mind provides solutions to keep one from losing one's grip. I knew that our askari had a very different body odour which was unpleasant to my smell. With both of us sheltering as near to the bottom of the trench as possible I asked Mutale whether the smell of the European was offensive to the African. He replied "Yes Bwana". Mutale had been with me since I had joined 'D' Company and was a pre war regular soldier. He was a member of the Bwemba tribe and a first class soldier. This living together under fire cemented our friendship for each other. He behaved so well under fire that I was delighted to recommend him for promotion to section leader and said goodbye to him as my batman with great reluctance. We corresponded with each other for a few years after the war until I lost touch.

Checking that the last planes had completed their attack we rushed from our positions to seize the hill. This time the Japanese reacted very quickly and were back in their trenches waiting for us. I decided that we should withdraw and prepare to assault the peak at dusk and this was agreed by Gillies. We arranged fire support from our mountain battery which undertook the task although our line of attack would be directly towards the gun firing position. We had seen their worth and had full confidence that they would drop their shells where they were needed.

The attack went in but once again the steepness of the peak prevented getting to grips with the enemy who fought tenaciously and continued to inflict casualties. We came under fire from a Japanese artillery piece and its muzzle flash was visible in the dusk each time it fired. I was able to give fire coordinates to our 3" mortars by shouting out the orders in Cinyanja so the Japanese would not know what I was doing. Looking back I saw a Medical Officer who had come to support only yards behind darting from one bomb crater to the next and tending one of the wounded right in the front line. Each time an attempt was made to clamber up the slope another askari was hit and we were not succeeding in knocking out the Japanese holding out in their trenches. Grenades thrown at their positions were flung back down the slope. Gillies decided to call off the attack and we withdrew to our forward positions while Gillies with company headquarters stayed on the next ridge in a laid back position.

Next day after daylight I sent a probing patrol forward which drew fire and showed the Japs were still hanging on. Later that morning the company was relieved by 'C' Company and pulled back to battalion reserve onto the ridge where we could observe our shell and mortar fire on the enemy held ridge.

'A' Company were now ordered to attack the ridge from the north end and seize Point 752 aiming to roll up the enemy positions along the ridge. This assault initially gained ground but was then halted. Further attacks were launched by 'A' and 'B' Companies without success and resulting in further casualties. The Japanese was proving to be as tenacious as we had been expected to believe. It was a further four days before the ridge was cleared and the battalion could resume the advance through Mawlaik and move down beside the Chindwin. We had counted twenty two dead Japanese and we had suffered fifty eight killed and wounded over a period of nine days

The Brigade had been given another battalion, the 1st 5th K.A.R. a pre war regular battalion, which crossed the river. The brigade thrust towards Kalewa now moved down both banks of the Chindwin River.

We were suffering casualties both from wounds and sickness. Lieut Ferraby was evacuated with malaria. We were operating in the worst climatic conditions where malaria and tick typhus was endemic. Casualties from both these diseases were as prevalent and serious as battle casualties. This in spite of rigid anti malarial precautions and drills. A drug for tick typhus had yet to come our way. Thus although battle casualties were as yet minimal the same could not be said for malaria and officers were being sent out of the line. It took time before any replacements arrived to fill their shoes.

One of the facets of a close knit unit was that any individual feeling the onset of malaria was loath to report sick. Once he was moved back through the medical chain he would end up back in India and the chance of rejoining in weeks or even months was remote.

Tommy Tompson and Bob Tait Bowie who had gone sick weeks before had still not rejoined. Accordingly the individual stepped up his ration of mepocrime and hoped to sweat the fever out. Sometimes this remedy worked at other times the individual was sent off. Tick Typhus was more insidious as the person affected needed rest if a full recovery was to be made. Rest was just not possible when the individual was on operations. A few individuals stayed with their units until they were so ill there was no alternative but to go sick. Some forty or so members of the brigade died of tick typhus during our period of operations because rest and medicine had been delayed. All very sad but emphasising the esprit de corps of members of the brigade. Many were still serving who had been with the battalion since before the war, had fought in British Somaliland and Abyssinia. Friendships had built up over the years, the battalion was family and home.

Our first major action in Burma was behind us we now pressed on heading for Kalewa and the 1st 2nd K.A.R. took the lead. Setting out down the track the valley opened up and we saw the bungalows of Mawlaik. It was a small village on the banks of the Chindwin.

Chapter Sixteen
The Advance Continues

The brigade was now firmly established astride the River Chindwin and the advance continued with our main objective being Kalewa where there was a river crossing and another road from Tiddim and the Kabaw Valley came through the Myttha Gorge to join ours in the town. However we did not tell our askari the general picture but rather the immediate tasks. Had we said our objective was Kalewa in their mind that would have been all that was asked of them.

We were still relying for all our needs to be dropped to us by the R.A.F. though brigade now had the luxury of twelve jeeps. The Mountain Battery with us had mule transport. These animals were lovely beasts capable of carrying the various loads which 'The screw guns' broke down into. At company level our sole transport was a so called mule. It was more the size of an ass and we felt cruel imposing the weight of a single point 303 ammunition box upon its back. This then was our only reserve apart from any extra ammunition and kit we carried ourselves.

Having passed by Mawlaik the battalion was now in reserve and we found a suitable location to take up a defensive position and dug in. The pattern where possible was to march about ten miles in the morning and settle for the night. This gave plenty of time to prepare defences and to suss out the surrounding territory. It was impracticable to expect to have barbed wire dropped for each halting place so we made use of local resources. Bamboo sticks were cut and sharpened. These were then stuck into the ground with the pointed end facing towards the enemy. This form of defence was very effective and easy to set up. At each long halt every askari cut and shaped some thirty sticks which he then carried tied to his back pack for use as soon as a new location was reached.

Our first company position was some nine hundred feet up a peak beside the road so we could protect the flank. It was a steep ascent but there was a sheer drop on part of the other side protecting most of that flank. Casualties from malaria and disease were causing concern and we received orders that mosquito nets had to be used except by sentries. This was an order we were suspicious about but orders were followed. That evening after dark an enemy patrol tried to attack the company position. There was the sound of grenades going off and machine gun fire. It is not easy to disentangle oneself with a rifle from inside a mosquito net and urgency did not assist. From then on we disobeyed orders and stayed ready to leap into our trenches should any firing take place close to hand.

Two days later after a further ten mile march we dug in alongside the mountain battery providing them with close protection. It was fascinating to see how their mules carried their loads over the rough uneven ground - they were magnificent animals. As we got to know these gunners our respect for their enthusiastic handling of their guns grew even more. At one time this battery managed to provide thirteen forward observers and their response was always immediate.

We had ample proof of the accuracy of their fire support as we passed through vacated enemy positions during our advance. The process of digging in had become a routine drill and the whole company split down to dig two man trenches around the company perimeter. I shared this task with my batman and everything had worked out happily with Mutale as my batman. I would dig for thirty minutes and hand over to him for the next thirty minutes while I walked round the position encouraging the askari in their work and checking on the sentries. Mutale was now doing well leading a section. My new batman proved to be idle and returning to carry on the task of digging our trench for the night I found that little if any progress had been made in my absence. This did not please me very much and I admonished him and told him to get on with it when it was next his turn. Unfortunately my orders were not complied with. This meant I had to dig harder to ensure our trench was completed. In spite of warnings this dilatory approach to helping to dig our communal trench continued. I was having to expend more effort on digging and my fuse was becoming shorter and I was being more abrupt with the other askari during my tours round the position. The African CSM saw what was going on and came to me and said "Bwana I will find you a new batman. This man is no good for your temper". Thus I was relieved of an idle soldier and everyone was happier as the new askari was first class at doing his share of the digging.

Although we had little transport we did have a first rate system for the evacuation of casualties and sick. Short runways were hacked out in selected open spaces and the ground levelled. Small L5 aircraft were piloted by American conscientious objectors and these aircraft acted as a shuttle to airfields further back. This ensured that casualties were evacuated rapidly to hospitals which could provide better facilities. They gave backing to our Field Ambulance which also deployed Field Surgical and Field Transfusion Teams forward to support the Medical Officer of the battalion leading the advance. This close medical support was a great morale factor.

A Special Boat Section now joined the brigade and carried out raids behind the Japanese lines. Paddling down stream in their canoes they would ambush enemy parties on the river. They had success one evening and brought back the sole enemy survivor from the crew of a boat who had been badly wounded.

As transport was at a premium Brigade decided to build rafts using bamboo and tarpaulins. These were then to be used as a means of bringing supplies down the river with us. Some one hundred rafts were made and loaded up. Unfortunately as this convoy was drifting down stream one morning it was shot up by a 'Spitfire' pilot who unaware of our efforts thought it was a Japanese river convoy. Half our rafts went to the bottom!

1st 2nd K.A.R. advanced against determined resistance. 'A' Company which had outflanked the Japanese position and cut the road to the rear had a hectic battle when the retreating enemy fought through the centre of their defensive position.

Soon after this 1st NRR took over with 'A' Company in the lead on the route forward which ran close to the river on its left flank. It was not long before the enemy were bumped sitting on a ridge which ran down to the waters edge and 'A' Company were held up. 'B' Company was sent off to make a deep encirclement to shoot up any enemy who withdrew. Major Beresford planned to try and bounce the enemy position after dark and a platoon of 'D' Company was given this role. Once this platoon had made a break the rest of the company would follow through to exploit the situation. A second platoon was held ready for immediate exploitation. I was to collect the third platoon deployed three hundred feet up the slope to the right and then rejoin the company.

Things did not quite work out as planned. The lead platoon was received by heavy fire from a number of positions on the ridge. This fire affected 'A' Company who joined in with a resulting brocks benefit isolating the 'D' Company platoon in the middle. Waiting for orders in my trench I was aware of the sound of rushing feet charging down the hillside beside me. The next thing I knew a body landed in the trench beside me. I was about to shoot this intruder when the askari who was from the platoon up the hill made himself known. It was apparent who these bodies rushing past were. I leapt from my trench and bellowed for them to fall in calling them all the names under the sun. It says much for the loyalty to their officers that what had been a terrified group of men fell in smartly in three ranks even though the fire fight was continuing and bullets were passing overhead throughout this phase. Having collected the platoon and told them their fortune I then led them back up the hill to their trenches. I was hoping that the Japanese had not taken advantage of what had happened and moved in to occupy them. Coming to the place where the ground levelled off a bit I halted the platoon and went forward with the European platoon sergeant and two askari. There were no enemy and the platoon settled down in their old trenches. I walked round and spoke to all the men and made it quite clear that I did not expect to have to repeat this action. The platoon followed instructions.

It is interesting to remember that this platoon had lost its officer and the Sergeant in command had only joined the day before. Disorientated in the dark and terrified the askari responded at once to the command of a voice they knew - rallied and from then on performed as required.

The European Sergeant had a limited knowledge of the language and the askari had not got to know him. Talking to the SBS team the following morning was an eye opener. We had looked upon them as a group of highly specialised and very brave men performing a task which we would not happily volunteer to do. It was therefore surprising when one of their NCOs commenting after this episode remarked "I would not have your job for anything", each to his own as they say.

There is another example of realising that the askari reacted differently to similar situations. A reliable junior NCO was lead section and rounding a bend in the track came face to face with a Japanese patrol. He immediately led his section into a charge and killed the enemy. A day or so later exactly the same incident occurred but this time on seeing the Japs he turned and fled with his Section. The explanation I believe was that the first time he was thinking ahead and fully alert and when the crisis situation happened he was ready. The second time he was surprised probably because his mind had been distracted and consequentially he panicked. Living with our askari over the years and speaking their language helped us in starting to have an understanding of their way of thinking and attitudes to life. After all these men were mercenaries fighting for Kingi George to earn money to buy cattle as a bridal dowry. The longer one served with them the more one grew to respect them and enjoy the privilege of leading them in battle.

After this set back the previous evening and not having had news of 'B' Company the colonel decided to leave 'A' Company in a holding position on the river bank and to take the rest of the battalion on a wide enveloping move. We set out the next morning and climbed for three hours to the top of the range on our flank. We spotted a Japanese patrol below us to a flank observing what we were up to but they were outside effective range. The climb was hot work and not knowing where we would next have a chance to replenish our water bottles I struggled on without a drink. As the day drew on I felt the first signs of heat exhaustion and had to help myself along by grasping tree trunks and pulling myself forward. It was not a nice feeling and I was much relieved some two hours later when we halted by a spring in the shade of some trees where our water bottles could be refilled. I took a long draught of water and at once felt normal again. While moving along the range close to the crest we had looked down some two thousand feet to the river below and watched our Hurricanes dive in to attack the Japanese who were holding up our troops. It was fascinating to watch this display of flying from above and increased our respect for the support the air force was giving us. This march had been more onerous than expected and taken a longer time. As a result we had not arrived at the proposed dropping zone in the valley but were still high up the mountains when we halted for the night. The drop in temperature was noticeable and I wrapped up in my gas cape to keep some warmth in my body and took a tot of rum. As we were operational we received a daily rum ration which the officers carried in old spirit bottles in their packs and issued to the askari each night. There was always a reserve as some of the askari refused the ration on religious grounds.

The next morning we arrived at the selected dropping zone and took up defensive positions awaiting the arrival of supplies. Late that afternoon a single Dakota flew in and dropped ten parachutes and some sacks. Imagine our dismay when the supplies proved to be hay for our mules and petrol. Major Beresford sent off a sharp signal enquiring how we were expected to fight without proper rations and ammunition. We spent another night on short tack before a replenishment flight arrived in the morning.

The battalion regrouped before continuing the advance in support of 'B' Company who were now in the lead. Meanwhile the remainder of the brigade staged a river crossing to join up with 1st 5th K.A.R. on the far bank. The river crossing that night went off successfully without any mishap and 1st NRR were now the only brigade unit on the West bank of the river. Our task was to take Kalewa which was about twelve miles ahead. As we advanced the mountain range which until now had risen sharply from the river bank fell away and we crossed an open valley with paddy fields. Beyond this valley the mountains closed in a little with a smaller range of hills interposed between the main route and the river.

A stream crossed the road and this was where the Japs had taken up a defensive line. A frontal attack by 'B' Company was held and the battalion deployed with 'D' Company in the centre and 'C' Company on the left.

'D' Company dug in on a small ridge which fell away sharply on one flank providing a natural defensive position. Gillies Shields decided that as we were now very short of Europeans the CSM and CQMS as well as myself would take out a platoon fighting patrol each. This order shattered the CQMS who was a little taken aback at first but once he realised he was expected to show his leadership capabilities got on with the task of determining his route.

These patrols enabled us to determine the enemy positions in more detail. Before I set out I pre planned some fire support from our 3" mortars based on intelligence from earlier patrols. I gave orders that the patrol would travel light and the askari would go bare foot to avoid making a noise as we moved through the bush and gave orders accordingly. I would wear gym shoes. Before we set out the African CSM came up and said an askari wished to speak to me. He did not know what the complaint was. The askari in question was a new recruit who had only been with us for two months. I asked him what he wished to say.

Askari: "Bwana I cannot go on patrol without my boots as I will hurt my feet"
Self: "How long have you been in the army ?"
Askari: "Eight months Bwana"
Self: "Before you joined the army did you ever wear boots in your village?"
Askari: "No Bwana"
Self: "And when you were first given boots in the army did you always take them off as soon as possible because they hurt your feet?"
Askari; "Yes Bwana"
Self: "And do you still take off your boots because you find it more comfortable without them?"
Askari: "Yes Bwana"
Self: "You will go on patrol without your boots"
Askari: With a grin from ear to ear "Yes Bwana".

This episode is another example of the pleasure it was to have such delightful men under command. They were prepared to try it on. But these little incidents were all part of inter relationship between the askari and his officer. It was important for the officer to hear the complaint and to give his reasons for his decision. Once the decision was made it was obeyed without any rancour and very willingly.

The patrol set out moving slowly and quietly through the bush heading for a small hill which was across the river line held by the Japanese. Earlier patrols had defined a crossing area two hundred yards away from a possible Japanese position and I intended to verify this information. I chose the hill for defensive fire from our mortars if and when I needed fire support. The approach went well without incident and we crossed the stream and started to make our way up the small hill feature when we came under machine gun fire from our right flank. The platoon was well dispersed and the fire was returned. Shortly after other parties of Japs in extended order appeared through the bush on the flank of their machine gun section. Two more machine guns entered the battle and a fire fight developed. I could not see what was happening to my front and other flank and it was obvious that the enemy were sufficiently strong to prevent us advancing. I gave the order to withdraw coming out with the last section and at the same time calling down fire on the selected target. The fire came down at once and prevented our withdrawal being harried by the enemy. We returned without any casualties.

In the meantime a new method of harassing the enemy had been developed by 'B' Company. Two askari asked permission to go out lightly clad to hunt a Japanese. These men set out and following the techniques learned as hunters of wild game crept up on single Japanese sentries and quietly killed them bringing back their identity disc. Seeing this tactic seemed practicable further such sorties followed with the resulting lowering of morale on the part of the enemy. These stalking patrols were followed by a flank attack on the main enemy position causing the Japanese to withdraw in haste. The battalion was gaining in experience and pursued the fleeing foe.

'C' Company was now in the lead and Kalewa was but a couple of miles ahead. The remainder of the 11th East African Division which had been advancing down the Kabaw valley were approaching Kalewa down a gorge through the mountains from our flank and their artillery was landing on the town. This fire held up our advance and when lifted 'C' Company joined up with friendly forces and Kalewa had been captured.

This was cause for celebration and medical comforts were freely dispersed. The askari found our celebration for such an insignificant town surprising. Companies deployed on ridges overlooking the river and 'D' Company was held in reserve alongside battalion headquarters.

We were expecting a supply drop and I was standing by the chosen drop zone ready to unfurl my orange umbrella when a jeep appeared

111

down the track with an RAF Pilot aboard. Just then a Dakota came over and I put up the umbrella. "Why are you putting up that umbrella" I was asked by the RAF visitor. I explained that this was the recognised signal for us to identify ourselves to all friendly aircraft. "Well no one has told us" was his reply. He told me he had come forward to be with us as a ground liaison officer and to look for likely sites for a forward air strip on the other side of the Chindwin.

Chapter Seventeen

Company Command

The afternoon after we had all celebrated the capture of Kalewa, Major Beresford called me to his office and told me to go and take command of 'B' Company that afternoon. I was to go by a certain route whilst the officer being relieved would return to battalion headquarters by a different route. There was not to be a physical handover.

I set off and arrived at 'B' Company headquarters where I was met by Captain Ken Scott the company second in command. Ken was a Rhodesian whom I knew and respected and I felt lucky to have him to help me settle in. I had been with the battalion for four years now and 'B' Company was the only company I had never served in so I was going to have to get to know the NCOs and askari quickly.

I sent for the platoon commanders as I wished to say hello and find out if they had any immediate problems they wished to discuss with me. We had hardly settled down for this preliminary get to know you session when the company area came under a session of heavy shelling. The phone rang and Major Beresford enquired as to what was happening and was everything alright. I replied we were undergoing a little shelling and it was nothing to be concerned about. I then replaced the receiver. The shelling continued and the commanding officer came on the phone again anxiously enquiring after us. I assured him we were fully under control and that I would let him know should we suffer any casualties.

I ordered platoon commanders to return to their platoons as I had no wish to have all the key members of the company in one place whilst we were being targeted. I said I would visit them once the shelling ceased. The shelling finished ten minutes later and a walk round the platoons showed the company had come through unscathed. I called the Commanding Officer and reported we were in good shape.

This episode was fortunate as I was able to demonstrate a lack of concern at the shelling in my conversation with the commanding officer which I believe helped the company to adjust to the unexpected change in command. The next morning we moved to a rest location near to a local Burmese village but not before I had taken a jeep into Kalewa to have a look round. There were a few houses but not nearly as many as we had expected. There was a lot of activity and I saw the engineers setting up a Bailey Bridge over the three hundred yard river obstacle. A ferry was being used to carry heavy equipment across the river.

Once we had reached our new location the day was used to get to know the officers, NCOs and askari. I first talked to Ken Scott who had a fund of experience and sounded him on the characteristics of the principle African NCOs. Then I spoke to the African CSM and with Ken we spent the rest of the day talking to every NCO. Platoon commanders were brought in when the discussion affected their command.

I wanted as quickly as possible not only to form an assessment of each NCO but to determine the strengths and weaknesses in every section. The African CSM stated his views on the platoon sergeants from his viewpoint. The platoon commander then had his say and strengths and any weakness were agreed. The Sergeant was then interviewed, complimented on his strengths and advised on any weaknesses if any, after which he was asked to state his own feelings. Having tackled the senior African NCO in each platoon in this manner he was now brought into the discussion and invited to comment on the attributes of his section commanders. Did he feel all his NCOs were pulling their weight or should any of them be downgraded? The section commanders were then interviewed and consulted individually and then we discussed every askari in that section. Was the man reliable under fire? Having determined the good steady askari the plan now catered to ensure that a soldier who was deemed possibly to be less reliable was placed with a reliable askari who was charged with taking him under his wing. Finally the askari themselves were talked to and told what was expected of them as part of their section team.

This series of interviews took the best part of the day but was very worthwhile as I had established an understanding with all the key NCOs in the company and persuaded them that they had my full confidence and backing. I went to bed feeling a great deal happier.

Orders arrived next morning the company was to embark on DUKW amphibians to be taken across the Chindwin. I was to report with the company to Brigade Headquarters for further orders. The DUKWs arrived later that morning and once the company had all embarked the flotilla headed upstream. The journey to the disembarkation point took two hours and the company then marched through soft sand along a dried river bed which was very heavy going. The daylight hours were passing by and we camped alongside our Field Ambulance for the night.

An air strip for L5 aircraft had been made and these planes were constantly flying out with casualties. This was their first day at this air strip and there was a back log of casualties awaiting evacuation.

We were told that these pilots had managed to fly out ninety five casualties that day. The site we camped in had previously been a company defensive position and was ready made. We had no need to dig trenches they were there already.

Marching forward next morning we arrived close to Brigade headquarters. I reported in and was told to settle down for the night. The following morning the Brigadier gave me the task of advancing some two miles forward to seize a prominent feature. The company was to dig in and protect the flank of the 1st 2nd K.A.R. who would pass through on the following day to cut the main road from Kalewa to Ye Yu.

The terrain immediately forward of the Brigade Headquarters position was open rolling grassland. The leading platoon set off in open order with company headquarters following. Steady progress was made and eventually the objective came in sight with thick jungle on the lower slopes to either flank. There was no opposition, the company dug in and placed bamboo stakes forward of the trenches. At dusk the silence was disturbed by the sound of two grenades going off on the far slope of the feature which was being overlooked by Ken Scott. It transpired a two man Jap patrol had appeared obviously seeking to find out what was going on. The outpost on that front threw the grenades which sent the enemy packing hopefully before they were close enough to gather any useful information. Apart from that incident the night passed quietly. Next morning it rained and we watched the 1st 2nd K.A.R. pass by.

In the afternoon new orders arrived from Major Beresford. I was to return to Battalion Headquarters with two platoons leaving one platoon to secure the hill. I left Ken Scott in charge and led the company back to 'Uncle Drunkle' who greeted me warmly saying "Thank goodness you are here. The guns are just behind us and we are to protect them and you are the first and only troops I have to do this job at present. 'A' and 'C' Companies are on their way but I do not know when they will arrive". I joined his party with my company headquarters and positioned myself in a trench a few yards away from him. The two platoons were sited on either flank. He was somewhat concerned that the other companies had not put in an appearance as the afternoon was drawing in. Sunset started and still no sign of the other companies. 'Uncle Drunkle' needed a little fortification and asked if I had any available rum ration. I handed over the bottle I carried in my pack and he took a swig. Handing back the bottle he jumped into his trench and proceeded to set out his rifle, revolver, grenades and machete along the parapet saying "If the Japs come I shall start from the right and work my way along through the weapons to the machete". It was getting dark rapidly and my two platoons were the only troops he had to hand. I could understand his worries. Fortunately the Japanese were sufficiently occupied elsewhere to be concerned about us and the night passed by quietly.

The 1st 2nd K.A.R. had cut the main escape route and established a strong battalion position and Brigade now called for a company to support this battalion by taking a position astride the road at the junction of tracks where the British had abandoned their tanks during the retreat from Burma in 1942. 'B' Company was given this task. A special unit of stretcher bearers had been raised and twenty of these askari were placed under my command for this task. I also had Roland, the RAF Pilot who was given permission to come with the company.

We set out at 1300hrs and collecting Ken Scott and the other platoon on the way reached our objective by 1600hrs without meeting any opposition. En route close to our objective we came across a Japanese food dump. Arriving at the road I selected a location where the road rose over a small hump. There was a precipitous drop into a dry river bed on one side and I gave orders for the defence. The platoons started to dig. Just then I heard the sound of an aircraft and an Artillery Observation Plane flew overhead. I raised my umbrella to show our position and the plane waggled its wing and circled around. It dipped as it came by and a message was dropped. This read - 'I will bring you a link so you will have direct call on the whole of the divisional artillery'. Good news indeed however when the plane returned a few moments later a further message was dropped. It read - 'Sorry the line broke'. The pilot waggled his wings and left us.

The company dug in with a will and I was pleased with the layout when we stood to at dusk. Not long after we had stood down there were sounds of jabbering coming up the road and Ken Smallwood fired his 2" mortar which made an unholy noise. Grenades went off and this little action went on for not much longer than five minutes before everything quietened down. We remained ready for further activity but the rest of the night passed quietly. The company followed the drill which was to bayonet any figure outside our trenches after dark. This meant I had to wait till after daylight before I could find out what had happened. It transpired a party of Japanese had come down the track and turned into the road where they had encountered our positions. I was not happy to discover that the road in front of our forward posts was littered with 36 Grenades which still had their safety pins in and others which although the pins had been withdrawn had not gone off. There were three Japanese dead but the rest of their party had circled off into the jungle and avoided further contact. The identification tags were removed from the Japanese and unit type and identity were noted and reported to Brigade. The teaching on the ship paid off. Verification and full details of the unit and its strength reached us from the UK within a week.

Roland took a small patrol down the road to Brigade and looked round for possible forward air strips for our fighters. It was now possible to take a more detailed look around the immediate company position than had been possible the evening before when the emphasis had been on digging in for the night. Two hundred yards back down the road towards the Chindwin another track joined from the South. It was here hidden in thick scrub and bushes that we discovered the tanks of the 7th Hussars which they had had to destroy and abandon in 1942. They had done a good job and the tanks were where they had left them.

I went round all the positions and emphasised that I was not pleased with the way the grenades had been handled and that I expected the pin to be withdrawn, the lever released, and for a count of two by the soldier before he threw the grenade. That evening just after dark two grenades went off - then silence. I wondered what the morning would reveal. Japanese stragglers had followed the party of the previous night and run into the company. On going round the company next morning I learned one Jap was grabbed by two askari who held him down and set off a grenade under him. He met his end quickly. There was another dead Jap on the road and it was thought another had been wounded and crawled away. A Corporal went off with another askari to track and deal with this man. He was found an hour later and had to be shot as he refused to surrender. This NCO had already volunteered to go out head hunting on eight occasions and brought back evidence of a dead Jap each time. He was put up for the award of the Military Medal.

That morning an Officer came along from a Gunner Regiment in the 2nd British Infantry Division. He told us his regiment would deploy for action in the paddy fields close by and that the 2nd Division was in the process of taking over from us. They were to press on to Ye Yu on the road to Mandalay. An hour later the whole artillery regiment passed by and we watched the guns line up and deploy ready to fire.

In the afternoon Colonel Derek Watson marched through leading the 1st 4th K.A.R. and heading for a range of hills to the South of the road widening the frontage of our bridgehead over the River

117

Chindwin. He was coping with an attack of dysentery and continuing to command his battalion.

There was a growing sense of feeling that our front line duties were rapidly coming to a close. Later in the afternoon there was a minor hiccup as I heard our mountain battery open fire and this caused a flap in the 2 Division Gunner Regiment. They began to train their guns in the direction of the sound of gunfire. I ran over to their lines and let the fire control officer know that the fire was friendly. At any rate a possible engagement between our own guns was prevented.

1st NRR were now concentrating in the Ingaung Chaung and 'B' Company was recalled with the duty of deploying one platoon on a hill overlooking the River Chindwin and blocking a track which might be followed by lone Japs trying to rejoin their units. I visited this platoon the next morning to say goodbye to Lieut Smallwood and the askari as orders had come through for my return to the U.K. I had accumulated over five years overseas service and so was eligible for a return ticket. We were about to go out of the line and I wished to have another go at the Germans on their own soil.

The route to Smallwood was across country but it crossed a main track on which lay the bodies of two dead Japs. Whilst with the platoon we witnessed the only air raid by the Japanese air force during our whole period in the line. Their target was the Bailey bridge at Kalewa and they had delayed their attack until the air defences were fully deployed. A heavy anti aircraft barrage was put up which prevented any direct hit on the bridge. One plane was obviously damaged and departed emitting a lot of smoke and the other five planes did not dally. The defensive fire was such they did no damage to the bridge.

The battalion had sent out a long range fighting patrol under Ken Scott to cut the Jap lines of communication some thirty miles to the rear. The patrol reached the road and set up an ambush which caught a small party of Japs. The enemy was disposed of, one Jap was taken prisoner, and the patrol set out to return to our lines. The prisoner proved to be very bloody minded and whenever the patrol halted for a rest attempted to get free kicking his captors and making a general nuisance of himself. At one halt he grabbed at a sten gun, wrestled with the askari and hit out against anyone close to him. His efforts were not only delaying the patrol but also creating sufficient noise to draw attention to their whereabouts. The patrol leader decided there was no alternative but to kill him.

I returned to Battalion Headquarters and said farewell to many friends. That afternoon I thanked the askari for their support and wished them well. The war in the jungle had been very much a company commanders war. The four weeks I had had in command had been a great privilege and a thrilling challenge. The company had responded to all the demands placed on them and willingly and cheerfully accepted the abrupt change of company commander.

Over the years I had formed a deep affection for the askari, learnt their language and characteristics, their strengths and weaknesses. They gave to their officers a simple almost child like trust. They had a lovely sense of fun and attacked whatever task was set willingly and with zeal and enthusiasm. Their natural hunting skills made them an enemy to be feared.They more than repaid the confidence placed in them. Soldiering with African soldiers was very different from service in the British Army. As an officer it is an honour and privilege to have command of men particularly in war. I knew I was going to miss the askari.

Next morning I left the battalion with a heavy heart. An officer of 1st 2nd K.A.R. was also on this party and we set off in a jeep down the road to the Bailey bridge at Kalewa. Our brigade bridge head over the Chindwin River had cut the road to Ye Yu some ten miles ahead of this bridge. It was now a hive of activity with military police controlling the mass of vehicles awaiting to cross over. We had to wait our time before we were given a space between these convoys moving forward. As we drove down this road which had seen the thrust of our advance we saw evidence of the accuracy of our medium artillery with clusters of shell holes astride the axis. We stopped at the battalion 'B' Echelon area for the last night of rough sleeping. The next morning we flew to Imphal and the joy of a proper bed for the first time in four months.

The jungle war was usually fought at close quarters as vision ahead was often not much more than thirty yards and this meant the lead scout was likely to be hit in the first exchange of fire. The Japanese made excellent use of terrain and had to be killed in their trenches. Often a position would be atop a precipitous rise with but a narrow approach so the battle was a very personal one. Such was the nature of the ground in the Kabaw Valley and beside the Chindwin that it was not practicable to operate as a battalion. Companies were given tasks and operated on their own to fulfil a general plan. As the advance progressed more battle experience was acquired and greater use was made of the field skills of the askari who themselves learnt that they were much better at field craft than the Japanese.

Casualties were light though sickness, malaria and tick typhus were a major problem. A number of our officers were evacuated sick. Curiously those who had avoided malaria in Ceylon were struck down in Burma and tick typhus also took a toll. I had suffered bouts of malaria every few months in Ceylon but kept fit throughout our spell in the line. Mepocrine was a daily dose and this undoubtedly helped as did DDT. Unfortunately the medicine to combat tick typhus only arrived after the Division had been relieved.

The whole of our advance had been supplied from the air and Hurribombers had provided air support. Their contribution was invaluable. In particular the 'Dakota' pilots flying the air drop planes ensured we always had ammunition and supplies. No matter how horrific the monsoon conditions we were never let down. This support enabled us to advance whereas had we been restricted to ground transport during the monsoon our progress would have been all but impossible due to the weather and the terrain.

There was one very important aspect which helped considerably to uphold our morale. Mail from the UK was delivered to us with the routine air supply. Instead of the delays of months experienced whilst we were in Ceylon in 1942 and 1943 letters now reached us within days. We were many miles from home but the links were so much closer.

We had been part of an Army which had inflicted a major defeat on the Japanese and anyone who fought with the 14th Army felt justly proud.

Chapter Eighteen

Return to the United Kingdom

The flight from the forward air strip to Imphal was in a Dakota, the sturdy aircraft which had delivered our every need in the way of ammunition and rations during our operational tour. There were metal seats running along the side of the aircraft and after take off we looked down on the jagged peaks and saw our simple road had been transformed by engineers into a main supply route. Bridges spanned the many chaungs which had been impassable torrents during the monsoon. The route was jammed with an endless convoy of vehicles heading towards the bridgehead at Kalewa.

The pilot in charge of the plane was probably about nineteen and seemed a mere boy to our seasoned eyes! After some forty minutes we landed at Imphal and went to a transit camp to await a flight to Calcutta. Next morning with our baggage we boarded a USAF 'Commando', which was a larger transport aircraft and set off over the mountains. Again there were no seats and we sat along the sides of the aircraft with all the baggage piled in the centre.

This journey was not without its excitement. The young American pilot had a pair of frilly ladies panties hanging on display beside his seat. He seemed only too pleased to let anyone who wished to to take the controls. This was not too worrying when the passenger, who was handling the controls, flew level and straight as the ground below showed a serried series of jagged peaks interspersed with deep valleys. However when an Indian Officer trying his skill as a pilot began to bank into a series of sharp turns with the wing dipping steeply first to one side and then the next all the rest of us cried 'Enough'. Having survived months in the jungle we had no desire to dice with death in this manner.

Some four hours later we reached Dum Dum airfield and were lifted into a Transit Hotel in Calcutta where we stayed whilst awaiting orders for onward movement. During this spell we collected our heavy baggage from Deolali where it was stored in a large hanger. We had last seen it at Chittagong in June and no matter how much I searched I could not find one of my trunks. I assumed it must have been stolen en route from Chittagong and accepted its loss.

We celebrated Christmas as best we could in Calcutta. I bought a pair of leather shoes for fourteen rupees in a market and they are still in fine shape to this day.

The next move was by rail to Bombay a journey across the country which took some forty eight hours. Arriving at Bombay we were amazed to meet up with Major Peter Beresford and Tony Fawssett who were off on a spell of leave. We shared a few drinks with them. For our part we were now despatched by rail to a transit camp at Poona where those due to return to the UK were being gathered awaiting a ship. Again by chance we bumped into Fetherby who had been evacuated sick from 'C' Company after the battle at Point 825. He was due to get married and we were able to give him support. I was also happy to give him news that he had been awarded an MC to send him off on his honeymoon in even higher spirits. It was in this transit camp that I first met 'Hippo' Phipps of The Bedfords who had been with the 1st Battalion of the 'Bedfords' with the 'Chindits'.

We spent about ten days at Poona before entraining for Bombay and boarding a ship to start the journey home. There were six of us in a small cabin, which would have probably been a single berth before the war. There were a series of sittings for meals and space was at a premium. A concert party was organised and time was whiled away reading and playing bridge. The ships in the convoy sailed independently via Aden to Port Said where we waited to gather as a convoy. Fortunately we were allowed ashore which was a pleasant change after our cramped living. After five days we set off once more and were surprised to find ourselves steaming on our own until arriving at Gibraltar where we anchored in the bay and listened to the depth charges being dropped throughout the night to deter enemy divers and mini submarines.

When we set forth we were under heavy escort with cruisers and destroyers heading out into the Atlantic and the change in temperature was obvious after our years in the tropics. During this voyage we were given a series of lectures about life in the UK to prepare us for what seemed to be a very different life with rationing, air raids and the war still being fought bitterly.

There was snow on the hills as we sailed up the Clyde and we lined the rails to savour everything we could see as the ships made their way slowly to port. It was night time before we entrained to journey south and it was noticeable how yellow our faces seemed compared with our compatriots who had not been East. We had not appreciated the long term effect mepocrine had had upon our complexion!

Arriving at Euston in the morning we decided to have breakfast in a hotel before continuing on our individual ways to our leave destinations. Egg and bacon was ordered and the waiter was very angry when I queried the peculiar tasting mess of dried eggs. This was my first encounter with this substitute and I found them perfectly foul. The waiter was convinced I was being awkward and did not believe I genuinely did not know what this dish was.

I arrived at my parents home in Bookham and completed reporting requirements before enjoying six weeks leave. The war had reached the stage when V2 bombs were targeting London. In the fresh spring mornings the skies were filled with the USAF bomber formations massing in the skies overhead in preparation for the daylight raids on Germany. There were Canadians and Commandos camped nearby and I met Peter Young by chance. He was now commanding a Commando Brigade and we enjoyed a drink together in a local pub one evening. I made a few journeys to London proudly wearing the Fourteenth Army insignia on my uniform. This acted as a magnet to any other member of the 'Forgotten Army' and we promptly celebrated properly. I took the opportunity to have some portrait photographs taken for the benefit of my parents.

It was during this leave that I met up with Lionel Hitchen who was working for the Ministry of Supply. We had known one another before the war and had a number of mutual friends.

The six weeks flashed by and I joined the 8th Suffolks, a training battalion stationed at Blakeney in Norfolk. The battalion received soldiers who had completed their initial training and gave them a further six weeks of field training. I was to be the senior training officer in one of the companies. These soldiers were being trained for the Far East and it was our task to indoctrinate them on Japanese tactics. The company was billeted at Salthouse and the officers were housed in a holiday home overlooking the sea. The battalion was staffed with a mixture of officers from local regiments including a number of 'Bedfords' and we all sported our own regimental badges.

Having spent so many years in the Far East I was despatched to the School of Infantry to attend a platoon commanders course. There were some one hundred and twenty students ranging from ten individuals like myself back from war service, some who had commanded companies over many months, to newly commissioned officers straight from OCTU. The course was divided into platoons which were required to double from place to place. We decided the best way of showing the powers that be that we were not a group of backward colonial adventurers was to give of our best. This we did and I received the highest pass grade of 'AX'.

On returning to the 8th Suffolks I learned the Colonel was anxious to set up a museum and gather equipment so our soldiers could learn what enemy uniforms and weapons looked like. One day I set off with 'Stormy' Tempest (Bedfords) in a truck to a USAF Base outside Norwich to see if we could gain photographs of air raid damage on German targets resulting from their daylight missions.

Arriving at the airfield we found our American hosts most hospitable. Apart from a collection of bombs of different shapes and sizes we were given a 'Surplus' .5 inch machine gun in working order. We were also given a selection of first class pictures of air raid damage taken after the raids by reconnaissance flights.

It was now time for a meal and we sampled the fare in their mess after which we were invited to go to the control tower to hear the debriefing of the wing leader on his return from the morning raid.

We stood in the background while the Station Commander was briefed on the target and awaited the arrival of the twenty seven B 17 four engine bombers to come into view. A little while later we saw the three squadrons heading to pass by the control tower. The lead aircraft then peeled off and turned to circle round for a landing followed in single line by the remaining planes. It was an inspiring sight. As the lead plane landed a jeep chased alongside until the door opened to allow the wing leader to jump out. The plane then taxied on to its dispersal area.

Meanwhile the jeep sped towards the control tower and shortly afterwards the commander strolled in still fully attired in all his flying kit. He saluted and then proceeded to pace up and down across the control tower room. Up and down, up and down and not a word was said. Eventually after a couple of minutes of this pacing the wing leader, still pacing to and fro murmured "Gee I'm unhappy, Gee I'm unhappy". This went on for a further moment or two which to those of us standing there seemed ages. He then continued "There was thick cloud cover when we arrived at the target area. We flew around trying to identify our target. I spotted what I believed was the target through a gap in the clouds and gave the order 'Let go'. Gee I'm unhappy". He then went off to attend a more formal debrief and we bade our farewells and headed back to the battalion with our spoils thanking our hosts for a fascinating day.

There are five things which remind me of my days at Salthouse. I found it almost impossible to be warm in my bed at night no matter how many blankets I cowered under that early spring. Then I was amazed to find that everything stopped at 10.30 am for a tea break of thirty minutes as we were still at war. When I looked back to our training schedule in India which gave us an hour or so on Sunday evening I found this attitude incomprehensible. Then I found myself going down with malaria at regular intervals. Shipped off to hospital I was used as a guinea pig to test new untried pills instead of the drugs which I had been given in India which I knew staved off the problem for months instead of weeks.

On one occasion I was lecturing on medical problems and talking about malaria when I began to sweat and shiver. I knew an attack was coming on so I closed by saying "You can now see how malaria affects a person as I am displaying the symptoms". I went off to hospital that afternoon. On another occasion I had prepared myself to take part in a battalion cross country race and in practice had moved well. On the day I set off with the leaders and kept going for the first four miles when I began to feel leaden and had to struggle to carry on with competitor after competitor passing by. I took ages to complete the course coming in after dark with malaria catching me up yet again.

As the evenings grew lighter with double summer time being used every evening we watched the passage of our heavy bombers flying in streams heading out to sea towards the enemy coast. The skies were filled with the steady throb of the engines and the display of aerial might took some thirty or more minutes to pass by. Just before the war in Europe ended our bombers flew past skimming the waves on their return from dropping urgent food supplies to the Dutch.

VE Day came whilst we were at Salthouse. I was in the training area preparing for a demonstration with a squad of soldiers. We returned to the company area to find it deserted and the mess staff told me everyone was at the local inn. Arriving there I found a celebration going on and 'Stormy' Tempest, a Bedford with one of the other companies joining in. A short time later a blue truck arrived with a WRNS Officer aboard. In the rear were some twelve WRNS and they were hauled in to join the party. It was decided we would celebrate later in the evening and the WRNS were invited to join us. News got around and the Carrier Platoon drove down from Holt with some ATS and others came along with members of the WRAF. After a drink in the pub everyone clambered aboard the Carriers which proceeded to circle the village green with their Bren guns firing tracer into the sky and thunder flashes being dispersed freely around. We had sufficient sense to cease this racket after a few moments and dispersed to our lines to celebrate with a dance which saw the dawn come up next morning.

I was given a spell of leave which coincided with VJ Day. I went up to London, marched up and down Piccadilly and Regent Street in the afternoon, and joined the crowds outside Buckingham Palace in the evening to cheer the King and Queen. At long last the war had ended and there was no need for an invasion of Japan with all the loss of life such an operation would have entailed.

The battalion regrouped to mobilise for a move to the Bahamas. Meanwhile my visits to hospital were causing the doctors to look at my medical fitness and I was advised that should I return again I would be downgraded. This was not at all to my liking and I discussed the matter with a Nursing Sister I met in London. She gave me a tin of a few hundred tablets saying "You are sensible enough to administer these yourself. I suggest you volunteer for a hot climate". I had applied to attend a course at The School of Military Intelligence as the new colonel of the 8th Suffolks had ordered us all to remove our Bedford badges. The only way I could continue to wear these badges was by seeking a staff job. The course was at Farnham and having passed I was posted to an appointment in the Middle East.

The journey out was by air in a Dakota which took two days with a flight to Istres, on to Malta for the night, and to El Adam and Cairo on the second day.

Chapter Nineteen

The Middle East - Palestine 1946

After landing at the airport at Heliopolis we were taken to a transit hotel and told we would be picked up the following morning. Having sorted my kit out I thought I would have a look at the city of Cairo. Strolling down the main street I found myself accosted by any number of urchins all anxious to sell me their wares. Their approach was aggressive but having seen traders in Africa, Ceylon and India I firmly rejected their pleas. The Egyptian tout is persuasive to say the least and can be very unpleasant. A few paces ahead were two Army Nurses in their attractive white uniforms. A boot boy demanded to clean their shoes and on receiving their refusal promptly slashed their white uniform dresses with his black shoe brush. He then ran off melting into the crowd before anything could be done. So much for this initial introduction to the locals.

The next morning with other prospective Intelligence officers we were taken to GHQ and briefed for the next two days on the organisation we would working for. We paid a visit to the office where copies of Identity records were held. These records covered the whole period of the war in the Middle East and I was impressed to be shown the photo of the son of a family friend, whom I had not seen since the outbreak of war, and who had been killed at the battle of El Alamain.

I was to be posted to Headquarters Palestine and Transjordan as an Intelligence Officer and would travel over night by train from Cairo to Jerusalem. The next morning I awoke to find the train was climbing through the twisting valleys up hill from Lydda Junction to Jerusalem. Even the small change in altitude provided a less humid atmosphere.

There was an officers mess about a mile outside the city which housed members of the Headquarters staff which was to be my home. The Headquarters offices were in the two top floors of the King David Hotel. The hotel stood on a ridge on the outskirts of the new city overlooking the walls of the 'Old City' across a valley. One complete wing of the hotel was taken over as offices for the civil government. The Governor at this time was General Cunningham, who had planned and executed the defeat of the Italians in Italian Somaliland and Abyssinia in 1941. The Army Commander was General Sir Evelyn Barker who had recently arrived to take command.

I shared an office with an ATS officer who was our branch administrative officer. General Barker came round to say hello and meet every member of his staff. He had been my Brigade Commander in France in 1939 and immediately recognised me. He proceeded to run through the names of all the key officers of the battalion at that time asking for news. He had earned our affection and respect for his leadership in the battles leading to Dunkirk. His memory was amazing and I was delighted to think I would be serving such a great man.

Two small incidents help illustrate his character. Some weeks later returning to the office one evening I was on the stairs near to the entrance of the building. An officer, who had been held captive by Jewish terrorists, came rushing in breathlessly having just made his escape. A plan was immediately hatched to return there and then to the place where he had been held with him as guide to see if any of his captors were still around. At that moment General "Bubbles" Barker arrived and seeing the officer welcomed him back. The officer then advised the general that the terrorists were planing to assassinate him. General Barker replied "Good luck to them they ought to be able to see me without too much trouble". It should be pointed out the general had an escort of Bedouin Arabs dressed in galabiers who besides being readily seen presented an awesome spectacle.

There was a small private cinema where the headquarters staff were able to see the showing of films when local cinemas were out of bounds for security reasons. I was attending one evening accompanied by Ursula Buchanan one of the branch civilian personal assistants. We were sitting near the back and the general came in with some of his staff. Having seated himself down General "Bubbles" looked around to see who else was at the cinema that evening. Seeing me with this attractive young lady he smiled and gave a splendid wink.

My work entailed liaison with the Palestine Police with whom we worked in close cooperation. The Superintendent in charge was Dick Catlin who was full of energy and who obviously ran an efficient office. It was therefore no surprise some years later to see him as the Police Chief in Malaya during the troubles and later in Kenya at the time of the Mau Mau.

Arriving in Palestine in March 1946 I had no previous antipathy towards the local population either Jew or Arab. In the first few weeks life was still fairly relaxed and I with others joined a French Society where we met local families and conversed in French in a local patois. We also made a number of trips round places of religious interest in our free time. The Old City surrounded by its imposing walls and with its narrow streets was fascinating with the shopkeepers vigorously promoting their wares. The Temple and the Wailing Wall, which at that time had not been opened up as it is today made a deep impression. I also visited Jacobs Well, Herods Palace and Bethlehem, Jericho and the Dead Sea. There was a sense of commercialism around the holy places which reminded one of the story of Jesus upbraiding the merchants in the temple forecourt.

One of the most interesting historical places was the tunnel dug through the mountains by the Jews to bring water to the besieged city. The tunnel was some eight hundred yards in length and twisted and turned deep under ground. A guide led our party through which entailed bending and ducking to avoid obstacles. Construction had begun from both ends and there were evident jigs in alignment when the two digging parties could hear the sounds of excavation ahead. Timing of undertaking this expedition was important as at times the flow of water through the tunnel made this passage impossible. It took about twenty minutes to progress from one end to the other. I feel fortunate to have been able to visit and see these places which are so deeply embedded in our religion.

Regrettably terrorist incidents began to increase and it was noticeable our Jewish friends became embarrassed when we met for our weekly social gatherings. Trips into the Old city were forbidden so I was glad I had had the chance to look around places of biblical and historical interest before these restrictions were imposed.

A common sight was groups of young Jews in shorts singing and marching in file behind their youth leaders with the Jewish Flag at their head. It was all too reminiscent of the Hitler Youth and was a rude reminder of things we wished to wipe clean from our minds.

Our work dealt with the machinations and plots of the terrorist organisations and as soldiers we had nothing but contempt for their evil works. There was the incident of the two NCOs who were captured, killed and then strung up with booby traps attached to their bodies. Then without warning bombs were placed in the King David Hotel and one hundred and nine Jewish and Arab civilians working in the Government offices were callously murdered. As a soldier I despised these people and it took many years for me to feel any sympathy for the Jews. Any terrorist of any race who seeks to attain any aim by murder and shooting people in the back is unworthy of being acknowledged a member of the human race.

We had in the course of our work got to meet a number of Palestinian Arabs and after a few months it was inevitable that I felt a closer affinity towards them. A party were invited to attend a celebration in Hebron of an Elder. He was expressing thanks for a return to good health after a serious illness. We sat around a long table while dish after dish of succulent food was presented for our pleasure.

The wife of our senior officer had the duty of receiving the eye of the sheep!

A bottle of whisky had been provided especially for us. Unfortunately it was dropped and broken before any guest had received this generous libation much to the embarrassment of our host. Such is the hospitality of these people that we were at pains to show this accident was not the end of the world.

There were other formal occasions when we met the Arabs as well at less formal parties in their houses. It was perhaps not unnatural that I felt less inhibited in their company.

Our work was principally counter intelligence and I had been directed to move my desk into the office with an officer who was dealing with the Army Formations. I left our offices which were at the end wing of the King David Hotel to move in with him. One morning there was the sound of an explosion in the road outside and looking out of the window we could see smoke. With my office companion we strolled down to the end of the corridor where there was a stair way and exit guarded by military police. The Brigadier Quartermaster General was there with two of his staff Bob Knight and Kinnersley-Taylor and we all discussed the event with the military police before returning to our offices.

I had hardly had time to sit down when there was a massive explosion and the building shook. Looking out of the window the YMCA building opposite was hidden in thick dust. I remarked "Why on earth would anyone blow up the YMCA?" Going into the corridor we saw thick smoke and dust at the end of our corridor and as it cleared saw the whole end of part of the wing at the end of the building had disappeared. There was no trace of the military police and this was where our clerical offices had been. We walked round the edge of the corner to the other wing to see how the rest of our staff were and led them out as orders had come to evacuate the building. In spite of the proximity of the explosion those in these offices were not hurt. They were very shaken but we were relived to see Mary Lachlan, Diana Methold and Ursula Buchanan and help them negotiate round the debris to safety. The explosion was not long after mid-day so we escorted them to their accommodation and stayed with them for lunch.

After that I returned and spent the next few hours digging in the debris to see whether we could retrieve any wounded. We did in fact succeed in digging out one of our clerks alive. As much of our paper work was classified I looked for and found our filing cabinets and made sure they were taken to a secure place. Six of our clerks were killed and five others including ATS girls were injured and hospitalised.

Searching for casualties and files - King David Hotel, Jerusalem 1946.

An off duty ATS girl had been on the roof of the building at the time of the explosion reading a book - it was entitled 'Did she fall'. Amazingly this young lady slid down with the roof as it collapsed onto the crumbling debris below and walked away very shaken but unscathed.

The work of rescue and removing debris took a few days and troops were brought in to help with this task. Among these working parties were soldiers from the 1st Hertfordshire Regiment commanded by Lieut Colonel 'Sox' Hose, DSO.

After the bomb we were provided office accommodation in another part of the building and there was much moving of files around. Pat Robinson and extra staff came up from General Headquarters in Egypt to help sort things out and reorganised our filing system. As I knew all my files by name and number and had personally retrieved them from the rubble I found this change irritating.

The aftermath of the explosion had left unsafe structures hanging from around the damaged area and the Royal Engineers were ordered to make the building safe. They set their charges and the sound of these going off reverberated around Jerusalem. Things did not go as planned and this cleaning up operation caused many of the windows remaining in the building to shatter. The Commander Royal Engineers was summoned before General Barker to receive an imperial rocket!

There was a formal military funeral for the soldiers who had been killed and we travelled to the cemetery at Sarafand. The escorts and pall bearers were provided by 'The Hertfords'.

Visiting HQ one day Colonel 'Sox' Hose came to my office and asked whether I would like to join his battalion. At that time there was a possibility that the battalion would become a part of the Regular Army. I wished to participate more actively in the fight against terrorism alongside soldiers and accepted his offer. Lieut Colonel Bill Peters, DSO, MC, who had been a company commander with the Bedfords in France in 1939/40 was at General Headquarters responsible for the posting of Infantry officers and he helped fix my posting. I joined the 1st Hertfords at Sarafand some two weeks later.

The battalion was part of 6th Airborne Division and employed on Internal Security duties. I was given command of 3 Company and settled down to the run of the mill duties of training and keeping the men fit and occupied and ready when called to take part in operations against the terrorists.

After a week or so I was sent off with my company to defend the railway workshops and the station at Lydda Junction. This was a likely key target for terrorists as they had attacked Haifa Station a few days previously. The station and railway engine repair shops were alongside country which provided plenty of cover for anyone wishing to attack this target. I felt my task was sufficiently important to ask for barbed wire which would be put in place to make it more difficult for anyone to rush the workshops and blow up an engine. My plea was backed by the Colonel and I received two thousand yards of wire released from reserve stocks. The wire was quickly erected and the whole position was more secure as a result.

Colonel 'Sox' was promoted and went to the Middle East training School and Major Phipps, whom I had met eighteen months earlier at Poona, assumed command.

Internal Security operations demand a high state of vigilance. Two thirds of the company were committed on duty at any one time with one platoon manning section posts and a second platoon ready to move on call at any time day or night to repel any attack on the engine workshops.

It was important to keep the soldiers happy in these conditions and the platoon off duty engaged in five a side hockey matches against company headquarters and the 9/12th Lancers who shared our camp. We also managed to play some cricket. Such was the state of tension we all kept our arms close at hand and I went to bed with a Sub machine gun by my side.

There was a detachment of Railway Police living with us commanded by a Superintendent. One evening he had visited our mess and a party developed. I went to bed before things had settled down and adjusted the mosquito net. I was dozing when I became aware of a figure stealthily creeping along the verandah. I rolled over and quietly gripped the Sub Machine Gun and pointed it towards the figure which was now entering through the door. Fortunately I identified the intruder as the Superintendent. I called out "Switch on the light" which he did and was taken aback to see the weapon aimed at his belly. He had taken drink and thought a thunder flash in my room would cause some amusement! He realised that had I not recognised his silhouette the joke would have rebounded badly on him.

There was a minor flap one morning when the sentry guarding the approaches to the station was in danger of being swallowed up among the crowds of Arabs seeking to travel on the pilgrimage to Mecca. As the crowd pressed forward in spite of his warnings he fired a shot over their heads. This had the desired effect and the crowd drew back. I arrived to find the Section commander had brought up reinforcements and all was calm and under control.

The company finished its tour of duty at Lydda and joined the battalion in Sarafand camp. Drafts of soldiers were returning home for discharge and the battalion was not receiving any replacements. One day we heard that two companies of The Black Watch were to join us. 'Hippo' Phipps decided that these officers and men would stay in their own companies and would retain their Tam-o-Shanter headgear. This approach worked well and I found I now had a Captain Cottrill, Black Watch, as my number 2. A battalion sports day was set up with inter platoon competitions in Soccer, Hockey and Basket Ball. The merging of the two very different set of troops worked very well and there was no friction at any level. In fact the link up was such a happy one that the battalion assumed the title of 'The Hertfordshire Watch'.

The run down of the forces continued apace and news came in that the battalion was to move to Egypt to disband. The 2nd Bedfords were in Greece and a draft from the Hertfords was to be despatched as reinforcements. The Military Secretary at Headquarters Palestine and Transjordan sent for 'Hippo', Ian Ross, Stan Chandler and me. Stan had been my platoon sergeant at Dunkirk. He had been given a Commission. On arriving in his office he suggested we volunteer to be available for posting to staff appointments. None of us were very happy at this idea and forming a solid front against the proposition requested to be posted to Greece to join the 2nd Battalion. Our request was accepted and we returned to Sarafand to move by train with the battalion to a transit camp at Heliopolis.

One of the hazards of these train journeys was ensuring the security of weapons. The Arab was adept at stealing rifles from soldiers sleeping in railway carriages. Loss of a weapon was a court martial offence and not only reflected upon the individual soldier concerned but also on the unit. Our soldiers were impressed that two men in each compartment would remain awake and a roster system of guard duty was to be set up. This order paid off and the battalion arrived with all its weapons.

We spent nearly three weeks at the Transit Camp winding the battalion down and organising drafts to go to different battalions. A party of nine officers under 'Hippo' with one hundred and thirty men were posted to Greece to the 2nd Bedfords.

Our time at the transit camp was fully occupied. I found that I was to be a Permanent President Courts Martial for a week to relieve the incumbent filling the post while he had some leave. Three of the four cases brought before me related to soldiers losing their rifles whilst in transit by train. The Arab is very skilful at thieving almost literally from under the nose of anyone. One soldier had put his rifle on the luggage rack and woke to find it gone in the morning. Another soldier had had his rifle removed from between his knees when he dozed off. The thieves were past masters at their trade and were known to ride the carriage roofs. Any carriage window left open was an invitation to these experts. The train travelling across the Sinai Desert became hot and sticky and windows were opened in spite of orders to the contrary and thus soldiers losing rifles were charged with negligence.

There were some officers under arrest awaiting trial. In one case the individual had sold off tracts of desert for thousands of pounds to local speculators as land for building upon!

We visited Cairo and found a night club which was renowned for the display of belly dancing and sat and enjoyed this art. There was a shooting range attached to this club and we tried our hand managing to win a number of trophies. We thought it would be nice to see whether we could invite some girls to join us for a party and I was asked if I had any contacts. I thought of Pat Robinson who had come to Jerusalem to help in the office after the bomb and called her. She accepted the invitation and promised to see if she could bring along some friends. The next evening four of us met up with Pat and Pam Plowman. They thought a visit to see the belly dancing sounded fun so we set off to the Kit Kat Club. The evening passed pleasantly and we had a good meal and after dancing went to the range to show off our shooting skills. Not one of us secured a prize possibly we were far too sober!

We took the girls home and said good bye as next day we were off to Port Said. Some months later when I met up with Pat again I heard that when asked in her office next morning after our party where they had gone that when she replied 'the Kit Kat Club' there was a shocked silence. She was then advised the Club was a high class brothel. The place was so tastefully decorated, the food so well served and the entertainment so good, the thought of other activities on the premises had never even occurred to any of us.

Arriving in Port Said next day with Jack Richardson I had time to purchase a book to despatch as a thank you gift to Pat for the pleasure of her company and for bringing a friend along to our party. One night was spent in a transit camp before embarking to sail to Piraeus.

Map 7 A   Greece

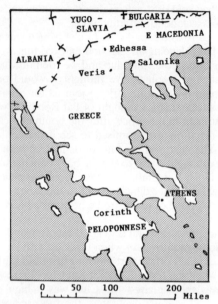

Map 7 B   Palestine and Egypt

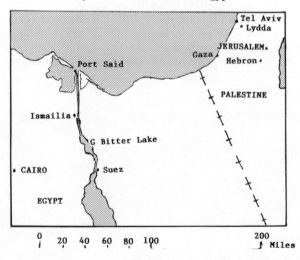

Chapter Twenty

Middle East - 1946 to 1947
(Greece)

The voyage from Port Said to Piraeus took three days and was uneventful. We disembarked and were given accommodation in a Transit Camp. We were told the ship to take us to Salonika would take us aboard the next evening and we would have the morning free. So Jack and I took the opportunity to go into Athens to see the Parthenon and the Acropolis which made a much greater impression on me than had the Pyramids. Jack took some photos which came out well.

Our transport to take us to Salonika was an old cargo ship and soldiers and officers camped out between the decks. We sailed close alongside the shore passing between many islands which appeared barren without much vegetation. The ship followed a line between marker buoys and we were told this was because this was the route which had been cleared of mines. After one night on board we came to Salonika and found transport waiting to take us to the battalion.

This journey took some three or more hours and the ravages of war were evident along the whole route. There were bomb damaged houses and railway engines and rolling stock left where they had been damaged. This was our first sight of war time destruction in an occupied territory in Europe. We were to see a lot more.

The battalion was stationed at Edhessa with companies on detachment in outposts at key communication points. There were Communist guerillas operating in the mountain ranges who raided into the surrounding territory after dark. The battalion positions were on the limits of the land dominated by the guerila forces. Our task was to act as a deterrent without actively engaging these groups to enable the civilian population to live a normal life. The roads from battalion headquarters to the companies were cut by night. Movement was restricted to daylight after a truck travelling to Naousa after dark was ambushed and shot at and one of our soldiers was killed.

The Commanding Officer was Lieut Colonel A.C. Young and Jack Richardson was to take over as Adjutant from Robson who had been with the battalion since Italy and was to go home for release. I spent a few days at Headquarters before being sent to Veroia to take charge of 'C' Company. Whilst at Edhessa I went out shooting one afternoon with the Colonel and Peter Francis. The guns had been provided to enable officers to relax from the day to day routine.

Arriving at Veroia I found the company billeted in huts alongside a railway line and that I had a caravan. Winter was fast approaching and the weather was becoming bitter and it was difficult to keep warm at night. Many of my soldiers had either been with me with the Hertfords or had gone through training in Norfolk with the 8th Suffolks. This was an advantage as we knew each others foibles. Brigade Headquarters was in the town and I called in to meet Brigadier Preston. His brother had commanded the 1st Bedfords in the Desert.

British Forces in Northern Greece were now ordered to withdraw from Edhessa and the forward outposts towards Salonika. The locals at Edhessa were very concerned to see us go. They told us the Communists would come and kill them. Once we pulled out the Communists quickly occupied all these mountain foot hills.

The Battalion now concentrated in an old school about four miles outside Salonika. Our numbers were decreasing with the continual release of drafts who had completed their service and 'C' Company was dissolved. I now went to command Support Company taking over from Dennis Peet who was going home. This gave me the chance to learn at close hand about the Mortar, Carrier and Anti Tank Platoons. We continued an active training programme and took part in battalion exercises.

Christmas was coming up and morale was raised considerably when we heard our regimental band would be with us over the festive season. The band arrived and Colonel Young took the whole battalion out on a route march one afternoon with the band playing at our head. This was the first time I had marched behind a band since before the war. The band also provided the gilt to a Guard of Honour for General Sir Miles Dempsey the General Officer Commanding in Chief Middle East when he visited Salonika. Support Company provided the guard under my command and the soldiers performed splendidly.

This time of year saw the migration of hundreds of wild geese and Hippo Phipps organised shooting parties at week ends to see whether the menu could include goose. Initial forays were not too successful as although with the mass of birds overhead it was all but impossible not to hit a bird casualties were minimal. Hippo decided the shot was not sufficiently lethal and a party sat in the mess in the evenings changing the size of shot in the cartridges. This labour of love paid off and the shooting parties came back with more than sufficient birds to not only meet the needs of both the officers and the WOs and Sergeants messes but also the cook house. The whole battalion enjoyed fresh goose for Christmas a great change from routine rations.

There was a delicatessen in Salonika which sold delicious home baked cream cakes which all of us sampled at one time or another. As there was a shortage of the essentials to make such fare it was obvious some form of black market was providing the wherewithal for the ingredients.

This was a time when units were experiencing the transition from a war time to a peace time environment with all that meant. Colonel Young was a brilliant administrator and he did much to ensure the niceties of change to peace time administration were understood and correctly applied. He was determined all officers were fully indoctrinated in mess etiquette. There were to be two formal mess nights each week when all officers would attend and guests would be invited. Some officers already had their 'Blues' with them and I had mine posted out to me from home. It was fascinating to see the change of attitude of my batman when my 'Blues' arrived. Instead of leaving my kit ready and departing to the lines he now remained until I was dressed and almost escorted me from my room to the ante room. Other officers who changed into 'Blues' had the same experience. A choir was formed by the officers which entertained our guests after dinner. All taking part sang lustily though I doubt many points were earned for technique.

Time passed and the band left us to do a tour of duty at Athens. News came in the battalion was to move to Egypt and we would hand over to the HLI. I was asked by the Colonel whether I wished to go as a staff officer to a liaison team with the Greek Army. I declined not realising the battalion would soon receive orders to close down and be placed in Suspended Animation.

We left Salonika and sailed via Piraeus to pick up other drafts returning to Egypt. The band was now in Athens and our bandmaster had acquired a landing craft and sailed round our ship for two hours with the band playing heartily. They gave a great concert and this gesture was greatly appreciated by one and all. Having taken on the drafts from Piraeus we set sail for Egypt.

Chapter Twenty One
Middle East - 1947 to 1948
(Egypt)

Landing at Port Said we were taken to Fayid where the battalion was housed in tents in one of the many camps round the shores of the Great Bitter Lakes. The Officers tents were close to the perimeter wire. Waking the next morning one young officer found all his kit and clothes had been stolen in the night. Such pilfering was rife and the colonel decided something had to be done. Next evening two bren gun teams were sited forward of our wire waiting for a repeat attempt. They were not disappointed. At about eleven pm two figures were seen approaching the perimeter wire. As the wire was crossed they were challenged and failing to halt fired upon. They promptly ran off into the desert. A trail of blood next morning showed that one of their number had not escaped unscathed. The battalion had no further problems of attempted thieving from then on.

The battalion was given the Guard duties for the Commander in Chief, Senior Staff Officers and the ATS and Civilian Ladies Mess. The latter task was not without its amusing side as soldiers, having fortified themselves in the N.A.A.F.I. Canteen, made attempts to cross the perimeter wire from time to time. Such episodes resulted in a frantic telephone call from the ATS Field Officer to the Battalion Field officer on Duty. "There is a soldier in our lines - help". A detachment of soldiers would then be sent off under the Orderly Officer to sweep the ATS lines to round up the culprits. This call for help came sufficiently often for us to reply in kind. One evening a party was in progress in our mess to which a number of ladies had been invited. The Field Officer on duty rang the ATS mess and asking for their Field Officer said "There is a female in our lines - help". The lady in question did not seem to see the funny side.

The Warrant Officers and Sergeants Mess was managed by WO1 Vernon French who had distinguished himself serving in the 1st Bedfords with the Chindits. He had the task of building the morale of his mess which was losing a large number of experienced war time members. Such was his personality that the esprit was evident and this reflected in the way the Senior NCOs behaved. He had nominated Sergeant Talbot a pre-war NCO of stolid character as Provost Sergeant who was quite splendid in this job. Sergeant Talbot had been one of my first Section Commanders when I joined the 2nd Bedfords at Shorncliffe in July 1939. The morale of the mess members was high and this affected the whole battalion.

The RSM decided to arrange a formal evening with officers and lady guests invited. I was encouraged by Colonel Young to invite Pat Robinson who was living in the ATS Camp. She accepted the invitation and met up with us again for the first time since our party in Cairo. There was little doubt Colonel Young thought Pat was a most suitable match for me and he encouraged our meetings and Pat got to know the Bedfords.

Orders came through for the battalion to disband and be placed in "Suspended Animation". The battalion was ordered to find an officer to take up a staff appointment at General Headquarters and I went along for an interview. I was taken on by Colonel Rose of The Buffs as a Staff Learner. I said goodbye to the battalion and joined General Headquarters Middle East as a Staff Captain in the Military Secretarys' Branch.

Officers working at General Headquarters Middle East were housed and fed in some eight messes and I was allotted to Mess number 2. Single Majors and Captains were accommodated four to a tent. There was a hard floor and we had a bed and a bedside locker. Life was not as comfortable as being in a battalion. Our batmen were German prisoners of war who were awaiting repatriation after being captured in the Desert Wars. The camp was sited in the desert and had a wire perimeter fence. We continued to experience the forays of thieves in these surroundings who would even go about their work in daylight. One Sunday morning an officer in a tent next to mine heard a ripping sound and saw a knife cutting the tent side. Leaping out of bed, bare foot and in night attire, he chased the Arab across the sands to the break in the wire through which he had entered our lines.

I found my job with the Military Secretarys branch was to process applications from officers applying for a Regular Commission. GHQ Middle East stretched from PAIFORCE (Persia and Iraq) and Palestine and Transjordan in the North and included Egypt, the Sudan, Abyssinia and East Africa, Greece, Italy, Tripolitania and Malta with subordinate Headquarters in each of these countries. Applications once checked for accuracy were sent to the War Office. Once sufficient candidates were in the pipe line a Regular Commissions Board came out from England to test and interview the candidates.

I had the interesting job of organising all the administrative arrangements for these Boards. This entailed finding suitable accommodation and mess staff, providing transport and liaison with the team throughout their stay. Candidates had to be summoned from throughout the region to attend these selection courses in batches of twelve. The candidates had to arrive before their course started and be called to my office and directed to the senior officer of their Arm or Corps for an interview for that officer to add his own opinion on the suitability of the applicant. This meant placing the candidate in a Transit Camp until the start of the selection course.

The Board was headed by a Major General assisted by two Lieut Colonels and a staff officer. The selection procedure took three days and during this time the candidates donned a numbered jacket, took written and physical tests and took part in group discussions. The whole programme was devised to see which candidate showed leadership qualities. As might be imagined this whole concept of selection was viewed with deep suspicion by many senior serving officers. Colonel Rose got permission for two commanding officers from within the command to attend as observers on each course and they sat alongside their opposite numbers on the team. This indoctrination paid off and those who attended in this capacity went back to their commands convinced of the validity of this means of selection. It was not long before word spread round that the system worked fairly for all concerned.

I was afforded the opportunity to sit in at different phases of the procedures on a number of courses and was fascinated how the character of the candidates was revealed in the answers to written questions and responses during the discussions and physical tests.

I recall two cases where candidates who had to answer forty questions in as many minutes clearly demonstrated their worries. The first was an Engineer officer who I knew and had had dealings with and whom I had found somewhat brusque and intolerant. His reply to the question 'What do you dislike most about the Army?' was "I dislike having to take orders from senior officers". The other case was somewhat different and the individual had a rather personal problem which preyed on his mind. In answer to the question 'Have you any problem which you worry about?' he replied "In that I am not like other men and only have one ball".

There was a common concept at the time that a regular officer spent his leisure time hunting, shooting and fishing and these activities were nominated by candidates in response to the written questions. Some candidates were genuine in expressing their interest in these activities whilst others had but a vague idea of these sports. Topics for discussion cleverly covered all types of sports and the genuine candidate in his responses showed his knowledge whilst the man with but a perfunctory understanding failed to enter into the discussion. Candidates were observed throughout their stay and notes were kept of each activity.

The physical tests also showed who was a natural leader. Each candidate was interviewed by the Lieut Colonel and by the General.

The Board team then sat down and discussed each candidate and agreed a final grade. On completion the General told each candidate his result.

I saw some two hundred and forty candidates pass through this selection procedure with two different Generals with their own teams. I needed no convincing the system was fair and accurate to the candidate and the army in selecting the right individuals.

I had seen a lot of Pat Robinson during the passing months and asked her to marry me. To my delight she consented and we planned to get married at home. I was due for leave in lieu of Python (LIAP) in September and Pat managed to take leave at that time. I had a few anxious days at this time as I thought I would be retained as a witness in a Court Martial of the mess manager. I had been appointed wines member and briefed that it was suspected that the German waiter was fiddling the books. At the time all liquor consumed was paid for in cash. The wines officer checked the bar stock each day and relieved the bar man of the cash. I had only been performing this task a few days when I noticed the bar man seemed agitated. After checking the bar and collecting the correct cash he said "What about your cash Sir". I pretended not to hear and walked away. The same question was raised the following night and again I ignored it but reported to the PMC. The following night the question was raised once more. By this time the bar man was very agitated so I asked him what he meant. He produced quite a tidy sum of cash and said "This is your share sir". I called over the PMC who was waiting for my signal and asked the barman to explain how he came by this money. It transpired that there was always a small surplus of liquor in each bottle of spirits and with one hundred or more officers these small amounts soon built up into a tidy sum. I should hasten to say the German barman received no return from this racket.

This was but the thin edge of the fiddle going on as delving deeper it soon became evident the mess manager, who received his share of these proceeds was also running other enterprises. He was selling ration cigarettes to local contractors and running the same racket in another mess for which he was responsible. It seemed that he would be charged and that I would be the key witness which would most likely delay my leave. The only other witnesses were the German mess staff. In the end it was ruled the case could not be pursued as it was not acceptable to have a prisoner of war give evidence against a British officer. The officer concerned was reprimanded, removed from his duties, and posted to Cyprus.

Our leave came up and we sailed home on 'The Empress of Britain'. Pat was in a cabin with a dozen ladies and I with eight other

Captains in a cabin somewhere above the propellers. Arriving home I met Pat's parents and we were married by special licence at St. Michael's Blewbury on 20 September 1947. Brigadier Jimmy Davenport my first Commanding Officer who was a friend of Colonel Robinson was one of the guests. Colonel Rose sent his telegram from Egypt, 'Well. Well. Well'.

I was very touched to receive a Silver Entree Dish from Lieut Colonel Young and the officers of the 2nd Bedfords with the officers badge of the battalion engraved upon it. As the regiment no longer exists this is now a piece of history. After our honeymoon I flew back to Egypt to attend a Pre Staff Course before settling down to study in my spare time for the entrance exam for the course at Camberley. Pat followed by ship.

Robin and Pat on their wedding day, Blewbury 20th September 1947.

There was a cholera epidemic in Egypt at the time and some diplomatic problem so mail was not getting through. I received no mail from Pat and she heard nothing from me. The result of this lack of communication was that she arrived at Port Said and I was not there to meet her!

We spent a few days in the NAAFI Club at Fayid in a tent until we found a native house alongside the Great Bitter Lake not far from the Commanding Generals residence. The facilities were pretty primitive. Water was brought round and siphoned into a tank on the roof which by the evening provided natural hot water for a shower. There was a cool box and we stored our drink alongside drinking water in old gin bottles. This led to confusion as to which was gin and which was water. There were three other families living close by.

Married quarters did not exist and to cope with the problem a number of family villages had been built made up of clusters of wooden huts. There were eight rooms in each hut. A married officer with a wife without children was allotted one room. There were four outside loos and wash rooms to each block so there were cases where there were as many as six families sharing these communal facilities. The loos were of the bucket variety which were removed each day for emptying by local Arabs. There was obviously competition between the Arab cleaner and the user of the loo to ensure the hot seat was not being occupied when the bucket was being changed!

Central dining and sitting rooms were provided for a group of huts where the families took their meals and gathered in the evenings. These facilities were quickly named 'Butlins'. Even then there was not sufficient accommodation to meet all needs and junior officers with but eight or more years service had to find accommodation elsewhere. About one hundred officers found accommodation in Ismailia some thirty miles away on the Suez canal.

An Officers Club managed by NAAFI was sited on the shores of The Great Bitter Lake. This provided temporary accommodation in rooms with mud walls and covered with tentage for the roofs. Meals could be bought and a dance band played music. Entertainment was not very sophisticated.

Two brigadiers arrived to join the Headquarters staff. One Pete Pyman was promoted Major General and became the Chief of Staff, the other Hunt later of Mount Everest fame became a Lieut Colonel on the General Staff. General Pyman had served in Europe under Montgomery and had adopted some of his former chiefs characteristics. Colonel Rose the Military Secretary was a senior officer in the old mold and inevitably tension developed between the two officers as there were certain confidential matters affecting senior appointments which were for the eyes of the Commander in Chief only.

On returning from leave I had been given a new job assisting Major Chris Waters in handling all senior staff orders and movement papers on behalf of the colonel. Chris was an able officer full of life and fun. One evening feeling that activities in the NAAFI Club were somewhat dull he decided to liven things up. In the company of a cavalry major the pair rode into the club on their horses to the cheers of the younger members present. This episode widened the cavern between the two branches.

We had only been living in our small house beside the Great Bitter Lake about two months when a neighbour was shot and killed late one night following a party at his house. As a result those of us living in the area were told it was unsafe and we were ordered to move. Temporary accommodation was found in a hotel in Ismailia while we searched for a suitable flat. Christmas was approaching and the South Wales Borderers Rugby team came on a visit from Cyprus. They beat all opposition and it was left to the GHQ team to redeem the honour of the forces in Egypt. I played in the second row and the game was fairly even until the last few minutes when we lost eighteen points to eleven. During a scrummage a knee came up and I bit my tongue which soon swelled up and in spite of treatment refused to reduce in size. I was admitted to hospital on Christmas Eve. Not an auspicious start to our married life! A Doctor came round and after examining the swollen tongue moved on down the ward. Later a nursing sister brought me some penicillin. After this we were left to our own devices over the next two days and I remember spending time making decorations for the ward. Medical treatment was a supply of medical comforts in the shape of spirits and champagne. This combined with enforced bed rest had the desired effect and my tongue healed. After four days I was able to return back to the hotel.

We eventually found a small flat on the outskirts of Ismailia with its own piece of sand at the back surrounded by a high wall. The flat was on the boundary of the "Out of Bounds" area. Our landlord belonged to the Muslim Brotherhood so we felt we were reasonably safe living in his property.

A sweet water canal ran alongside the Suez Canal and carried water which helped irrigate the fields which grew produce. The canal was used by the local people for all purposes, not only did they wash themselves and their livestock in the waters they also used it for all toiletry requirements. There were so many bugs and diseases carried in the waters that we were advised that should we fall in we would need some dozen needles to protect against infection!

The working day at Headquarters was from 8 am to 1 pm every day, and continued from 5 pm to 8 pm on Monday, Wednesday and Friday. The bus from Ismailia started at 7 am and on a long day got back by 9 pm. There was insufficient time to return home on the long days and time did drag on as the only place to go and relax was the Club on the shore of the Great Bitter Lake.

There was a saddle club and young officers working at General headquarters were encouraged to join. A special class was arranged and we went off riding in the mornings before work. On free afternoons we would ride out into the desert and ascend the local hills. After I married I was taught sailing by Charles Brewis of The Welch Regiment. Having qualified I was able to take part in the sailing races which were managed by the joint Army/R.A.F. sailing club at Ismailia. Pat acted as crew and we spent nearly every free afternoon enjoying racing on Lake Timsah. At week ends when we were not racing we joined with others and took picnics across the other side of the canal.

Sailing on Lake Timsah in 1948.

Charles Brewis had lost a leg below the knee but this did not prevent him enjoying life to the full. He lived in a fourth floor flat in Ismailia. One Sunday we were at a drink party. The Sunday papers were there and we read of a court martial case in the Royal Navy. The accused claimed they had mixed up a cocktail and had not been responsible for their actions. The amazing thing was that the contents of the mix were printed in the paper. This was too much and we decided to try it out. We were sensible enough to reduce the volume of the mix very considerably. Even then the effects were startling and I retired home to bed. What was worse I woke later with a raging thirst and as soon as I drank water the effects of the mix made themselves felt again. What it might have been like had we tasted the full measures I dread to think.

On another occasion we had gone out to a club in Ismailia. There was a sleazy manager who irritated Charles who made some remark after a singer had finished her piece. The manager implied that an Englishman could not render a song in another language. I was encouraged to disprove this statement and gave a rendering of J'Attendrai which received applause from the clientele. The manager not to be beaten then challenged me to sing a song in a second language so I responded with a song in Greek which was received by the other customers with even greater applause. This was too much for the manager who said something to Charles who promptly stood up and saying the place was not to his liking jumped out of the window. There was a ten foot drop to the street below. I felt I should make sure Charles with his gammy leg was all right and followed him. He was unhurt. We returned and collected our wives and repaired home.

Charles was posted to the South Wales Borderers Regiment in Cyprus and I was now assisting Colonel Deeds in work to do with drafting orders for senior officers throughout the command. I got to know many names of senior officers but only met a few of them.

I was continuing my studies to take the entrance examination for the Army Staff Course. I had attended a pre staff course which set a number of test papers and provided guidance. This was to be the first written exam following the war and competition was fierce. The exam was in February 1948 and after the first paper listening to comments by fellow officers I felt I had missed a lot and my thoughts were somewhat sanguine as to my chances. The next papers were much more to my liking until I came to the Military Law which I hated. The die was now cast and I had to wait to hear the results.

The results were a long time coming. I was sitting in the office one evening in late August and Chris Waters the Deputy Assistant Military Secretary received a signal listing the names of those from the Middle East who had passed the exam and selected to attend the next course. "There are only eighteen names for the whole command" he said and started to read them out. I sat listening and as each name was read out felt sure that there could not be any more to come. At last my name came up and Chris let the whole office know. The relief was wonderful and I went off to tell Pat in person.

The romantic novelist Denise Robbins was married to an officer on the staff at G.H.Q. She used the desert background and the hot winds blowing off the desert as the background for a novel entitled 'Khamsin'. One or two of the characters in the book were clearly individuals she had met in the social round.

Field Marshal Montgomery paid us a visit and we were all ordered by the Chief of Staff to parade in front of the offices of the Commanding General to cheer.

On another occasion there was a flying demonstration by a De Haviland 'Vampire' jet aircraft, which was test flying in desert conditions. The R.A.F. locally were still flying 'Typhoons'.

I was due some leave and went to Cyprus in September where we stayed with Charles Brewis who was now serving with the 1st Battalion of The South Wales Borderers. We had a great break enjoying sailing, swimming, visiting Nicosia and Kyrenia and seeing the old Crusader Castles. We sailed back to Port Said on a Corvette and I continued my work in the Military Secretary's office. The experience as a staff learner had been interesting and earned me a good recommendation which ensured a place on the next staff course. I handed over my job in December to return home to attend the 1949 Army Staff Course at Camberley.

Chapter Twenty Two

United Kingdom - 1949 to 1954

This was our first move as a family and we hired a local firm to pack up our glass and china and hoped it would arrive in the UK in one piece. We moved out of our flat to a transit camp in Ismailia the day before we were due to embark at Port Said. We were joined by Derek and Barbara Tewkesbury of the Bedfords who were also returning home. News came in that our ship the S.S. 'Orbita' which was sailing from East Africa had broken down and would arrive two days later. This was not an auspicious start. Eventually when we boarded Pat was accommodated in a cabin with eight other wives and children. I found myself once again with five other Captains in a cabin deep in the bowels of the ship at the stern with the noise of the propellers as a back drop.

We set off from Port Said heading for Limassol in Cyprus to pick up more passengers. When we arrived the seas were so rough the floats, which had brought the new passengers out from the shore, were rising on the waves and falling in the troughs to such a degree it was decreed unsafe to transfer people and baggage from the floats to the ship. The embarkation was cancelled until the next morning when the storm had passed by and a more seemly loading could take place. Jack Walliker of The Welch Regiment embarked at Cyprus with his wife. He was due to attend the Staff College as a fellow student and our paths would cross in the future.

Our next port of call was Malta. Our passage was further delayed as the ship broke down once more and hove to whilst repairs were carried out. The original schedule had forecast our arrival in the UK in time for Christmas. These delays meant that we would still be at sea for the Christmas festivities. A party of civilian dock workers had joined the ship at Malta. They were not amused at the dilatory progress of the ship. They had plenty of cash to spend and took advantage of the reduced bar prices. Some of their number celebrated to good measure and attempted to break into the female only accommodation. The Ship's Officers managed to prevent any incident from getting out of hand but they had their hands full.

Our journey home continued with further delays while more running repairs were carried out in the Irish Sea. It was rumoured we nearly drifted ashore near Dublin! We arrived at Liverpool in time to be home to celebrate the New Year. In spite of these delays we had managed to occupy ourselves during the voyage with on board entertainment and plenty of bridge.

The Staff Course started on the 6th of January so we had little time to sort ourselves out into a small flat at Beech House, Bagshot. There were no married quarters available in 1949 for students and we had had to negotiate a place from Egypt. Pat's parents had kindly gone to to see the owner, Nods Moore-Anderson, on our behalf and clinched a deal so we did have a pied a terre. Our baggage arrived and we were delighted to find our china and glass all in one piece.

The flat was minute but the house was set in lovely grounds with a lake and Nods from the start welcomed us warmly. She loved parties and was a delightful host and invited us to meet her friends. It was a coincidence that John and Averill Barrow from the Regiment were frequent visitors. Two other Bedford officers Geoffrey Warland and Tony Gauvain had lived in the flat in earlier days so there were strong links with the regiment.

There were some two hundred students on the staff course and we soon discovered that the pattern of work would put us under pressure. Projects had to be completed and handed in on time. The Commandant was General Dudley Ward who had served in the ranks in The Bedfords. There was a lovely story about his application for a Regular Commission when he was serving as a Sergeant at the Regimental Depot. The adjutant at the time was a Captain Denning, whose brothers all attained jobs at the top of their professions. He had a fierce reputation and interviewing Sergeant Ward turned down his request saying "Sergeant Ward you are a very good sergeant but you must appreciate that you have reached your peak. Application is refused". Captain Denning finished his career as a Lieut General and Sergeant Ward as a full General. The Deputy Commandant of the Staff College was Brigadier McLeod.

The time table proved to be hectic. Monday evening was sufficiently leisurely to allow us to join a Scottish Dancing class, the thing to do as General Ward and Brigadier McLeod were keen participants. For the rest of the week the candles were burnt till the small hours until the Friday when groups would meet socially with wives to get to know each other.

It could not have been more than two weeks before we were invited upstairs one Sunday evening by Nods to meet some guests. Pat found herself sitting next to a General who was working in the War Office but failed to catch his name. He enquired where we had been stationed and hearing it had been General Headquarters Middle East asked a lot of questions about life and accommodation. Pat answered forthrightly and told him the conditions were pretty awful and more-over that the RAF looked after their married families much much better than the Army. A week later I found a letter in my box at the Staff College from the Director of Personal Administration at The War Office. The letter asked me to confirm in writing the comments made by Pat at the party if I could verify them. It assured me my name would not be broadcast. Biting the bullet after talking things over with Pat I set down the list of complaints which she had raised. I heard no more officially but some four months later a friend of mine working in the War Office met me and said "You certainly stirred things up about officer accommodation in the Middle East. Your name is circulating round every office in the Ministry". So much for confidentiality.

Among the young friends of Nods who visited Beech House were Jimmy Stuart Monteith and Ashton Cross. They had fought at Anzio together where Jimmy had been seriously wounded and lost both his legs above the knees. Jimmy was remarkably active in spite of his disability and did much to promote BLESMA, the British Limbless Ex Servicemens Association.

There was an American student in our group called Samuel Sneilson Neill who with his wife Marthalina came from the Southern States of the USA. One Summer Evening Nods kindly allowed us to invite some of our fellow students round to a drink party. Nods joined our party with Jimmy and Ashton Cross. Marthalina was a well built lady of formidable stature. She was happily partaking of a glass of whisky clutching a flower in her free hand. I introduced her to Ashton Cross who was standing with the lake behind him. Advancing towards Ashton twirling the flower at face level Marthalina demanded of the shaken Ashton, in a pronounced 'Southern drawl', "Say, are you a Surrey Dook?" Ashton recoiled in front of this approach and replying in the negative escaped sideways only avoiding falling backwards into the lake by a miracle.

The year spent on the course provided in depth teaching on all aspects of military organisation and tactics. Students were grouped into syndicates of ten made up of individuals from the different Arms and Corps. This encouraged exchange of views and working together on exercises. Visits were made to Industry and to Fleet Street to provide an insight into industrial relations. There were visits to the Royal Navy and Royal Air Force as well as a battle field tour. The battles studied were the 'D' Day landings, the airborne assault on the Mieville Battery and the armoured break out from Caen. This visit was more personal as some of the Directing Staff and fellow students had themselves taken part in these actions and no attempt was made to gloss over errors and mishaps. We found the French food quite wonderful after the restrictions of rationing at home.

Our course was the first since the war to have been selected following an entrance exam and the Commandant kept us all under pressure. We heard that anyone who failed to meet the standards expected would be sent back to duty at the end of the second phase of learning. As a result there was a great deal of soul searching. Eventually when the time came two of our number were failed and returned to duty.

The Scottish Country dancing proved very popular and Frank Coutts, KOSB and Sandy Leslie, Black Watch two fellow students often accompanied us with the pipes. Pat Hunter Gordon assisted as an instructor. His wife, who had been a Ferranti, displayed all the family genius for developing new ideas. She was experimenting with 'Paddipads' and sought advice from the married families among the students. She patented the system and did well from this product.

Apart from learning how to work as part of a staff team the Staff College course brought one into contact with officers from other Regiments and Corps. The social activities were an escape valve after the pressure of producing written work to a tight schedule. It was very much a case of following the adage of 'Work hard and play hard'.

During this year we met up with Pat's cousin Conn Hackett, who after service in the Indian Army, was now with The Carbineers and ADC to General Sir Ouvry Roberts. Nods Moore Anderson was always making up parties to attend the different dances and enquired whether we could find a partner for Kaye her niece who was visiting from Canada. Pat suggested Conn and sent off an invitation. Fortunately he was not required by the General that weekend and joined our combined party. Conn set his cap at Kaye and we attended their wedding the following year.

On completion of the course Rouse, a fellow student drew up a lovely certificate which was presented to all who had attended the dancing classes. The certificate was a PhD (Passed Highland Dancing) with a splendid characterisation of Frank Coutts playing his pipes with a learned owl, the staff college symbol, looking somewhat askance. It is one of my proud trophies.

The year came to an end all too soon and we all departed to staff appointments. Weather wise it had been a lovely dry summer which made all the outdoor work more pleasurable. It was a year of making new friends. Paths would cross in the years ahead and these friendships helped later in staff appointments in working together and sorting out problems.

I was to meet Sam Neill some fifteen years later in the U.S.A. and met up with Pat Patterson in 1955 in Malaya. Of the students on the

1949 course Jack Harman, 'Monkey' Blacker and Frazer became Generals and Pat Patterson, Max Sawers and Abraham made Major General. Many others attained command all at a time when the Armed Forces were continually contracting.

Some fifty percent of the course were given second grade staff appointments I with the remainder found myself appointed as a General Staff Officer Grade 3 to the Operations Branch at Headquarters Western Command at Chester.

There was little time to find anywhere to live as there were no married quarters available for a young Captain of two years married status. We had to vacate our flat at Beech House and Pat went to live with her parents at Blewbury. This was the first time we would live apart during army service. After three months I found accommodation in the wing of a large house at Littleton some four miles in the country.

Life as a junior staff officer entailed detailed work and I well remember the advice offered by a senior Lieutenant Colonel Ordnance Officer when I asked about controlled stores. "The regulations are there for guidance. Your job is to interpret them for the benefit of the units you are serving". It was an adage I never forgot.

On the social side I was given permission to form a Headquarters rugger team and arrange a few matches. I enjoyed the inter branch shooting on the local .22 range as well as the annual Command rifle competition. I also started a Scottish Dance club and passed on the teaching I had been given at Staff College. Once a month we all attended the local parish church in Uniform when our senior Chaplain took the service.

It was an interesting introduction to peace time soldiering in England made more interesting when Churchill returned to office and directed the UK Army to be prepared for any expected threat from Russia. I had the task of preparing and submitting a weekly state report on the capability of forces in the command to the War Office. Each week saw an improvement. Coloured pins in a map of the Command showed the strength of mobile forces as compared to the total numbers of men on station. Briefing General Nickolson one day on the operational situation looking at the map display he commented on the large number of immobile troops at an Ordnance depot; "There is a mass of immobility we will have to do something about that".

During the two years at Chester I experienced a variety of tasks ranging from determining the scale of issue of controlled stores, recommending Staff cuts to meet a fourteen per cent required reduction, collating the bid for cash to pay civilian staff and with a senior member of the Command secretariat meeting trade union officials.

I served under two great Generals. The first was General Simpson and his successor was General Nickolson. The Brigadier General Staff was Jack Churcher who had a sharp tongue but was wonderful to work for. John O'Neill a Gunner, who had been in the Indian Army, was my immediate boss. Rollo Price, South Wales Borderers, his opposite in the Adjutant Generals' department was always trying to catch him out. Rollo would call on the phone pretending to be the Chief of Staff and tell John to bring him a document. One day John was completely taken in and taking the relevant paper knocked on the General's door saying "You asked for this paper, Sir". The General who had no sense of humour told John not to waste his time and to get out of his office. Brigadier Jack Churcher in the next office heard the rumpus and coming out told John to check with him next time before going direct to the Chief of Staff and then went in to the General and took the heat off.

We were able to get our own back on Rollo later. The Tatler had intimated they wished to have a picture of the staff with General Nickolson shortly after he had taken over command and Rollo was responsible for all the arrangements. A phone call initiated in our office purported to be from the Tatler and required him to arrange a separate photo with a named group of officers. He took the bait and phoned around those listed. We felt we had evened the score.

It was at Chester our son Guy was born on the 3rd of January 1951. The arrival of this infant took longer than anticipated. It was almost thirty six hours after leaving Pat at the nursing home that I was given the news at home at 6 pm. I went down the road to tell a medical friend and we drove around the local roundabout twice in celebration. After visiting Pat I went to the annual Sergeants Mess Dance where my fellow officers were waiting to hear the news. Such were the celebrations that one wife increased the weight of the baby each time she spread the news. Before the party ended the child was at least sixteen pounds in weight.

The christening was performed by our Chaplain the Rev Canon Pike. Pat's Uncle, Dalby Hackett, and Lionel Hitchen were kind enough to agree to be Godparents. Lionel came up for the service with his wife Louie. The two years at Chester passed very quickly and in January 1952 I was posted as a Training Major to the 1st Battalion The Hertfordshire Regiment (Territorial Army) at Hertford. There were no quarters and we found a small house at Great Amwell which had been let to John Salazar the adjutant who was moving on.

The Hertfords were one of two territorial battalions affiliated to the Bedfordshire and Hertfordshire Regiment which provided the regular permanent staff. The Hertfords had served with a Guards Brigade in France in the 1914 - 1918 War and numbered their companies following the tradition in the Household Brigade. Battalion Headquarters was at Hertford with company detachments at Cheshunt, Watford, Hemel Hempstead and Letchworth. The appointment of Training Major was a new one and had been authorised to help cope with the extra load caused by the need to train National Servicemen completing their 'Reserve' training commitment.

Lieutenant Colonel Ivor Grey, a Solicitor in London, was the commanding officer and his second in command was Robert Humbert of Humbert and Flint. The Adjutant was Captain Tony Ward-Booth whom we had first met in Egypt when he visited Fayed on a Regular Commissions Board. Major Joe Townsend was the Quartermaster. Army quarters had been built in Hertford for them. All the TA company commanders had seen active service during the war. They were an enthusiastic team well supported by their junior officers and Non Commissioned Officers.

'TA' Ball 1952. Pat, Robin and the Humberts.

The TA volunteer came to his drill hall in the evenings after work so I spent most evenings visiting these halls. There were also week end activities covering exercises and shooting competitions. In addition brigade headquarters ran training days for regular permanent staff at Bedford.

156

There were some ten schools each with a combined Cadet Corps and we helped take their Certificate 'A' examinations. This was an interesting task and the local schools welcomed us most hospitably. It was fascinating to see the different way each school was run and get a feel of their atmosphere. This close contact helped me determine my choice for Guy a few years later.

At this time with the National Service Reservists there were some eight hundred men on the strength of the battalion. The commitment required each man to perform so many drill hours outside annual camp and to come to camp for fourteen days each year. Colonel Grey decided that it was more efficient to call up the National Service element for a days training rather than try and manage a training programme spread over innumerable evenings and this system worked well. Week end camps were run outside Annual Camp usually making use of the facilities of the Army Training area at Stanford in Norfolk.

Apart from tactical training emphasis was placed on ensuring the battalion had a good Regimental Band and a Corps of Drums. They played a major role during the celebrations centring round the Coronation of H.M. The Queen beating the retreat round all the County towns and supporting the Honour Guards.

The officers mess ran a series of mess nights and an annual Ball, which was most popular in the County. Past members of the battalion were very loyal with their support.

In my second year I spent three weeks attached to the French Army on an exchange posting. I travelled to Paris by train with three other officers where we were briefed by the Military Mission to whom we were to report on the regiments we would visit. This whole visit provided an interesting insight into the way the French army was building itself up after the earlier defeats in the war. I spent time with the 62nd Regiment of Infantry at Soissons and was impressed with their keen approach to training. The 1st Chausseurs at Verdun were not so efficient and my stay with them was more social! I came away with a feeling of awe of the battles of World War I. The cemetery at Verdun with row upon row of crosses and the memorial on the crest of the hill behind stretching many hundreds of yards, each spur of which housed the bones of unknown dead retrieved from different areas of the battle field. Not far away the Trench of Bayonets where the soldiers manning the trench had been buried alive and left there. Fort Douamont where soldiers had endured weeks of bombardment and fought underground manning turrets firing weapons somewhat akin to a battleship on shore. The ground round these forts was littered with unexploded shells and there were still cases being reported of civilians straying in these areas being blown up.

Whilst at Verdun I was driven one Sunday to the frontier at Halstrof and visited the area 'C' Company of the 2nd Bedfords had occupied in the Maginot line in 1940.

At the end of the visits I reported back to the Military Mission spending two days in Paris where I was joined by Pat who came over to join me. Our return journey home was very rough as it coincided with the East Coast floods. Pat coped with the swell of the seas better than I did sitting in the lounge facing some very sick nuns. I stayed on deck and just managed to reach dry land without disgracing myself.

The annual camps were the climax of training for the year. The battalion set itself up with an Officers, Warrant Officer and Sergeants mess and mens dining hall and found the staff to man them. In those few short days the unit functioned together in a way impossible for the rest of the year taking part in training at all levels and learning to function as a team. Our first camp at Shorncliffe required all effort to be given to ensuring the tents were not blown down in a gale. Vehicles and Carriers were tethered to the guy ropes and all mess tents were maintained. After this start the weather turned dry and hot. Our camp next year on Salisbury Plain provided a heavy down-pour of rain at the time of the Brigadiers Inspection!

Apart from the training side the second year was different as the 1st Hertfords and the 5th Battalion of The Bedfordshire and Hertfordshire Regiment were due to have new 'Colours'. This involved a series of meetings with General Sir Reginald Denning, Colonel of the Regiment, Brigadier Longmore Colonel of The Hertfords, Colonel The Lord Luke of The Bedfords, the two commanding officers, training majors and adjutants. H.M. Queen Elizabeth the Queen Mother, Colonel In Chief, had kindly consented to perform this task. It was now General Denning's responsibility to set the machine in motion and ensure detailed planning for the event.

It was eventually agreed the ceremony would be at Hertford with both TA battalions providing four guards. In addition any surplus officers and men would be on parade supported by representative bodies from the Home Guard battalions, each school Combined Cadet Force and Old Comrades Branches.

The task of coordination fell upon the Hertfords. Tony Ward Booth was to make all the arrangements for the guards from the two battalions to be fed, form up and march to the parade area at County Hall Hertford. My task was to handle all administrative arrangements covering the forming up of the remainder and marshalling them on the parade ground, spectator seating, loud speakers, car parking, floral decor for messes and programmes. There would be some two thousand on the parade and some four thousand spectators to be seated.

There was also the question of ensuring that there were sufficient swords for officers. Some of the swords presented were somewhat ancient and needed resilvering. The design of the programme for the day had to be agreed. All these problems were met whilst the officers had to polish up their sword drill.

Came the day and we were lucky with the weather. H.M. The Queen Mother having handed the new Colours to the receiving officers, took the salute at the march past and then met all the officers posing for a group photograph. After which her Majesty took tea in the officers mess set up in County Hall for the day. She then walked round escorted by General Denning and met members of all messes not in the least concerned that she was some forty minutes behind the time when she was meant to leave.

Just as The Colonel in Chief was about to leave General Denning called me over and I was presented as the officer who had managed the administrative side of things. Her Majesty was gracious enough to spend a few minutes discussing the day and commenting how much she had enjoyed it all and how well it had all gone. I felt very honoured.

Time was passing and I received orders to hand over to Major John Harrison, who had been my company commander at Bognor for a short time in August 1940. My two years with the Hertfords had been energetic but most enjoyable. Our daughter, Oonagh, had arrived just before the Summer Ball but this did not prevent Pat from attending this function.

I had got to know Ivor Grey and Robert Humbert well and admired them both for the time and effort they put into their part time soldiering. We kept in touch and became good friends.

I had served in England for five years I was due for an overseas posting. I was to be Deputy Assistant Adjutant and Quartermaster General at Headquarters 35 Infantry Brigade in Hong Kong sailing in February 1954.

Chapter Twenty Three
Hong Kong - 1954 to 1956

Leave was spent in packing up for the move, visiting parents and getting rid of our car, which was sold for the measly sum of £35. Although a 'Disturbance Allowance' was given to help defray costs it seemed that the loss on the sale of a car was the heaviest burden on the pocket when changing an appointment. One was always down financially on every move overseas. Curiously enough I was to find later in life that industry were far less parsimonious in assisting staff for a move.

We were to embark on 'HMT' Devonshire at Liverpool so a night was spent in a hotel in London prior to travelling by train to the embarkation port. As an officer it was my responsibility to make travel arrangements for my family to the port of embarkation. Seats had been reserved on a train to Liverpool and a porter collected our luggage from the hotel. The children were aged three and just over a year and it took time to get them ready for the journey so we were not left with too much spare time to catch our train after dressing and eating breakfast. Our porter with our baggage headed off ahead of us to the train. We caught up with him and he looked nonplussed when we told him we had reserved seats. We headed along the platform but could not find our carriage. Eventually we got aboard and the train pulled out.

Settling down we discovered that this was a special troop train for soldiers and their families which our porter had taken us too. He had not listened to my directions. For my part I was unaware a special troop train was leaving the station at about the same time so could not warn the porter. More disturbing was the fact there was no refreshment car as all the families aboard had been told to bring their own food and drinks. In spite of this we survived though poor Pat must have looked pretty harassed when we arrived at Liverpool. Seeing us loaded down with hand baggage and small children a WRVS lady came to help carry our daughter Oonagh. This was a most welcome relief.

The voyage to Hong Kong via the Mediterranean and Red Sea took six weeks. We had acquired sea sick pills. This was just as well as we ran into a fierce storm in the Bay of Biscay and the ship hove to to ride out the worst of the storm. On top of this the children of a Medical Officer travelling with us were found to be suffering from measles! Apart from that the rest of the voyage was uneventful, though a storm in the Indian Ocean was sufficiently rough for sea water to be scooped into our cabin through the port hole by the air catcher even though we were on 'A' deck. The childrens pots served well in bailing out the water rushing around the cabin floor. We were allowed ashore at Aden, and Colombo. Colonel Wilbur Bickford who was the Provost Marshal and an old family friend of Pat's father looked after us at Singapore and we all enjoyed swimming in fresh water.

There was a group of young officers sailing with us and it was fascinating to observe the activities of the odd Lothario in their midst. One young man in particular drew attention to himself chasing after unattached married women. He was not deterred when the object of his affection left the ship at one of the ports of call. No sooner had this amour left ship than he turned his attentions elsewhere. He continued in this vein throughout the voyage in spite of many pointed comments from his seniors and peers. He was due to disembark at Hong Kong and was earmarked to join a Gunner Regiment. The day before the ship was due to arrive in Hong Kong a delegation of subalterns came to me and the only other major on the ship and told us they intended to take him down a peg or two. They had prepared an operation order which defined individual tasks in detail. The plan involved a snatch party who would take the target to the bathroom where he would be stripped. Whilst he was held down he was to be liberally painted front and rear with gentian violet. 'Lover boy' was to be drawn on his chest and back. Copies of the operation order classified 'Top Secret' were passed to interested parties.

The whole action passed off as planned without any hurt to anyone other than pride. We complimented the subalterns responsible on their ingenuity.

The next afternoon as we steamed past Hong Kong island the RAF came out to welcome us and by late afternoon we tied up at Kowloon.

Initially the family lived in The Four Seasons Hotel on Boundary Road Kowloon and I travelled out to Sek Kong in the New territories each day.

Chinese tailors are adept at copying and I found a lad named Man York in Nathan Road who was setting up in business. Giving him my Saville Row suits as a guide he produced two beautifully cut light weight summer suits for me for the sum of about £8.35. Brigade Headquarters was in huts at Sek Kong sitting in a valley nestling below Tai Mo Shan the highest mountain in the New Territories rising to nearly 3000 feet with mountains on three sides. The valley led down to the Pearl River. A families village of semi detached bungalows lay on the lower slopes below the mountain providing housing for about two hundred families.

There was an airfield and runway which ran down the valley with the service camps sited alongside. We became used to the 'Vampires' of 28 Squadron screaming down the runway to take off as a routine event. The noise factor was somewhat different when there was a squadron scramble and at such times no telephone conversation was possible. There was also a Gunner Regiment and a Field Ambulance sited alongside the runway. The brigade commander was Brigadier 'Tiger' Urquhart who was due to leave for home on promotion later that year. There was a British Infantry battalion the 1st Norfolks commanded by Lieutenant Colonel Turner Cain, the 2nd/2nd Gurkhas commanded by Lieutenant Colonel Gordon Richardson whom we had met when he was GSO I Training at Headquarters Western Command in 1950. The Gurkha Engineers were operating as Infantry and the 7th Royal Tank Regiment were under command. Douggie Moir and Walmesley Cotham of the Tanks had both been at staff college on the 1949 course. We were already finding friends.

27 Infantry Brigade known as the rival firm was made up of three British infantry battalions. There was a Royal Artillery Brigade with three Field regiments and all these forces were stationed in the New Territories Divisional troops and a Heavy Anti Aircraft Regiment were stationed around Kowloon and on the island.

As DAA & QMG I was responsible for planning with my commander the programme for the Annual Inspections of the brigade units. The Gurkhas take great pride in their turn out and so as inspecting officers we would take a clean pair of starched shorts with us and change in the offices before appearing on parade. It would not have done to step out of a vehicle with creased shorts!

The Gurkha follows instructions to the letter. During the inspection of the 2nd/2nd Gurkhas I decided to test procedures for a fire alarm. On being told there was a fire in a certain building and before I had time to ask what action he would take the Gurkha Officer sounded the alarm and set the full battalion fire drill action in motion. Everything stopped and the Brigadier who was inspecting troops elsewhere found he had no one around. It took a while to restore calm but Brigadier 'Tiger' Urquhart took the whole episode as a joke.

I was a guest one evening at a mess night with the 2nd/2nd and was regaled with the story of an incident when the battalion had been entertaining a Provincial Governor in India. It was the custom when Liquors were being served for a Gurkha orderly with a large rams horn wrapped round his arm which contained snuff to follow the waiter serving drinks. On this particular evening the orderly lifting the flap on the horn realised that the horn was empty. Not in the least put out he offered the snuff to the principal guest. "Will you take snuff, Sir?". "Yes, I think I will". "I am sorry Sir, there isn't any". The orderly then processed round the whole table repeating the question and answer. I treated this as a good anecdote and would probably have forgotten about it until when attending the farewell parade of the battalion a few months later a similar incident occurred.

The Governor and a number of Chinese members of the press were gathering in the mess after the formal parade where drinks were being served. I was in conversation with the President of the Mess Committee (PMC), Dudley Spain, when the Mess Manager, a splendid Gurkha soldier came up and addressed him. "These Chinese gentlemen Sir, am I to offer them a drink?". The PMC replied in the affirmative whereupon the immediate response was, "And if they accept Sir, shall I give them one?"

These anecdotes are in no way told to disparage these splendid soldiers but rather to show how they are determined to be sure they do what is required in the most efficient manner.

Lieutenant Colonel Richardson finished his tenure in command and was relieved by Lieutenant Colonel Bill Vickers who had been one of my Directing Staff at Staff College.

The local Chinese held a number of ancient beliefs. Depression was likened to a heavy load on an individuals shoulder. It was believed this burden could be removed by a passing vehicle if the sufferer got close enough for the vehicle to knock the devil off his shoulders. A dangerous game of last across and all our drivers were warned to watch out for any desperate attempts to dash out in front of a vehicle. We were returning to Hong Kong one Saturday after work when a bus stopped to disgorge passengers. Our driver slowed down to about eighteen miles per hour and was signalled to pass by the bus driver. We had all but passed by when a local woman ran out and tried to dash across our path. She had miscalculated and was hit by the bonnet. Fortunately an Army ambulance was coming by and the injured casualty was rushed round to the Field Ambulance. Regrettably she succumbed to her injuries.

There were a number of exercises and Brigadier Urquhart tested each rifle company in turn. The exercise would be planned by the 'G Operations' staff who would set out in the morning with the brigadier. I would man the office with my staff captain until the evening when we would report and act as umpires through the night returning to the office early next morning. This seemed to me a brilliant way for the front line soldier to be aware that a staff desk job did not preclude active participation in unit exercises.

HQ 48 Gurkha Brigade - Hong Kong
Back row: Captains ?, Pearson, Roberts, Bell, Reverend Cooke, ?
Seated: Major Glanville, Brigadiers Waldron, Urquhart, Majors Dyer, Medley.

There were brigade study days and I remember one in particular when Brigadier 'Tiger' required all present to consider the implications on morale of having to withstand tactical nuclear weapons. We were all very aware that casualties from a tactical nuclear weapon would be very heavy. He had invited the Rev Cook to address us at the end of our deliberations. The padre spoke quietly on the need for an anchor, a belief in the Christian faith to help the individual face up to the challenges these modern weapons of destruction posed. This period was a fitting close to an interesting study day. There were in addition exercises organised by Land Force Headquarters.

It had been impressed upon us as students at Staff College that it was important to keep in touch with all units under the command and not to stay stuck behind a desk. I took this teaching to heart and made a plot to visit every unit once every ten days or so letting the Adjutant know beforehand and paying my respects to the commanding officer. As a result I got to know the key personalities and hopefully prevented any problems developing.

There was a Hong Kong Police Station at a road junction in the valley which we had to pass on our journey to Sek Kong families village. One afternoon as I was being driven home by my Gurkha driver a truck with a Chinese police driver was approaching from the side road in a somewhat erratic manner. My Gurkha driver slowed and stopped as did the policeman. We had right of way and my driver started to move forward. At that moment the police truck suddenly surged forward accelerating all the time hitting our jeep in the side and driving us sideways off the road. This incident had been witnessed by a Police Inspector in the police station. He rushed out, upbraided the learner driver and gave him the sack on the spot. Towards the end of the year the plot was for 35 Brigade to move to Malaya to be replaced by 48 Gurkha Infantry Brigade. In effect when the change in designation took place it was merely a change of title. Brigadier Urquhart left to return to England on promotion. I was sorry to see him go as I had found him an understanding and helpful person to work for. Brigadier Waldron assumed command and Lieutenant Colonel Alford with the 1st 7th Gurkhas replaced the Gurkha Engineers. The 7th Royal Tanks were due to return to the UK and were replaced by the 7th Hussars, and The Kings Regiment under Lieutenant Colonel Scott replaced The Royal Norfolks whose RSM WOI Chatting had been a Bedford.

Although the New Territories were lacking in real estate it was still possible to take part in exercises without covering the same ground each time. The peace treaty after the Korean War was not yet complete and relations with China were taut. The hills near to the frontier were covered in many yards of barbed wire set out in great depth and defensive positions had been dug behind this obstacle. There was a major flap one day when it was thought the Chinese were moving forces in a possible move against Hong Kong. Defensive positions were manned and we waited to hear whether our families would be ordered to evacuate. Luckily after two days the flap ended and normal routine continued.

There were the usual sporting activities such as cross country running where British soldiers held their own. However there was a 'Khud' race each year in the Brigade. This consisted of the runners starting in the valley and running to the top of a selected hill and then down again. The hills all rose steeply from the valley so it was hard going to reach the peak. The downward run was also difficult because of the steep descent. The Gurkha is a hill man and used to moving on rugged hills from youth. He is short in stature but his thigh muscles are well developed and this enables him to descend a mountain leaping in great bounds at great speed. In the khud races there was not much to choose between British and Gurkhas in the race to the top of the peak. The downward leg was a very different story as the Gurkhas bounded down like leaping gazelles leaving the British soldiers way behind. It was an amazing sight to watch as a spectacle.

Map 8   South East Asia

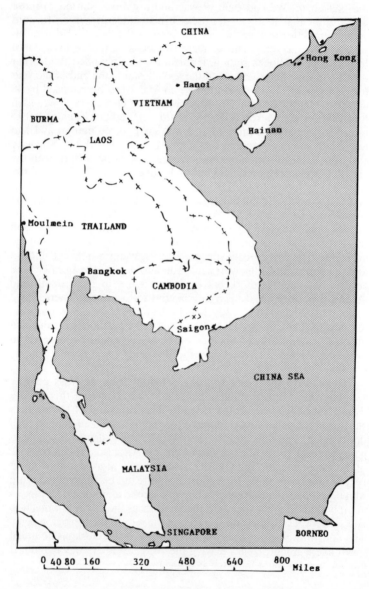

Once when we were on an exercise Brigadier Waldron decided the staff should climb the local peak acting as hares to our Gurkha soldiers. In spite of a fair start we only just started our descent when we saw our soldiers coming over the peak behind us. They overtook us at speed bounding gracefully and in full control from boulder to boulder, ridge to ridge.

Once in a while the Gurkha signallers would have a social evening and we would be invited to sit and watch them perform their dances. One was given a tumbler which was promptly filled to the brim with rum. A bottle of lemonade was placed within reach. It was important after drinking the rum not to be distracted in conversation, nor should one continue to quench ones thirst and leave the glass half empty. Any glass partially emptied was immediately topped up with more neat rum. The drill was to take a sip of rum and promptly refill ones glass with lemonade. This action slowly reduced the alcoholic content. When it was time to leave the contents of the full glass were downed in one after which one promptly stood up and thanked one's hosts before making a hasty exit. Even then such was the strength of the rum it was straight to bed as soon as one reached home.

Dashera was an annual religious festival of the Gurkha Regiments. A selected soldier was trained to perform the task of severing the neck of a bull with one stroke of a large kukri. This act was ceremoniously performed before the assembled battalion and families. It was the most significant event in the year as if the neck was not severed in one blow this meant misfortune in the days and months ahead. A post was set in the middle of the arena close to the Regimental Truncheon of the 2nd 2nd Gurkhas. Nearby rifles and weapons were piled so that the act of propitiation brought blessing on the arms. During the evening proceedings the sacrifice, feasting and drinking would take place with the officers and their ladies watching the ceremonies. It was the custom before the bull was beheaded for the Gurkha Major to report to the commanding officer. He then suggested the ladies withdraw to the powder room which advice was followed. The ladies were thus saved having to watch the formal beheading of the bull and other sacrificial animals.

It was important to ensure we maintained good relations with the local Chinese farmers who worked the open lands in the New Territories. The Chinese have a deep sense of caring for their departed forebears and graves were sited with great care to ensure all the spirits were favourable to the departed and revered relative. It was thus very important that the correct procedures should be followed after a tank had run over a hill side grave during an exercise. The army land agent made all the preparations for a formal apology to be made to the family and their village elders. This entailed Brigadier Waldron and myself turning out in full dress on a very hot day to support the District Commissioner also in full dress with his plumed hat, and the District Officer and Land Agent in Top Hats, Morning Suits and Tails. This gathering of officials in full regalia out in the country was somewhat incongruous in the boiling heat. The whole party sat down facing the assembled villagers whilst the District Commissioner offered apologies. The Brigadier said his piece and cash reparation was handed over. The party drank tea and the matter was happily concluded to the satisfaction of all concerned.

Brigadier Waldron at a Propiation Ceremony at Chinese Village Sheung Tse, New Territories 20th February 1956.

The massed bands of the brigade beat retreat at Sek Kong and in Kowloon. The Brigadier received a request for a special private performance on the island and I met the Managing Director of Jardine Matherson on the island with the Band Presidents of the Kings Own and 2nd 2nd Gurkhas. He had kindly invited us to dinner afterwards with our wives. Travelling down in the afternoon I was wearing shorts and took more formal dress to change into once we had finished looking over the ground and agreed the pattern of events.

We arrived and our wives were taken off by our hostess. We finished our work and returned to the house to change to find our wives had gone off with our clothes. Our host promptly set us at ease by discarding his office dress and reappearing in shorts and open neck shirt. He was a Scot and was delighted to listen to the Gurkha Piper. The evening was made even more interesting as the brother of the Dalai Llama was a guest of the house. We also tasted eggs which were one hundred years old.

The Beating of The Retreat went off without a hitch so everyone was happy.

There were many social functions which took place. We were invited to drinks on a visiting Royal Navy cruiser. Seeing her across the water from Kowloon we caught a boat which took us alongside. The only means of boarding appeared to be a ladder dangling down the side. Pat set off climbing hand over hand clothed in her formal evening wear and I followed. This activity obviously took the members of the crew who greeted us by surprise when our heads appeared over the rails. Still the Army behaved differently from the Royal Navy. The laugh was on us as on coming aboard we saw the ship was tied up alongside and we should have approached through the docks!

My tour in Hong Kong was broken by two visits to Malaya to attend the annual Gurkha Brigade conference. On my first trip I flew by air to Singapore and then travelled by train which had an armed escort due to the threat from communist guerillas. The journey from Singapore to Kuala Lumpar was through the night. Travelling north to Sungei Patani the next day it was possible to see the wired in village enclaves constructed to protect the local population from intimidation.

I had further evidence of the measures taken to reduce the effects of ambush on roads as I travelled to Ipoh after the conference ended to stay with Pat Patterson an old friend from Staff College. He was stationed there with his Gurkha battalion. Wide tracts of jungle had been cleared on either side of the road to reduce the chance of close and sudden attack.

On my second trip a year later I flew to Penang via Kuala Lumpar and saw the territory from the air. I was at the conference as the administrative representative for the brigade and as the only officer attending who was not a member of the Brigade of Gurkhas felt privileged to be included in their regimental deliberations.

It had been a fascinating experience to serve with a Gurkha Brigade and the two years in the New Territories had passed by very quickly. Brigadier Waldron had a very different way of working from 'Tiger' Urquhart and expected to see everything that came in. I found this tight control very inhibiting. The few months under his command were frustrating. I was now due a tour with my regiment in Germany.

Chapter Twenty Four

Germany - 1956 to 1958

We travelled home on the 'Empire Fowey' a much more spacious ship than the 'Devonshire'. We were fortunate enough to be given a roomy cabin as I was to act as a staff officer to the permanent Ships Commandant to help with organising entertainment during the voyage.

We picked up a rear party of the 1st Battalion The Northern Rhodesia Regiment at Singapore. The battalion had completed a tour of duty in Malaya fighting against the communist guerillas and had acquitted itself well. I appreciated the opportunity this presented for me to talk to the askari as I had not forgotten my Cinyanja which I had learnt during the war. Those I spoke to were happy to talk of their experiences in the Malayan jungle. It was twelve years since I had left the battalion in December 1944 and there were no soldiers with the rear party who remembered my old soldiers.

The rear party was to be taken to Mombasa so our route after Colombo took us past the Maldives. We had a very clear view of the sandy beaches backed with palm trees shading the huts of the local villages sailing so close inshore that the local people could be seen following their daily chores. A typhoid scare caused the ship to hove to off Zanzibar before we eventually made Mombasa. This diversion South meant that the ship crossed the Equator so the full initiation ceremonies for King Neptune were laid on for the edification of those unaware of these traditions. Pat and the children received the appropriate certificates signed by King Neptune.

This all added interest to our trip. I believe we were the last troop ship to sail North through the Suez Canal before Nasser closed it down.

Arriving at Port Said late in the evening I had the task of receiving the 'official' Gully-Gully Man and arranging his tour round the ship for his performances. My son Guy was brought up in his dressing gown in a semi sleepy state and could not fathom how so many baby chickens kept appearing from all round his person.

We picked up drafts at Malta, always an imposing sight from the sea with the fortresses standing on their cliffs rising sharply from the clear blue sea. Sailing along the North African coast towards Gibraltar we were entertained by schools of porpoises. As many as thirty or more of these graceful creatures would crest and dive alongside in the wash from the ship's bow creating a pattern of joyous symmetry. It was a picture so beautiful to the eye that the observer was magnetised by patterns of movement and just let the pleasure soak into the mind.

We sailed past Gibraltar and North along the coast of Portugal where there were myriad local fishing boats plying their trade and thence home to Southampton.

A spell of leave enabled us to visit Pat's family at Blewbury and my parents at Bideford and allow the grandparents to see the grandchildren. Guy was now five and little Oonagh three and they had changed considerably in the twenty eight months we had been away.

We bought a Hillman Estate and set off to join the 1st Battalion of The Bedfordshire and Hertfordshire Regiment at Goslar near the Harz Mountains. We drove across England to Harwich and then on from The Hook of Holland to find Vernon French the Quartermaster had a quarter ready for us in the town alongside three other officers houses.

The battalion was quartered in an old German Airforce barracks about a mile outside the town which provided spacious accommodation and plenty of space for sporting activities.

The border with East Germany ran North South some six miles to the East. The border had a continuous high wire fence overlooked by watch towers manned by armed East German border guards. The ground behind the wire on the East German side was ploughed at regular intervals so any foot prints would be easily observed. Behind this marked area were differing booby traps to catch the unwary. In parts of this obstacle designed to prevent escape to the West dogs were left loose between two lines of barbed wire. Any person scaling this obstacle then faced being caught by the dogs. On top of all this no farmer in the East was allowed to farm nearer than half a mile from the border. Even then he had to be accompanied by an armed soldier. All residents within the border region had to carry additional personal identification passes. Such was the rigid regime imposed on Germans living in the Russian Occupied Zone. In contrast the farmers in the West farmed unattended right up to the demarcation line.

This was my first experience of living in Germany and it soon became very evident the locals were very happy we were there to protect them from the Russians! Goslar itself was a lovely old town with many historic buildings and the Harz Mountains were close by.

Life in a battalion was active to say the least. All week days were taken up with training of one sort or another. Inter unit games, which everyone not participating in would travel miles to support, took place on Saturday afternoons. Usually on Sunday mornings there would be a Church Service followed by drinks in the mess. The rest of Sunday was taken up socially being entertained or entertaining. There were some eighteen National Service Officers with the battalion at that time and they would join the marrieds at lunch parties.

We had a saddle club and Tony Ward Booth, the Adjutant, ran an equitation class for all officers. I joined in after a gap of seven years since riding in Egypt. Tony Hunter our Commanding Officer was an accomplished horseman and I set out with him and two of the wives one Sunday afternoon on a cross country jaunt. Returning to barracks about two hours later I had lost all use of any riding muscles and knew I had no proper communication with my horse. As we entered the barracks the colonel said 'Lets go round the hunter trials course'. I knew Tony W B had told us we were in no way ready for this and remarked in this vein to the colonel. 'You're not scared are you?' - I replied 'No' and off we set. My horse was kind enough to take me over the first three fences with no assistance on my part whatsoever. I was clinging on as best I could. At the fourth fence my steed decided he had had enough and stopped short of the fence and I slid forward onto his neck. I managed to retrieve my seat and wheeled round preparing to urge him forward. The horse moved forward towards the fence but this time stopped even more sharply. I catapulted over the jump landing on the far side breaking my arm. The Colonel came back and was telling me to mount up for another go when Hugh Overy our medical officer arrived in his jeep and took me off to hospital after finding I had broken my arm. He had seen us ride past his office and sensing first aid might be required had followed us.

My arm recovered and I continued riding and had great pleasure from this pastime. Tony Ward Booth ran a course of instruction for all the National Service Officers. The battalion entered competitions and Angus Robertson won the Mounted Infantry Cup.

The battalion also did well at rifle shooting winning the British Army of The Rhine competition. We improved our signalling skills and hardened our feet for marching.

Although the battalion was one of many first line units stationed in Germany as part of NATO I found that I only had nine regular soldiers in my company. The rest of company strength was made up by national servicemen. They would arrive with the battalion after their initial training and our job was to teach them all the many skills to enable them to work as part of an efficient front line team. These men had been drafted and so it was important to encourage each individual, find strengths and weaknesses, and develop the raw

172

material into a soldier who was fit and who knew what his role was in his section and platoon.

The training cycle started with teaching the individual weapon skills, radio, driving, anti gas, shooting, marching and games. After the basics the soldier progressed through section and platoon training to company exercises and eventually to take part in higher formation exercises as a part of the battalion team. Those with leadership aptitude were given stripes and became section commanders, some becoming platoon sergeants. The individual was now capable of looking after himself in the field and was a useful member of his platoon.

This training cycle repeated itself each year and each year ninety per cent of the junior non commissioned officers were a new intake as were the majority of the soldiers as the previous men had completed their time and had been released.

There was great rivalry between companies in sport and a soldier interested in football or hockey would be encouraged to help the man who organised the company team so that when he left the understudy could take over the task. This system worked well and individuals were given the chance to develop their leadership skills in this way.

The key to a good company is the company sergeant major and in CSM Brinkley I was indeed fortunate. He had a quiet but authoritative manner and a dry sense of humour. Before I joined the company had been on an exercise in dreadful weather. It was pouring with rain, the men were cold and hungry and at long last the ration truck came up. Lining up there was the noise of mess tins banging together. The company commander ordered CSM Brinkley to tell the men to quieten things. His response in an initial bellow was - "Now listen here you lot you are making too much noise if you don't quieten down I won't bring you out on an exercise again". The soldiers laughed and did as they were bid. The Colour Sergeant, CQMS Nicholls was also a good man. A strong team at the top made my task so much easier. When CSM Brinkley left the company we held a company party and the soldiers presented him with a tankard. His relief was CSM Cotter another first class Warrant Officer.

I was on an exercise at Sennelager one morning preparing for a major demonstration when a jeep drove up enquiring for me. I was handed a message to say my Father had died. John Barrow who was commanding the battalion by now gave me leave and I set off back to England. I handed over the company to David Carter and recommended he should be in charge for the demonstration. I returned some ten days later to find the battalion still carrying out field firing exercises at Sennelager. David as I had anticipated had done well on the demonstration before the hierarchy of the British Army of the Rhine.

The ranges at Sennelager were always in demand. One day exercising with Hugo Ironside of the 3rd Royal Tank Regiment we found ourselves in the target area of a mortar shoot. We had set up an enemy position with our two headquarters for his squadron and my company to attack. I had brought along two young soldiers who were being a little unruly as I wished to have them under closer observation. We were preparing the position when I heard the familiar sound of an incoming bomb followed by the explosion as it burst on the ground. This was followed rapidly by two more bombs. I shouted to Hugo we were under fire but his mind was on other things and he made some comment to the effect I was imagining things. Not long after this another group of bombs came down and Hugo agreed we should get away from the target area as fast as possible. We collected all our soldiers and kit in a hurry whilst Hugo got on the radio and called for the shooting to cease. Further bombs landed close by a cross track as we hastened off the range. Somehow a Belgian unit had been given the same range for a live shoot as us for our dry exercise. Fortunately no one was hurt and a few young National service soldiers could boast that they had been under fire including my two scallywags.

During the winter we went skiing in the Harz every week and John Salazar ran courses to teach the soldiers to build and live in a snow hole. One week my company had set off up the mountains for ski training with the company sergeant major. I had business to attend to in camp and met up with the company during the lunch break. There were two ladies enjoying their lunch one of whom I recognised as Lady Pyman the wife of the Corps Commander who was accompanying the Generals sister. A worried company sergeant major came up and enquired as to who the ladies were and I informed him. Lady Pyman was very much at home on the slopes and disappeared to the more difficult runs. The Generals' Sister however was a novice and stayed on the nursery slopes with the young soldiers. They all clustered round and were questioned as to their state of morale, was the food good, did their officers look after them etc. This got back to CSM Brinkley who now reported things to me. He also let the men know who the ladies were.

That afternoon the Generals sister was left on her own. There had been no order to them to avoid her the young soldiers simply felt that their good will had been taken advantage of. Subsequently I was told their comments had all been favourable.

Later that Winter I went with Pat and Derek and Christine Milman, Tony and Boo Ward Booth to Austria for a skiing holiday. It was great fun and our skills were much improved. On the last day of this holiday a message came through to say Pat's Mother had died so we had to rush back to Goslar so Pat could travel home for the funeral.

On our second winter at Goslar the battalion was tasked with providing administrative support for the Corps Winter Training School. Extra cooks arrived and we found billets for soldiers attending this training. The barracks had a vast amount of spare accommodation both in the cellars and the loft space. Either I or David Carter would walk round the whole company block daily to check tidiness. The passage in the cellars between 'A' Company and the company alongside was boarded up with a barricade. One morning David Carter appeared from his rounds escorting an attractive young German girl who it appeared had squeezed through this barricade to avoid an inspection in the other company. The German Police were sent for and it transpired this young girl had been brought into the barracks by a cook from another regiment. He hid her in the cellars when told his room was to be inspected. The young lady left the camp with the German Police and the cook was dealt with.

On the training side I often took the company to the Seesen training area which was some thirteen miles away in the Harz mountains. We marched out and back and most weeks we spent three days out of camp setting tests for the sections and encouraging the platoons to work together as a team.

The RAF College Cranwell brought their cadets over to be tested in an Escape and Evasion Exercise and the battalion was asked to provide a company to act as the enemy ground troops tasked to prevent them reaching a neutral land. This was great fun and by dispersing the men widely in small packets managed to make the whole exercise that much more realistic. Both sides learnt valuable lessons.

There were innumerable battalion and higher level exercises. In the second year company commanders devised a battalion exercise and ran it. This all increased our confidence and capability. Our training expertise had greatly improved at all levels and morale was high.

News now came through that the infantry were to reduce in numbers and we were to amalgamate with the 1st Battalion of The Essex Regiment. Not unnaturally initial reaction was one of shock and

Map 9   North Germany

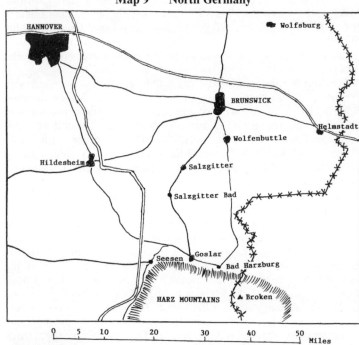

Goslar, Germany 1957.

a wake developed later. Once the order had sunk in everyone set to determined to make the amalgamation of the two battalions work.

Socially the mess held parties inviting representatives from other Regiments. In return we were invited to attend their parties. One evening John Kitto drove Pat and me and 'Boo' Ward Booth up to a party at Luneberg. This was a four hour drive and John ever keen on his food made sure we ate a substantial dinner in a hotel en route. There was a splendid meal laid on by our hosts awaiting us on our arrival at their mess! We set off on our return journey at about 3 am after a great party.

Anxious about petrol we had urged John to fill up before we set off for home but he pressed on. We had passed Brunswick and were driving along a road which ran close to the East German border not more than ten miles from home when we ran out of petrol and the car rolled to a stop. It was pitch black and in full mess kit I set off down the road on foot to find a garage. Whenever a car came along I waved it down hoping for a lift. Not a single car drew up. Seeing my red jacket they may well have thought I was from across the border.

After a mile or so I found a garage but could get no response until daylight. I then walked back to find the others asleep in the car. We made barracks in time to change and be on first parade.

Christmas activities followed army tradition with the officers serving dinner to the men in the mess hall. The officers played football against the Warrant Officers mess after which the married officers looked after the single subalterns as the officers mess shut down so the staff could enjoy a break. Dinnin, Taylor and Plackett arrived and tucked into the turkey. Plackett then disappeared whilst the rest of us continued with the festivities. He was back to partake of the Christmas Pudding though he seemed to be having to force feed himself. Once again he disappeared while the rest of us carried on. He returned to the fold later but by this time red blotches were appearing round his face.

We found out later that he had been invited to two other families and had not wished to offend anyone by refusing an invitation. Hence his disappearing act while he progressed from house to house partaking of a full helping at each home.

Formal Church Parades were authorised for special occasions such as Armistice Day. Colonel Hunter nominated a company to provide readers, and sidesmen for a service run by our padre, Padre King, each Sunday. It was customary for officers and members of the warrant officers and sergeants mess and their families to attend these services and repair to their messes for a social gathering afterwards.

The Army Chaplains corps ran courses for officers and men at Verden and vacancies were given to the battalion. I attended a course with Tom McMillen and we found other company commanders and commanding officers on the course with us. The Divisional Commander, General Hackett, took a personal interest and sat in on some of the group discussions. It seemed to us that officers in the Royal Navy had a closer link in managing church activities than was prevalent in the Army where the padre had his allotted time without any officer being present. After attending one of these courses Tom McMillen and I asked permission to run our own company morning prayers once a month and this was authorised.

I also found myself attending an Ecumenical Gathering of Officers of the NATO Countries near Flensburg where the role of the chaplains and their relationship within their units was discussed. I had been selected as I spoke French and was staff qualified. The British Army of the Rhine was represented by four infantry majors and a Chaplain Grade IV (Captain). The Americans sent four full Colonel Chaplains and the Belgians their Chaplain in Chief. Fortunately our chaplain spoke German and French fluently which helped as all the talks were in German though we joined with the Americans for the discussion periods. By the end of the week my German had improved a lot.

The course aimed to assist in understanding the part religion played in the national ethos of its armed forces. Each nation had to give a presentation and I was given the task of taking the stand. I prepared my short talk and received the blessing from our padre. My theme was that a British soldier enlisted to serve God, Queen and Country and that in our long history our army had never been an aggressor. My argument was weakened as the timing of the course linked with the Suez crisis and invasion of Egypt. Our padre supported my presentation and a German Student stood up and facing towards me said "Spoken like a true soldier".

Goslar was a happy station and the morale of the battalion increased as its members became more proficient. General Hackett our Divisional Commander attended our final dinner night before the battalion disbanded. It was a memorable evening. The Colonel, John Barrow, raised his glass and gave the toast to the 1st/16th and having drunk threw his glass over his shoulder against the wall. To a man his action was immediately followed by every officer. We had said goodbye to a regiment raised in 1688 in a fitting manner.

The next morning I paraded the company ready to embus to go to Dortmund where they would become 'A' Company of the 3rd East

Anglians. I wished them well and thanked them for all their hard work and requested the Sergeant Major Cotter to carry on. Instead of moving the company off to embus he stood them at ease and then called for a National Service Corporal by name. The Corporal came forward and saluted and presented me with a shooting stick on behalf of all ranks. For a moment I was taken aback and at a loss for words. The worth of such a gesture can not be measured. I felt very humble and proud.

"Dinner Night" 1st Bedfords, Goslar 1958. Tom McMillen and Robin Medley.

Chapter Twenty Five
Soldiering in the U.K.

I was posted to the War Office to The Military Training Directorate to work for Brigadier Buchanan Dunlop who was the Director of Boys Training. It was a small branch with two staff officers. My task was to handle all policy matters affecting junior soldiers and apprentices and look after the Junior Leaders Regiments. I was also responsible for looking after the Army Outward Bound School at Towyn in Mid Wales and for liaison with The Outward Bound Trust. Another task was liaison with the offices of The Duke Of Edinburgh Award Scheme. Major Stephen Youens who shared an office with me was responsible for managing the Army Apprentice Schools at Arborfield, Chepstow and Harrogate.

The brigadier reported direct to Lieutenant General Lathbury the Director General of Military Training whose deputy was Major General Jack Churcher. The latter had been my Brigadier at Chester in 1950.

There were but few married quarters available and initially the family stayed with Pat's Father at Letcombe Regis and I found hotel accommodation in London during the week. The office was at Chessington but later moved to London.

It was some months before we found a house to rent having spent many hours at week ends travelling to look at possible lets in Berkshire, Surrey and Kent. One afternoon after an abortive sally over to Kent we looked in on General Churcher at Camberley on our return drive back to Letcombe. Rossie Churcher was marvellous and said she would tackle a local agent on our behalf. A few days later she rang Pat and as a result we acquired a let in Park Road, Camberley and subsequently bought the property. We heard Rossie, General Jack and the whole family had trooped round the house on our behalf and helped clinch the deal.

Settling in at the office required a deal of reading past histories on file and I was glad of the time away from home to attend to this chore. The War Office is mainly staffed by civilian civil servants who provide the continuity. It was a complex organisation made up of a vast collection of different branches all performing their own role. It was important to discover the departments who needed to be approached to help sort out a problem. Omission by lack of knowledge would add extra days or perhaps weeks before an answer was given.

The whole process of placing a request for dress or equipment took time for all involved to either accept or reject an argument. It was important to state the requirement clearly and present a well reasoned case. Having circulated all concerned it now needed the agreement of the Ministry Department responsible for controlling expenditure of funds. As a matter of principle the junior members of staff adopted delaying tactics asking for further clarification by inter office memo. Eventually after a few months had passed I would take the case up a level in the strata and this usually resulted in reaching an amicable solution.

Two examples of this bargaining are worth setting down as they give an insight into the need for diplomacy and determination on the part of the army officer involved.

The Apprentice Colleges and Junior Leaders Regiments had a full programme of physical training and sports. The young soldiers were only issued with two pairs of vests and shorts which did not allow for the time required for washing dirty linen. As the Royal Military College and the Officer Training School at Aldershot were entitled to three pairs I set about submitting a case for an extra pair of shorts and a vest for Apprentices and Junior Soldiers. The file went off and after six weeks I telephoned to enquire how things were progressing to be told it was awaiting to be dealt with among a host of other files. Time passed and the file returned with a query which was answered and the file returned awaiting an affirmative answer.

These transactions took time as the file would depart to registry and be sent on to the marked destination where it would be placed with other incoming files in the in tray. There was always a danger that before the file had been seen further files would arrive and be placed on top of those files already there.

Time passed until it was judged some decision was merited. Ringing the lady handling the case I was told after a pause that the file was there but that it had not been processed as yet. I asked to visit the lady that afternoon and my request was agreed. This entailed travelling across London to another office building. Entering the office the lady read all the pertinent papers. She then said she needed convincing of the validity of this request - they already had an issue of two pairs of items why could they not play games or do physical training in their underwear? I humoured the lady and carefully explained the effect of this approach. Accepting my line of argument she now agreed formally to the request and the units were authorised to have a third vest and pair of pants on their equipment table.

At this time it was recognised in our department that we would accept a period of up to six months negotiation before taking a request to a higher rank.

Another example of these delaying tactics was when we were applying for a list of equipment to be used in adventure training exercises for all our boys units. The request went off and again the gambit of calling for more explanation followed with the file journeying to and fro. On this occasion I was not getting far after six months so I rang the next senior man in the chain who agreed to meet me to negotiate. Arriving in his office he proceeded to go through the list agreeing each item in turn in a very pleasant manner. Moreover when he came to the request for rucksacks he changed my demand from a run of the mill rucksack to a much more expensive Bergen rucksack. Six months had passed since this bid had been initiated and he was feeling generous.

Not long before I went to Boys Training the spotlight had been focussed on these units as a young soldier had committed suicide at the Infantry Junior Leaders Regiment at Plymouth. A detailed review had followed which resulted in a change in the training syllabus. These units were now run much on identical lines to boarding schools. Half the instructional staff were from the Army Education Corps and fifty per cent of the curriculum was devoted to education. The rest of the day was devoted to all forms of military training. There were plenty of sporting activities and a whole range of managed hobbies for out of hours leisure time.

This curriculum meant that the officers and staff responsible were totally committed throughout the day with duties continuing until lights out. They were fully stretched during the term time and needed a reasonable holiday break to prevent them going stale. Negotiation with the financial department for three holiday breaks and for three return railway warrants was made more difficult as the other services did not manage their boys units along the same lines. They had not asked for as much leave between terms.

One morning a senior executive officer from the Finance Branch, whom I had worked amicably with years earlier at Western Command, came into my office and handing me a file said "I never expected you to deal like this when you know the battle we are putting up to support your case for eight weeks leave. Your units are issuing more than the agreed three return railway warrants in the year. You have not kept us informed." I was astounded as this was the first intimation I had that anything like this was happening and I assured him so. I asked him to leave the file and said I would deal with the problem.

Reading the file I found that two of the units were in fact allowing their charges extra railway warrants at a half term break. This perk was completely unauthorised and contrary to the Directors' guidance.

I drafted a letter to the commanding officers concerned to this effect and that the practice would cease forthwith pointing out that the whole case for our request for eight weeks leave was in jeopardy. The letter was typed and I took it to the Brigadier explaining the background. He signed the letter at once. I went with the file with this instruction to my colleague in the finance department. He read the instruction and realised that he had misjudged our actions. His attitude is understandable as some officers did try to get one over their civilian counterparts.

All major decisions in the War Office are dealt with by committee. The committee responsible for determining policy detail on 'Boys Units' was headed by the Director General of Military Training a Lieutenant General with Major General members from the Adjutant General and Quartermaster Generals departments and Heads of Arms and Services as appropriate. It fell to our branch to ensure all pertinent matters were presented to this committee for their approval. I acted as secretary when the Army Secretariat were otherwise engaged. Sitting in on this committee gave me a very good insight into efficient management. Points of view were discussed for the subject under review and a decision arrived at.

It seemed inevitable that if a major problem blew up it was bound to be on Friday afternoon. These Friday problems were usually of a political nature which took immediate precedence. The brigadier had been summoned to go and see the Director General at about 1600hrs on an October evening. He was kind enough to ring me at about 1640 hrs asking me to hang on as we had an urgent task to resolve by Monday pm. He returned to say the Minister, Mr Soames, wished a paper on setting up a new Junior Leaders Unit as he was concerned the existing units were over capacity and the Army was losing recruits.

Our task was to examine and recommend how to resolve the problem. This entailed determining the location, equipping and staffing requirements for a Junior Leaders Unit and stating when it would be practicable to accept the first intake. The brigadier discussed the task and told me to come in on Monday with my proposals in writing. He would also return with his ideas set down.

It was a busy weekend and I was pleased to see that my ideas were closely allied to the solutions favoured by the brigadier. We were both emphatic that ample time was needed to ensure that accommodation, equipment and personnel staff were fully set up to start training as soon as the intake of recruits arrived. The 1st of May was chosen as a fine early summer day would be a happier introduction to army life than a damp winters day. It also would give just enough time for all the negotiations over staffing, provision of equipment and preparation of accommodation to required standards. All proposals to meet the different requirements would have to be presented formally in writing to the War Office Committee under the Director General Military Training for approval before any action could be taken.

The first priority was to determine a suitable location. Eventually a decision was taken to modify Tonfanau near Towyn in Wales. The camp was large enough and close to country suitable for adventure training. The Army Outward Bound School, which ran courses for apprentices and junior leaders was only just down the road.

It had been decided that the unit would be All Arms taking in volunteers for the Royal Armoured Corps, Royal Artillery, Royal Signals and the Infantry. Staffing would be the responsibility of the Directors concerned who had many other demands on their resources. It was my job to draft and obtain agreement to an establishment table which shared the burden equitably between the four Directorates and at the same time provided a balanced rank structure. In view of the peculiar nature of this new unit we sought and obtained agreement for the commanding officer to be a Colonel. The Confidential reports of all officers nominated were seen by my brigadier and all the Arms Directors were most cooperative. As a result the unit got off to a good start and there was a long term benefit to all concerned.

The unit had to have an equipment table listing all those items needed to permit it to function. I went to the Infantry Directorate and borrowed a copy of the Table for the Infantry Junior Leaders Regiment and used this as a guide in producing the list of items for the table.

The DGMT's Committee approved the recommendations put to them and there followed a series of visits to the camp at Tonfanau with the different staffs responsible for the necessary works services. Later key staff for the unit arrived and visits continued to help make sure the pieces of the jigsaw were fitting together.

Initially I stayed at a local hotel and the prospect of Tonfanau camp being re-established was something they were very interested in. A few extra army families would bring trade into the locality and our proposal met with their approval.

These visits to units were important as a bond developed between the key members of staff and our office and we gained their trust. They were a useful means of keeping in touch and I would aim to be out of office visiting one of the units for at least two days each fortnight

The opening date in May was met by dint of hard work and cooperation between all Headquarters and all War Office staffs involved. I travelled up by train the day before the first intake were due to arrive. Changing at Barmouth I was advised by locals at the station that the first young soldier had arrived at Tonfanau Camp. This young man had arrived a day early as the first intake was due the next afternoon. On being met later at Tonfanau Station by Colonel Lake, the Commanding Officer, and Captain Desmond Barry the Adjutant they were taken aback when I said I already knew their first recruit had arrived. The bush telegraph was very accurate!

The Army Outward Bound School at Towyn was now being run by Brigadier (Retired) John Howard who had been in the Training Directorate before taking up this appointment. He kept himself very fit and swam in the sea every morning before breakfast throughout the year. His predecessor had been Lieutenant Colonel Churchill an army commando who had been held in Colditz during the war. Visiting the school for the first time I was provided with swimming trunks on a cold blustery day and expected to enjoy this dip. It was not so much the cold of the sea but the waves picked up large boulders which seemed to be constantly hurled against my shins. It was a painful experience. I hope the honour of 'desk warriors' was not besmirched?

One of the young officer instructors at the Army Outward Bound School in those days was Chris Bonnington who later earned fame as a leading mountaineer. We travelled down to London on the train together. He had been commissioned into the Royal Tank Regiment and had volunteered for an appointment at the Army Outward Bound School as he revelled in adventure training. I have followed his exploits with interest ever since.

Another episode happened on a Friday afternoon and the brigadier was away so the ball was in my court. The Prime Minister, Harold MacMillan, wished to move the Army Outward Bound School to Fort William and General Lathbury wished to be briefed on the matter with recommendations. Although the terrain was suitable the major problem rested in the remote location of Fort William. The Junior Leaders regiments were located across the breadth of Southern England and travelling time would add hours to the journey and reduce the time available for training in proportion. It was also not felt sensible to send junior soldiers on cross country journeys lasting as long as thirty six hours.

I went over to the main building and stated the reasons why this proposal was not beneficial to our training needs and the General thanked me and I fell out. We did not hear further on this problem.

The Army was asked to assist the Outward Bound Trust by providing a few Instructors and these were found by calling for volunteers. It was interesting as the army representative to liaise with their office and to attend their Annual General Meetings.

Another interesting link was with the Duke of Edinburgh Award Office as all our junior soldiers and apprentices were encouraged to participate in the scheme. One of their staff accompanied me on a visit to the Royal Engineers Junior Leaders Regiment at Dover. We then went on to visit a Borstal.

Two years at the War Office flashed past I had been lucky to have an interesting task covering a wide range of subjects which required working with many different branches. I experienced how the top level decision process worked through the committee system where all departments involved were represented. Committee members arrived having previously received all relevant papers relating to the agenda. I sat in on these meetings as a stand by secretary and saw how the General ran things. It was all instructive and I met any number of senior officers and saw how things worked at their level.

The 'Boys Units' were the only part of the Army which were expanding at that time. Brigadier Buchanan Dunlop was an inspiring man whose knowledge of the use of written English was brilliant. He trusted me and I found him easy to work for. His approach was based on his long experience in command and on the staff. He appreciated that it was impracticable to get everything that would be nice to have. Together we would list the twelve priorities which we wished to work for during the twelve months ahead and set them in order. He then told me to work on the first six expecting we would at least get three requests through the system and aiming for the first six. Any further accomplishments were a bonus. This ensured the main thrust was not diverted by taking on too many projects and we succeeded in obtaining eight or nine of the items on the list.

I learnt a lot from him and was privileged to have him as my chief. He retired and took the written exam for entry into the Civil service at Principal grade earning the highest marks in the English paper.

My next posting was to the 4/5th Essex as second in command. I finished at the War Office on Friday afternoon. The next morning a jeep arrived and took me to join the battalion in camp on Dartmoor.

One advantage of having a home posting allowed me to take part in Regimental functions at the Depot at Kempston Barracks Bedford. I was also introduced to members of the 2nd 16th Wartime Officers who met socially for a dinner every year. This group centred round Bill Whittaker who I had first got to know in September 1939 and was in the battles in France and Belgium. We had many shared memories.

We kept in touch with our old friends Lionel and Louie Hitchen.

Chapter Twenty Six

The 4th/5th Essex and Headquarters 53rd Welsh Division

The battalion had its headquarters at Gordon Fields, Ilford with companies in West Ham, Dagenham, Chelmsford, Malden, Braintree and Epping.

I joined the battalion on Dartmoor at the start of the summer training camp. A TA Officer, Don Garrard, had just taken over as commanding officer and there was much that needed to be done as numbers were dwindling and there was some dead wood. The camp showed up the weaknesses. The Corps of Drums was down to three drummers and three boy soldiers. On his visit the Brigadier got hold of me and indicated his displeasure and told me to do something about it as a matter of urgency.

The weather could not have been better and this meant that all the volunteers returned home after camp and spread the word. They were encouraged to bring in recruits and I personally worked on the Corps of Drums, even initially joining their ranks during practice sessions. Recruiting went well to such a degree permission was granted for a weeks camp eight weeks later at Stanford.

The 'Drums' had gathered thirteen new members, most of whom had served as drummers in earlier days. There was a brigade competition and the battalion entered our new Corps. They performed very creditably after such a short time and the brigadier was gratified to see them on parade in strength.

Over forty new recruits went to the second camp where they benefited from the instruction of the regular Permanent Staff Instructors. Once again we were able to impress the brigadier by having a 3" Mortar Section fire live ammunition after five days training.

Over the next two years we nearly doubled the strength of the unit. Don Garrard was a strong minded individual and he weeded out a number of volunteer officers whom he felt were not pulling their weight. As a result over the next two years numbers not only increased but morale rose considerably.

Life with a TA battalion meant visits to drill halls in the evenings, exercises at weekends as well as dealing with paper work during the day. The peak of the year was the summer camp. Each week I would have a session with the Permanent Staff Non Commissioned Officers and I wrote to the Commanding Officer of the Regular battalion to keep him informed of our activities.

The Regular battalion came back to the UK from the Far East and were good enough to let us have a platoon to come to the annual camp, which was in Wales. This platoon acted as a demonstration unit and mixed splendidly with the TA volunteers.

My time with the 4th/5th Essex was drawing to a close. I was due a further posting and was told I was to go to West Africa on promotion. At this time President Nkruma decided to go it alone and cancelled all British Army assistance with the resulting loss of jobs. I found myself posted to Headquarters Wales responsible for training.

My main task was to ensure that any unit wishing to cross into Wales had stated its requirement so that any clearance of land for training could be agreed with any farmer or land owner who might be involved. These negotiations were carried out by the local Army Land Agent.

Unfortunately there were those who felt these rules were too hidebound and trespassed on land. There was an incident when I accompanied the Land Agent to the local offices of the National Farmers Union in Newport to be told of a serious complaint. Some vehicles had driven onto a farm near Chepstow and waged a minor battle using blank ammunition causing havoc among a pedigree herd of cattle. The farmer had rushed out and requested the soldiers to move off his land to be impolitely told to b-- off.

We went to the farm at Chepstow and were shown the area and heard that two pedigree cows had aborted as a result of the noise of thunder flashes and blank ammunition. I apologised profusely whilst the Land Agent sorted out the initial stages of compensation. Whilst this was going on we were offered tea and delicious fruit cake and the farmer who had suffered serious loss could not have been more hospitable. He had noted markings on the vehicles which gave a lead as to the identity of the unit involved. Returning to the office and checking training applications none had come in applying for clearance to train over private land in the Chepstow area on the day in question. Not long after this a further complaint came in from a farmer in Herefordshire and it became apparent that this incident related to the same unit and once more no training request had been received.

The evidence provided gave a clue to the identity of the unit which had caused these upsets and their presence in Wales at the related times was confirmed. The Commander Wales was General Frisby and he directed the commanding officer of the unit be ordered to report to him in person.

I met the commanding officer, who obviously was totally unaware of the mayhem his men had caused or that he had infringed Army

Regulations. I escorted him to the Generals office. The door shut and the sound of the verbal rocket could be heard through the wall. The General ended by saying "You and your Regiment are persona non grata and will in no way ever come to Wales to train again". A very chastened commanding officer retired hurt from the Generals office.

The Headquarters Mess had at one time been the Depot Mess of the 24th Foot and one was greeted at the entrance by a splendid stuffed grizzly bear bearing a tray on which visiting cards could be left. The time came for General Dick Frisby to retire and he was dined out. After dinner the bear capped with a spiked helmet and wearing a drum majors sash was escorted in by Dick Sheldon and me both wearing helmets and sashes. The President of the mess then read out a citation making the bear an honorary member of the generals regiment much to his amusement.

On another occasion after a dinner night the bear was smuggled into the back of a van belonging to Jimmy Rice-Evans a popular retired officer. As the snout of the bear could not be totally concealed diversions ensured that Jimmy got to the drivers seat without passing round the back of his truck. As Jimmy departed we could see the snout showing through the back flap.

I was President of the Mess and seeing the bear disappearing I realised our prank had perhaps been over exuberant and was anxious to know that driver and bear had reached home safely. The thought of Jimmy being stopped and asked to explain why he had a stuffed bear in the back of his van after midnight was not a happy one. I rang Jimmy's wife Elizabeth pretending to be the General and imitating his gruff tone of speech to be told Jimmy had as yet not arrived home. I explained that the mess party had resulted in placing the bear in Jimmy's van and I was anxious it was returned next day undamaged.

Jimmy arrived home and found the bear after Elizabeth told him the general was concerned about it. It returned safely to the mess the next morning. It was some two months later that I confessed to Elizabeth that the general had not originated the message about the bear. We both had a good laugh.

Each year there was a four day competition for the territorial battalions which consisted of trekking some eighty miles across the mountains, a river crossing and a range firing competition. I had the happy task of planning and proving the route. I knew the general would ask about the hazards to be faced so once the route had been plotted on the map I would set off and walk it. It was wonderful to be free to walk across wide stretches of mountain lands in mid and South Wales. The routes selected ranged from the mountains round Lake Bala to

Cader Idris to the rolling Sennybridge ranges and the Carmarthenshire Black mountains. I enjoyed every moment of this freedom absorbing the glorious scenery.

Once a route looked good the Land Agent cleared it with all the land owners and farmers involved. It was important that good will was retained as even disciplined teams competing for a trophy would at times trample over growing crops in their desire to do well. In three years damage of this nature was minimal and the land agents followed close on the heels of the last group and negotiated a settlement on the spot.

General Douglas Darling took over from General Frisby. He was reputed to be a fire eater. He was energetic but charming to work for.

My time at Brecon was coming to an end and I received an assignment to the High Commissioners staff in Kuala Lumpar. This sounded interesting as it was the time of confrontation with Indonesia. Heavy kit was packed and marked and our daughter Oonagh sent to board at The Royal School Bath. Our son Guy had settled into Haileybury.

Three weeks before we were due to set out a phone call came from the War Office to say the job was an administrative one and not the Operational one intended. I was to relax and I would be found a more appropriate appointment.

I had only just returned home from the office one evening about three weeks later when the phone rang it was Jimmy Rice-Evans. "I have just had news in of your next job, you are going West". Residing in Wales at Crickhowell I asked whether the appointment was at Pembroke Dock? "No, you are being posted to America to United States Headquarters Continental Command at Fortress Monroe, Virginia as an Exchange Officer and British Liaison Officer with local rank of Lieutenant Colonel."

Colonel Peter Robinson, Pat's father, had been living with us over the last few years but did not feel up to the upheaval of coming with us to the USA. The only relative to turn to was Major Conn Hackett. It was Conn who had stayed with us when I was a student at the Staff College and who had married Kay the niece of Nods Moore Anderson after our introduction. Conn had retired from the army in 1958 and was working for Gallaghers in Belfast. They kindly agreed that Colonel Peter could live with them. Thus after six years living with us Peter packed up and we put him on the train at Abergavenny for his journey to Ireland. We were sad to see him go.

The Services at that time allowed two return flights for school children to visit their parents overseas. The only close relatives remaining in the United Kingdom were Colonel Peter, the Hacketts and my mother, who was well into her eighties and very frail. She was not up to visiting the children at their boarding schools so they were somewhat isolated. The Easter holidays were only a few weeks away and we decided to forego the free passage and wait for the summer. Our friends from the regiment Gus and Gillian Robertson kindly offered to have Guy and Oonagh for this holiday which helped resolve that problem.

We sailed aboard the 'Queen Mary' sailing from Southampton in late February. Chris Lee of the 24th Foot was also aboard accompanied by his wife Belle. They were off on attachment to the Canadian Army. The voyage was very different from our many previous trips on troop ships and we all spent a relaxing few days sitting at the Pursers table. He organised entertainment and received our support in helping to get things going.

After five days we sailed up the Hudson River in bright sunshine the rays of the sun reflecting in a myriad of brilliant colours from the windows of the skyscrapers. It was a sight to enjoy and retain in ones memory.

Travelling on the 'Queen Mary' to the U.S.A. - March 1965.

Chapter Twenty Seven

United States Continental Army Command - Early Days

Docking at New York we were met by the British Movement Staff officer who helped with our hand baggage, briefed me on where we were staying and took us to a hotel.

Our room was on the sixteenth floor and was not very impressive. The noise of traffic in the street was very obvious. We had our first taste of American TV with the constant interrupts for commercials. Sleep did not come easily.

Next morning we took breakfast at the fast snack bar adjusting to a different culture before the Movements staff escorted us to the main railway station and saw us on our way.

The railway journey to Washington took four hours and the first impression was of a mass of junk and litter lying alongside the track. It was not long before we became aware that 'Ladybird' Johnson had made beautification and care of the environment her main mission. Her drive and enthusiasm were to have a major impact on the national conscience. Returning on visits some years later there was a general tidier display.

At Washington we were met by a member of the British Army staff and housed in a hotel. I was to spend the next forty eight hours being briefed before flying down to Newport News to join Headquarters United States Continental Army Command on the staff of The Deputy Chief of Staff for Unit Training and Readiness. Two of the officers at Washington were old friends. David Owen and his wife Margaret we had known in Egypt in 1947 and met up with again in 1959 when David was commanding The Royal Artillery Junior Leaders Regiment at Hereford. The Colonel responsible for handling movements Peter Huyshe had a daughter at The Royal School Bath and we had met in Westward Ho where our respective parents had houses.

Two days later we left Washington National Airport and arrived fifty minutes later at Patrick Henry Airport, Newport News. We were met by Lieutenant Colonel Chuck Watson and his wife Elizabeth. He had been nominated as my sponsor to ease my arrival. The choice was typical of the thoughtfulness of the Americans as Elizabeth was English by birth. They arrived at the airport with two cars to ensure there was ample room for our baggage as well as ourselves. Having collected everything we drove the twelve miles or so to Fortress Monroe to the quarter allocated to us in Ingalls Road.

The Watsons helped us in with our clobber and showed us round our apartment, which already had my name board at the entrance in bold print. On the dining room table was an iced cake. The cake was beautifully decorated with the British and American Flags and the inscription "Welcome to Fort Monroe". Next to the cake were a bottle of Scotch and a bottle of Gin. The fridge had been stocked with food. We could not have been welcomed more warmly. Having satisfied themselves that we knew how things worked and knew our way around the Watsons left us to sort things out and to recover from our journeying. I had to be in the office by 0800hrs next morning.

This welcome was really heartwarming and we both felt it augured well for our stay in the US. Number 94 Ingalls Road was an upper floor apartment in a block of four quarters. The quarter had some basic furniture hired from the Quartermasters department as normally American officers moved around with all their own house furniture. We had been provided with beds and dining room furniture but it was up to us to acquire any extras. Normally in these circumstances one would purchase furnishings from the outgoing British officer. Unfortunately for us there had been a gap of nine months since the previous incumbent had left and he had disposed of all unwanted furniture so we had to start from scratch. Over the next few weeks we acquired carpets, a love seat and a recliner taking advantage of the periodic sales. Eventually we felt we had achieved our aim in presenting a homely atmosphere.

The morning after our arrival was taken up with administrative tasks such as having my photo taken for my identity card and meeting all the officers in the Training Division. I was briefed by General George Duncan, the Chief of Staff, on my role as the British Liaison Officer to the Headquarters and was interviewed by General Grey who was in charge of Unit Training and Readiness. As an exchange officer I would be one of his staff officers. I had been allocated to Colonel Horace Brown Jnr who ran the Training and Evaluation Branch. Of the six officers in the branch Horace Brown, Butch Charlton, Rayleigh Dunn, Cliff Norwood, and Nell Gerringer came from the Southern States and they all spoke with a soft 'Southern' drawl with the words rolling along seemingly in an endless stream. Patti Hodge the branch secretary was also from South of the Mason Dixon line and for the first forty eight hours I had difficulty in understanding anything that was said. Slowly my ear became attuned to this new language. It was only a few weeks later by which time we had all got to know each other that my American colleagues admitted that they had great difficulty in understanding what I was saying during those first few days. Such is the difference in our common tongue.

I had been given an identity card with my picture on it which would serve very much as a passport. This was the first time in all my travelling I was a foreigner in a foreign land! That first day was spent being introduced to the officers in the other branches in the Training Division of which Training and Evaluation Branch (TA&E) was part. That evening we were invited to the Officer's Club to dinner where we met Colonel Murphy the Colonel in charge of the Training Division and his wife as well as all the other members of TA&E with their wives. This was the first of a number of formal welcome parties.

TA&E 1966. Robin Medley, 'Patti' Hodge, Colonel Horace Brown,
'Nell' Gerringer and Lt. Colonel 'Jesse' Thomas.

Colonel Horace and his wife Chick were keen members of the James River Hunt which was holding a meet the next day. We were invited to go out to 'Hill Top' to follow the hunt and watch proceedings. Pat declined but I accepted the offer to be told to be up and ready to be picked up at 6 am the next morning.

The morning was bright and fresh and cold enough to warrant wearing a British Warm. I took a camera and binoculars with me. We drove to the meet which was south of the James River near Surrey.

The ground was very flat with a few open areas interspersed with trees and shrubs. On arriving at the meet I was introduced to a local civilian and his wife. He was to look after me and drive me from point to point in his car. The hounds and members of the hunt warmed up with stirrup cups and my host started upon the bottle of bourbon he had brought with him. After some thirty minutes the hunt set off and we drove off with the other followers to find a suitable place to watch what was going on.

My host was obviously entering into the spirit of things and by 1030 am had already consumed half his bottle. I had been watching the hounds through my binoculars and was taking the odd photo. This caused my host to remark "With your camera and binoculars you are just like all you Brits and your b...... Queen". This remark coming out of the blue as it did took me by surprise but I was not prepared to let it go. In a flash I decided to hit him reasoning that if I was court marshalled for defending Her Majestys' Honour it was a worth while price to pay. Having made this appreciation I hit him in the stomach and said "I don't care what you say about us Brits but no one, I repeat no one says that about my Queen". A look of utter surprise came over his face. There was a moments hesitation then he stepped forward hand outstretched. Shaking hands he said "I apologise I should not have said that. I like you." We became very good friends from that moment and met on a number of other occasions when I was supporting the hunt.

It was some twenty years later when Colonel and Frannie Dix were staying with us in Wales that this incident was talked about. The Dix's had also been invited to this particular meet as guests of Horace and Chick Brown and had heard that I had hit out and wondered what it was all about. Having told them the background they recognised the individual involved and commented they were not surprised as he had a reputation for drinking quite heavily. They were highly amused at the explanation and thought I had been more than justified in my action.

My first task work wise was to read in on the regulations governing training. I was seated opposite Rayleigh Dunn an Armour Corps officer whom I was to understudy. This was a historic time as the Vietnam War was just beginning to blow up and the first combat troops were being despatched to Vietnam from Hawaii.

One morning I was asked by Colonel Charlton if I had any experience of jungle warfare - had I served in Malaya? I replied my experience was in Burma fighting the Japanese during the war which was not so different. It transpired a staff officer was coming down from the Pentagon the following day to discuss our proposals on a sixteen hour training programme to be used for units and individual reinforcements due to be sent to Vietnam. I was told to come up with a proposal.

In reading reports coming back from Vietnam it was evident that units over there were often subject to being ambushed. I put together a programme which laid emphasis on anti ambush drills, jungle shooting drills, perimeter defence and health and hygiene topics. I had been given help by Colonel Jeanne Treacy of the Medical Corps for the latter topics. I had proposed eight hours be devoted to anti ambush drills. Shown this split Colonel Charlton asked why as much as eight hours had been allotted to anti ambush drill. I explained four hour split between drills when mounted in vehicles and four hours for moving on foot. Time was allotted for instruction, demonstration and practice. "I'll buy it" was his response after my explanation. The same applied to each of the other subjects covered.

The next day these proposals were presented to the officer from the Department of the Army who had flown down from the Pentagon in Washington. He accepted our recommendations.

The next task was to have these printed and issued. After the draft had been approved by General Gray I took it to the Adjutant General's branch for printing and publishing. Imagine my consternation when on reading the instruction in print I found that additional asterisks had been inserted by the Adjutant General's staff which destroyed the sense of what had been written. I was unaware the Adjutant General's branch was all but omnipotent and could override any instruction and change wording according to their whim. I was very angry and went over to see the officer I had dealt with and said the whole context had been changed. I objected to a document signed and approved by my General being altered in this way without any consultation and directed it be corrected there and then. It pays at times to be ignorant of the way things are managed.

We had been at Fort Monroe about two weeks when Chuck suggested that he would take us to see Yorktown. The senior action officer in the branch said "I hear you are going to visit the place where the Germans were beaten by the French". I did not know what to make of this remark until it became obvious it referred to our proposed visit to Yorktown.

The displays at Yorktown were beautifully laid out and I then understood the whole point of the comment. The regimental standards of all the British and French units which took part in the battle were on display. The British forces taking part in the defence of Yorktown were the Highland Light Infantry, the Royal

Map 10   Chesapeake Bay - USA

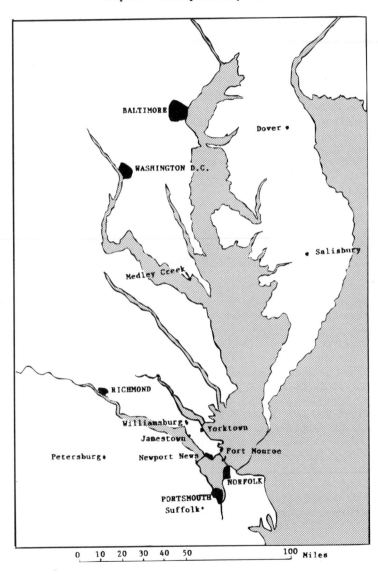

Welch Fusiliers, three Hannoverian battalions and three Hessian battalions. The flags on the American side were predominantly French - hence the comment from my American colleague. It is interesting to remember that a large part of the regular forces serving the British King at that time were from Germany.

The whole presentation of the battle of Yorktown was admirable. Many of the earthworks remain and the visitor centre provides the visitor with a detailed description of the way the battle was fought. One interesting aspect which I have not heard being taught in our history lessons was the intervention of high winds which prevented Lord Cornwallis evacuating his forces across the York River to join up with his other forces at Gloucester on the other side of the river. The evening the evacuation was due to take place the wind rose and waves three feet high swamped his boats forcing him to surrender. Had this act of God not come about it is interesting to surmise what might have happened if all the British forces had grouped at Gloucester before heading North.

In those first few weeks I was taken to Portsmouth to visit the memorial hall to General MacArthur the hero of the war against the Japanese. It was a fascinating memorial to one of America's great Generals.

There was much to see in close proximity quite apart from Yorktown where the demise of British Jurisdiction of America took place. It was only some thirty miles across the peninsula at Jamestown where the first British settlement was established in 1607. Between these two places was Colonial Williamsburg where the first seat of Government had been established. In many ways these few square miles represent the ancient history of the United States and the close links to Britain.

Jamestown exhibition centre had two pavilions one for the old world, and one for the new once America gained independence. Outside stands a statue of Queen Elizabeth I with the flags of the USA and Great Britain flying from tall flag poles by her side. The old pavilion has wax figures depicting how companies were formed in Britain with the Queens blessing to explore the new world. It lists the names of the first one hundred and nine colonists who arrived at Jamestown in April 1607. This was the first colony from England to survive and expand after the 'Lost Colony' at Roanoake Island. It tells of the raids by the Indians in 1633 when a great number of settlers lost their lives, of the expansion of the farms and the creation of Williamsburg with the Governor's Palace, its seat of government and its university. The tale ends with the revolt against the taxes imposed by London and the fight for independence. The new pavilion takes the visitor forward to the current times.

Meanwhile outside on the river bank tied to a quay are replicas of the three sailing ships which brought the original settlers across the seas. Walking the decks of these small craft one can only wonder at the fortitude and courage of men who braved the oceans in winter months to pursue their ambitions. Leaving behind a known way of life and possibly relatives to head for the unknown in search of a dream. It was not long before women followed to help establish family life.

Close by the shore stands a replica of the original triangular fortress with its high walled wooden stockades and its gun positions. Inside in a central position the Church which also served as an Assembly Hall. Other houses were built alongside the walls and the stocks were there to ensure any transgressor met his or her punishment. Not far away there is an Indian hut showing how the local indigenous people lived. At all these exhibition places there are individual guides dressed in authentic period costume. Many of these guides are volunteers from William and Mary College at Williamsburg. They delight in mounting and changing the guard and help the visitor obtain a clearer understanding of life in those days.

The original site where the settlers landed is on an island a mile or so downstream from the exhibition centre. Here it is possible to see the ground sites of the early buildings, the church where Captain John Smith worshipped. There is a lovely statue of Pocohantas, the Indian princess who saved John Smiths life and a tall wooden cross giving thanks for reaching a pleasant land. Again there is an exhibition hall and not far away a craft shop manufacturing and blowing glass following the methods used by the early settlers.

There was so much to see and take in in these exhibitions that it needed a series of visits to absorb it all. Rockefeller set up a fund to restore Colonial Williamsburg as a site of historic importance. A number of houses were restored to their original state and furnished appropriately. The gardens were set out in the pattern of the times. The main buildings open to the public were the Governor's Palace and Gardens, the Government buildings, the Jail and a tavern. Bruton Parish Church where George Washington worshipped is still in use to this day. There were individual houses showing different standards of living. All these places had guides dressed in period costume who were knowledgeable in all aspects of life at that time. The main street through old Williamsburg is closed to motor traffic throughout daylight hours and apart from authorised buses which follow a set route all other transport is horse drawn.

We spent many hours exploring this lovely town. The old jail was used well into this century. There was a main cell for holding as many as twenty or thirty prisoners. In one corner perched high above a series of eight or so steps was the loo in very public view - hence the expression 'Going to the throne'. There was the usual well run exhibition centre at Williamsburg. Perhaps the most striking aspect was the introductory film which showed the arrival of the early settlers, the expansion of the farms and trade with England. It portrayed the agony of decision when the tea tax was imposed with families and friends split, some deciding to fight for independence others leaving their possessions and returning to England. The story was told so feelingly that the observer felt drawn in to the action and felt sympathy for the agony of decision forced upon the citizens of that time.

We spent many hours at these three locations often acting as escort and guide to senior officers from the UK visiting Headquarters CONARC. We were almost unofficial tour guides and were able to take some American friends from Washington and show them around. All these exhibitions are well managed and well presented. They represent the early history of the country and fortunately are all within easy reach of each other and they were all within easy driving distance from Fort Monroe.

Meanwhile Pat was being invited to visit Norfolk to see the Azaleas in bloom by Mary Kaye Whittaker one of our neighbours who was kind enough to take her under her wing.

Another early trip was to Richmond where we visited the State Capitol buildings. The lady guide asked us where we came from. It was too complicated to say Abergavenny or Camberley so we relied "London, England". Her response was - "Now I want you folks to understand this is the capitol of the USA right here in Richmond NOT (said with emphatic emphasis) that place Washington, THIS is the capitol of the USA". We were beginning to appreciate there was a strong sense of independence and individuality south of the Mason Dixon line. Those living in the Southern States proudly displayed the Confederate flag on their cars.

In spite of these sentiments which were directed at the seat of government in Washington it was evident all these individuals were intensely proud of being Americans.

Chapter Twenty Eight

Further Episodes in the USA

I found that having two different tasks and wearing two hats helped considerably. As the Liaison Officer for the British Army I was one of a small group who came under the direction of General Duncan the Chief of Staff. The other liaison officers at the Headquarters were from the Canadian Army, the US Navy and the US Air Defence Command. They were all housed in one building in quite spacious offices. Lieutenant Colonel Buckingham, the Canadian Liaison Officer, sported the Canadian and American Flags behind his desk. I applied for the privilege of having the Union Jack behind my desk and this was granted. It stood in the TA&E office crossed with 'Old Glory'.

Patti Hodge our office clerk felt if I could fly the British flag she should have permission to fly the Rebel Flag of the South. I jokingly told her that she could not fly one flag on its own but that perhaps she might consider the flag of the Irish Republic! This was some years before the troubles in Ireland blew up again.

Whenever a British Officer from any of our Services visited the Headquarters I was invited to act as aide and sat in on all the briefings. This helped me to learn the role and organisation quickly. I was also invited to attend briefings on new equipments and to see demonstrations of hovercraft.

One day Captain Knight, the US Navy Liaison Officer, invited me to go with other members of the staff for a visit to the US Navy at Norfolk for a trip on a submarine. We went over to Norfolk and embarked on the U.S.S. Ranger. Once on board we were divided into groups and taken round to be shown how the ship was operated. We sailed out to the training area in Chesapeake Bay and commenced a series of dives. It was a fascinating experience.

It came for the time for our group to be in the operations room. The Captain explained the drill for bringing the ship to the surface using the periscope to check the bows and stern were clear before ordering the opening of the hatch to the conning tower. He impressed on us the importance of following these sequences and then told me to man the periscope and give the order to surface.

Facing forward I gave the order to surface and waited for the bows to appear. The moment the bows cut clear I called out as instructed "Bows clear, Sir". I then swivelled the periscope round and waited for the stern to show. A few moments passed and once satisfied the stern had risen out of the water I reported "Stern clear, Sir". Facing about I waited for the bows to reappear for the second time so I could give the order to open the hatches - there was no sign of the bows appearing. I waited and waited for what seemed an age and still nothing. As a land lubber I had not realised that the ship had been brought up rapidly and the bows had come out of the water steeply before crashing back down and causing the stern to rise at a more sedate pace thus delaying the reappearance of the bows. The Captain queried as to what was happening implying a sense of urgency. There was still not a sign of the bows. "Come on what is going on?" he said. I replied much to the glee of all present "I've lost the bows, Sir". Shortly after the bows did appear and the required drills to open the hatch were correctly followed.

We must have dived and surfaced at least six times and we were able to experience this activity from different parts of the ship. We were now entertained to a meal from the galley. It was of a high standard and there was more than enough to fill the hungriest belly. Returning to port we thanked our hosts and I was given a certificate as an Honorary Submariner of the US Navy. It had been a most interesting day and I came away with the greatest respect for the submarine service.

Captain Knight could not have been more friendly and he ensured that he took me along to various establishments when he was off on a visit.

My other hat as an action officer with TA&E was livening up as was the tempo of events in South East Asia. All this over the weeks ahead was to have a major impact on the branch and ensure I had a more and more interesting role to play. At this time I was not as yet aware how things would evolve.

It was of course normal that my background had been vetted before I had been accepted for this job. The British had not endeared themselves all that much with the Fuchs, Burgess and Maclean episodes so it was not unnatural that the Americans wanted to be doubly sure of any foreigner working in their midst before revealing highly classified material. Initially, looking back, I was given fairly innocuous tasks. I went off to Camp Drum in New York State on my first visit to a training exercise accompanied by a Chemical Corps Officer.

We arrived on the post in the late afternoon and were shown our rooms in the officers quarters. Having dumped sleeping gear I followed the usual drill I was used to in the British Army, collected my companion, and set off to the control office for the exercise. We were welcomed though I sensed a feeling of surprise at our appearance. We sat in on the full briefing and then repaired to the mess where we enjoyed drinks and a meal with the officers who would umpire the exercise starting next morning.

Returning to my room I found a paper directing me to report the following morning. My early arrival at control had been accepted gracefully.

The next morning I was taken under the wing of the chief umpire and we set off in a Huey helicopter. It was just as well as the training area was vast and the troops were scattered over a wide frontage. This means of transport not only provided a panoramic view from the air but it also saved time and it was possible to visit more units than would have been possible travelling round by jeep.

One interesting aspect was to monitor the use of helicopters to insert combat troops into selected areas of the battle field. We watched the pick up of an infantry company and tagged along behind the formation of thirteen planes on this sortie. Flying at speed close to the ground with trees flashing past was an exhilarating experience.

We spent the whole day flying and only landed at dusk. As part of the exercise a company was to be inserted deep in enemy territory after dark using helicopters. After dinner the chief umpire handed me over to his number two and we now set forth by jeep to monitor events. The fly in did not take place until 0230hrs by which time we were all feeling weary. My escort drove off the range and found a cafe which stayed open all night and we tucked into bacon and eggs. After this we drove back to base arriving there in time for a quick shave and more food and coffee before the chief umpire collected me to accompany him again. The wash and shave had cleared the cobwebs away and we carried on until the end of the exercise at mid-day. I said my farewells and we flew back to Fort Monroe arriving later that evening.

It had been a fascinating introduction and I was glad I had managed to hold my own over the whole period when the other umpires had worked in shifts. I put in a report on my observations some were complimentary others were more critical. General Duncan, the Chief of Staff, thanked me for this report.

As an 'Exchange Officer' whenever I was sent off on a visit I received a posting order for temporary duty which was the formal authority for me to claim allowances to cover my expenses. I was delighted to discover these allowances were of a more generous scale than those granted in the British Army. This was helpful as my rank as a Local Lieutenant Colonel whilst giving me the badges and status of rank did not include a rise in pay.

As the only British Officer on post it fell to me to entertain formally and the British Army Staff in Washington were kind enough to allow me a slice of entertainment funds commensurate with the size of the Headquarters I was working at.

The US Army is very rank conscious and mixing of different officer ranks socially was not the usual custom at that time. Hosting parties in our home we invited mixed groups from among the officers I worked with in the Training Division. Later I discovered that as the British officer I had a very free rein and this approach was accepted. Another facet of interest was the open attitude of the Americans. As an Exchange officer I came under the command of Major General Gray the Deputy Chief of Staff Unit Operations and Reserve Forces. He was invited to our first evening drink party with Lieutenant Colonel Rayleigh Dunn, who sat opposite me in our office, and some twenty other couples. I was recharging glasses standing alongside Rayleigh when the General asked him how I was getting along and settling in. Rayleigh replied "He's sharp, Sir, he's a real professional". I was amazed that this conversation was happily carried out in my hearing but it showed a refreshing openness. It was a while before I fully appreciated the meaning of Rayleighs' comments and that he had been very complimentary.

Office hours were from 0800hrs to 1300hrs and continued in the afternoon from 1400hrs to 1700hrs. The office was some six hundred yards from my quarter and I walked to and fro continuing after I had acquired a car. Apart from some of the general officers no one else on post walked, they all drove to work!

Buckingham, the Canadian Liaison Officer came over in the second week and said let me take you for a driving exam. I had practised and was happy I could handle the automatic drive and manage the reversing test. However the written test proved my undoing as this was where I had my first problem with interpretation of the written American language. I made a wrong assumption and my response was incorrect. It was also evident that finite detailed knowledge of braking distances and speeds were essential. I retired hurt, read up, ensured I knew the required details by heart and then returned to the fray. Having passed the written test I was now taken out onto the local roads. I stopped at major roads and turned as told but found myself in earnest conversation with the instructor carrying out the exam. He was so fascinated to hear I was English he bombarded me with questions all round the circuit. I am satisfied I did drive properly and that my being passed was not out of kindness.

Pat meantime was settling into our new home. There were a number of functions run by the wives of the different departments. As a Liaison Officer I came under the aegis of the Command Headquarters Group. I also came under the Chief of Staff Operations and Reserve Forces as an action officer in TA&E. So Pat found herself invited to meet a host of new faces having to try and remember names. These coffee mornings were very formal with hats and gloves being worn. Our neighbours were friendly and Mary Kay Whittaker who lived below us in our apartment block took Pat under her wing showing her around and being generally kind and helpful.

There was a formal department evening once a quarter which could be likened to a dinner night in a British Army mess. The only difference was the wives were invited and entertainment was organised by a nominated officer.

We had been on post about two months when we were alerted for our first evening. To my horror the officer responsible for organising the entertainment, Colonel Dix, came round to my office and said "The British Officer attached to this Headquarters always takes part in the entertainment and we have a role for you". I was taken aback but felt I had to make the best of things and comply. I was to play the part of an American Officer in Paris in 1918 enjoying himself in a night club and ogling the dancers. We had a rehearsal and seven of the wives had dressed up as Can Can dancers and practiced their routine. On the night I sat besides the floor with my binoculars. I also had my camera with me and was able to take a picture of the ladies in full display. This action had not been scheduled during the rehearsal however the picture came out well and was well received. I took part in all the entertaining whilst at Monroe and had a lot of fun and extended my circle of friends at the same time.

The first reinforcements for Vietnam were being despatched from Hawaii and reports of actions were coming into the office which made interesting reading.

I went off with Major Price, another Chemical Corps officer, on a visit of inspections. This time we accompanied General Paul Freeman who had his own four engined transport plane. Our first stop was headquarters Third Army at Chicago where I spent time with the Operations staff. Next morning we flew to Fort Leonard Wood to an Engineer Training Formation. Instead of being met by the Operations Staff Officer I found myself being taken to the Post Exchange (the equivalent of our NAAFI) to be briefed by the Post Exchange Officer. My description as British Exchange Officer had led to this misunderstanding. My companion soon sorted things out and we had a good laugh.

On again to Fort Riley where the 1st Division was stationed. There was a ceremonial parade of representative units of the 1st Division which was inspected and addressed by General Freeman. After the parade I was taken to the ranges to see rifle practice and was amazed to see a long line of at least one hundred soldiers on the firing point under a single range officer. There was no one assisting individual soldiers improve their techniques. The next day we flew to Fort Carson, Colorado Springs to spend two days watching the 5th Division on an exercise.

General Freeman had been received formally with a Guard of Honour at each location and we stayed in the plane until the formalities ended before exiting to meet our hosts. This tour was most interesting though I was unaware at the time the 1st Division was mobilising to go to Vietnam.

One morning a week or so later I was told to assist Rayleigh Dunn in monitoring the Air Cavalry Division in its preparation for movement overseas. A report format had been prepared which showed how every unit was completing all the required tasks. Reports came in daily and the progress chart on each unit was updated.

On the social side we were invited to a drink party with General Freeman. This formal invite was followed by further invitations from the other General Officers on post. Following these social invites came my participation in highly classified meetings in the operations planning room as Rayleigh Dunn was posted and I now handled the daily updates on the state of preparedness of the 1st Air Cavalry Division. It would appear I had been formally cleared by the Americans to handle Top Secret material.

I went with Colonel Horace Brown to Fort Benning to visit the 1st Air Cavalry Division which was being formed round an experimental formation which had formulated tactical doctrine over a period of two years. Unfortunately the experimental formation only had two infantry regiments and was also short of artillery. At the same time the posting policy dictated that a large number of individuals, all of whom were highly specialised in this new tactical role, had completed their two year tour. These persons were posted away. Thus the division which was due to go overseas in the near future was not only short of formations and units but was also being denuded of trained specialists.

The new infantry element were taken from an active division which was being broken up. The soldiers were in less than a month trained as parachutists and how to work from helicopters.

Our visit showed that the units and individuals were approaching their training with dedication and enthusiasm but it was evident that time was not on their side.

On returning to Fort Monroe Colonel Brown asked me to submit my views and recommendation on readiness of the division in a memorandum for the Commanding General. This I did, saying the division was not ready even though I was aware some of the formations were already embarked on ships. I added a rider that if movement could not be delayed the division should not be deployed into an operational zone for at least three months and further training was necessary. Colonel Brown agreed my comments and initialled my report which went off to the 'Head Shed' as the Commanding Generals office was named.

Three days later Colonel Horace Brown came into the office waving my memorandum and saying "Rob, you've got an OBE for your memo on the Air Cavalry Division". I asked what that meant as I knew the US Army could not award a British Decoration, explaining the letters stood for 'Officer of the Order of the British Empire'. Colonel Horace said as he did not know the meaning he would find out. A couple of days later he came back. "Rob, I've found out the meaning of OBE, it means 'Overtaken by Events', the Commanding General has already said the same thing to the Pentagon himself". In spite of this high level recommendation the Air Cavalry was despatched to Vietnam and became operational on arrival. Regrettably the soldiers at the front learnt the hard way.

Training establishments throughout the USA had expanded to absorb and train the drafts of young men called up for service. These drafts were needed to meet the demands of an ever increasing force in Vietnam. Individuals were sent overseas as reinforcements and replacements for battle casualties. Others were drafted to units under training in the USA prior to overseas deployment.

The length of the overseas posting to Vietnam was twelve months. This allowed the draftee to undergo routine initial training before moving overseas, serve his twelve months and have about three months back in the USA before discharge.

Major Schreiber a West Point graduate, who had been in the Training Division at Fort Monroe, received a posting to a staff appointment in Vietnam. After six months on the staff he was sent as the XO (In British Army terms as the Second in Command) to an infantry battalion. The reasoning behind these changes was to give the individual the widest possible war experience. In these early days of deployment it was felt the opportunity should be seized to gain as much experience as possible within the twelve month limit. One wonders whether disruptions such as this were overall beneficial to the units let alone the individual?

There was a rapid turn round of individuals at Fort Monroe. Cliff Norwood, Rayleigh Dunn and Charles Watson all left TA&E Branch within a few weeks of each other and apart from Nell Gerringer I was the sole 'Action Officer' left in the Branch. Jesse Thomas arrived but the work load had not decreased and the pressure was on.

All our telephones within the office linked up and at his request I joined in on the line when Jesse was calling a subordinate head-quarters. He was speaking to a Lieutenant Colonel Action officer at Fort Macpherson, Atlanta one afternoon on some requirement or other and this matter needed further clarification the following day. The phone rang and Jesse signalled for me to listen in. The colonel from Atlanta started straight in "Now listen here Thomas I have looked you up in the Army list and I out rank you by three days. You will address me as Colonel when you speak to me from now on". It seemed to me that individual was pretty insecure.

Operational reports were now coming in from units fighting in Vietnam and these came to me. Studying these reports it became evident that extracts from them could be used to produce training guidance for units earmarked for Vietnam. This policy was agreed and a quarterly pamphlet was printed entitled "Operations - Lessons Learned" and issued under a USCONARC Training Directive Number. I gained permission for a copy to be sent to the British Military Staff in Washington and subsequently further copies were made available for UK Training Establishments.

I had the simple task of determining suitable material from the incoming reports and editing as appropriate. Once satisfied I passed the draft to the Adjutant General's department for printing and issue. The printing and publishing of these training documents was carried out most efficiently. It was an example of how the American system works at high speed when the need exists.

Another example of this rapid response to meet a new tactical requirement was the rapid introduction of a small pack carried multi barrelled mini mortar. This equipment was produced in numbers once a demonstration of the prototype proved its worth.

Chapter Twenty Nine

USA - Holidays and Observations

Life was different. Quite apart from the language which caused initial problems in the office we found that we had to come to terms with a new vocabulary and different expressions. There were times early on when starting to drive off in the car I found myself initially on the wrong side of the road. Fortunately this mistake was rapidly put right. It was strange to find a car overtaking on the inside. The rule of prohibiting parking on main roads was something which kept traffic moving and also reduced accidents. It is a regulation which could profitably be introduced here.

We needed time to search for and buy furniture and sheets for the house and shop opening hours seemed so sensible compared with the UK. The shops did not open before 10 am and then stayed open in the evenings until 10 pm. Staff worked a two shift system and many of the major stores remained closed on Mondays. On Saturday mornings many young ladies would go shopping with their hair in curlers under a scarf. We learnt this was deliberate so as it let friends and neighbours know that the young lady had a date that evening.

There was a general attitude of competition and seeking to get on in life and improve prospects. In the military those who had not already earned a degree were encouraged to study to do so.

There seemed to be fewer written letters and instructions than would have been customary in the British Army and more use was made of signals. This was due to a more restricted attitude and tighter control from above. It took more time to get agreement from other departments for a written instruction as it appeared decision making was not delegated to the same degree as in the British Army.

During a visit to the Infantry School at Fort Benning I went with a senior instructor to listen to a Captain giving a lecture to a course of some hundred or so officers. We entered a separate room at the back of the lecture hall screened by a one way glass window which shielded us from view but we could hear every word of the lecture. On the shelf in front of us was a very detailed script for this particular lecture which gave timings for each phase of the lecture allowing the odd joke to be inserted at the named time.

We sat listening in and I noticed my guide becoming more and more agitated. Eventually he muttered "If the bastard deviates once more from the script I'll have his guts for garters". This tendency to set everything down in detail was general. It was caused in part by the enormous expansion of the US Army first of all for the war in Korea and then again for Vietnam. The reductions after World War II meant that for the Korean War the level of experience was at Captain and Major level and by the time the Vietnam War came along this experience level was now at the Colonel rank. There had not been time for adequate training of middle piece officers to cope with rapid expansion of the army and there was a dearth of experience at the lower levels. I was to see more examples of this problem as the months passed.

On the social side we had noticed that some families seemed to live very compartmentalised lives with husbands and wives moving independently in their own circle of friends meeting together solely for formal parties. The children would return from school, raid the freezer for food and then go out to meet up with their peer group. There did not seem to be much integration as a family group.

This way of life did not apply overall and there were a number of families whom we got to know who enjoyed doing things as a family. Saturday evening was often a cook out evening when the man of the house was in charge of the bar-b-que and all the family and friends joined in. We had more in common with these families and made some good friends. Over the months ahead these friendships blossomed and we have maintained contact through the years.

The early landings in Virginia in 1607 had initially taken place close to Fort Monroe at Kecoughtan near Hampton. Each year this historic event was celebrated with a formal parade. Not long after arriving at Fort Monroe I was invited to attend this ceremony. The Guest speaker was Admiral Beloe of the Royal Navy, who was Deputy Commander in Chief South Atlantic Command at Norfolk, Virginia.

Seated before the formal speech making I was astounded to see. marching on from a flank and playing lustily, a military band dressed in scarlet tunics and wearing busbys with pipes and drums to their rear in Highland dress. I wondered why I had not been forewarned of the presence of British troops.

The band drew closer and as they wheeled about I noticed wisps of golden and red feminine hair creeping from below the busbys onto their necks. I enquired of the person sitting beside me where this band came from to be told "The Warwick High School Grenadier and Pipe Band". They played and performed remarkably well and marched tidily. Later I was approached by Mr Lyle Smith their musical director to give time to assisting them with their drill as this was a task undertaken by the previous British Liaison Officer. I was delighted to have this opportunity of meeting these youngsters who not only played well but were enthusiastic to be sure their foot drill was correct. This delightful work brought me into contact with the parents and we enjoyed attending the school concerts. I found this aspect of liaison very worthwhile.

I was invited to give talks to local groups and was interviewed on the local radio to talk about 'Dunkirk'. A friend in the Training Division taped this interview and gave me a copy. The amusing side was the interrupts of the person asking the questions at the end of a description with the term "Oh my, oh my". The interview was favourably commentated upon and helped fly the flag.

I had been given a contact in Alexandria by Angus Robertson of my regiment named Bob Pomeroy. Angus had met Bob who was the United States Air Force liaison officer at the RAF College Cranwell where Angus was the British Army representative. Bob had among other things acquired a 'Warming Pan' which he had not been able to fit into his baggage when he returned home to The States. It was arranged for us to take the warming pan with us. This we did and after I had passed the driving exam I telephoned Bob who invited us to drive up to Alexandria and stay the week end.

The drive was about one hundred and eighty miles and we managed to find our way to Alexandria without too much hassle. The Pomeroy residence was set in woodland with plenty of space between the houses. We recognised the house as a Morris Minor was parked on the road outside. I rang the door bell and it was opened by Bob who was wearing a bowler hat and carrying an umbrella. We were warmly welcomed by Bob and Carol his wife and the warming pan was handed over. The Pomeroys had three children and this visit was the beginning of a delightful friendship.

There were a number of changes taking place at Fort Monroe. Colonel Whitaker was taking his retirement and moving to the West Coast. This was our first experience of observing the cleaning organisation parties which ensured the quarters were passed as satisfactory. Mary Kay had six sons and we gave three of them beds and also gave the family meals on their final days. We were sad to see them go as Mary Kay had been really kind in taking Pat around and introducing her in the initial weeks.

The Whitakers moved out and their quarter was taken over by George and Hanna Sgalitzer. He was a Doctor who had transferred to the regular forces from the National Guard. George was an Austrian Jew and Hanna was from Czechoslovakia. They had gone to China in 1937 as medical missionaries. Seeing the Japanese invasion of China they had left China and settled in the USA where George had to

211

retake all his medical examinations. Subsequently George, who was in the National Guard, was called up for duty with the regular army. He decided to make the army his life and stayed in.

George had brought a grand piano with him and this only just fitted into one corner of his sitting room. He was an accomplished pianist and used to perform regularly at medical conventions in the States. We could hear him playing in the evenings as the sound came clearly through the block central chimney stack. We would show our appreciation by clapping. George was an anglophile and a royalist and he always finished his repertoire by playing 'God Save the Queen'. As a surgeon with the Recruiting Command he travelled widely and we always had a post card from him on these visits with the first five bars of 'The Queen' written with his message. Colonel Vern Reaugh an Infantry Officer had moved in next door to us on our level. He had been posted to the office of The Deputy Chief of Staff Logistics. One evening not long after he had settled in he held a party for his officers and the jollification resounded through the walls. George meantime was playing below and the music was audible. The time came when George started to play 'The Queen'. There was a bellow from Vern next door - "Quiet you lot. The British Liaison Officer lives next door and Colonel Sgalitzer is playing the British National Anthem. Stand to attention". The hubbub ceased and in dead silence George finished playing.

Over the months George and Hanna and Vern and Elaine became very good friends.

Lionel Hitchen came over to the USA on a business visit and stayed with us over a week end. The Reaughs' entertained us all to lunch. Vern had fallen asleep preparing the meal and set the kitchen on fire. It took him all night to clean up and prepare another meal!

We discovered that there was a regular 'Happy Hour' in the Officers Open Mess on a Friday evening and we decided to go along. The only person I recognised was Pete Peterson from the Operations Division and we asked if we might join him and his wife. He explained they were due to meet some very old friends who had arrived on post that day so when they arrived they would break away. It did not work out like that as by the time these friends, the Sullivans, arrived we were well into our third round of drinks and were invited to stay. Bob Sullivan was coming to CONARC to take over as Provost Marshal and was accompanied by his wife Nicki. He had served in Ireland and the UK during the war and had a deep love of the British Isles. They had been delayed in arriving by ensuring that their son Bob junior was properly asleep before they left him at the hotel. We soon established a firm friendship with the Sullivans.

We seldom went to 'Happy Hour' but on another occasion we were drinking with friends when my attention was drawn to a large man with enormous bushy eyebrows. We eyed each other up and he started talking saying that I was the first person he had met whose eyebrows were a match to his. It turned out that Bob Smith was the editor of the major local newspaper who had become renowned in media circles in the Eastern States. Yet again a friendship was born which continued many years.

We had enjoyed sailing when we were stationed in Egypt and thought it would be fun to join the Fort Monroe Sailing Club. We found most of the members owned motor boats of varying sizes, and that we would have to attend classes on small boat navigation run by the local Coast Guard. The instruction was over six evenings and finished with a written test paper. To begin with we were fascinated by the pronunciation of the word 'Buoy' which came over more as 'boo-ee'. However we both qualified and joined with Colonel Murphy and his wife when the flotilla went on a week end trip up the Elizabeth River.

Returning across Hampton Bay we ran into a fierce storm and the waves were running quite high to such a degree that Mrs Murphy became somewhat anxious. Her concern increased when she heard Pat was not a strong swimmer. There was but one solution and I brought out the duty free and we all fortified ourselves. It was drenching with rain and besides providing a distraction from the pitching boat it helped warm the cockles a little.

It was now August and Guy and Oonagh were due to come out for their first holiday. They travelled separately as Guy had to attend his first Combined Cadet Corps camp after term ended. Universal Aunts met both of them in London and helped see them to the airport. We were amazed how both of the children had shot up in height since we had last seen them in February.

The local children had been on holiday since early June and were deeply involved in their own groups so it took a while before our two were fully accepted. Apart from the weather, as the temperature was in the high eighties and humid as well, the culture shock took a while to get used to. It was not too long before Oonagh took part in a tennis tournament and beat her first opponent before succumbing to a youngster with a powerful service. She was introduced to sleep overs by the Dix girls. They both enjoyed the facilities at the club swimming pool.

We had decided the children were our first priority and Pat let this be known to our friends. We turned down a number of invitations to drinks and parties on this score which surprised some, however there were those who appreciated what we were doing. Our friendship with these families became firmer.

I had observed that my American colleagues seemed reluctant to take their leave entitlement. The odd day would be taken but the idea of leaving the desk unattended for longer periods seemed to be deemed unacceptable. General Fyffe the British Military Attache in Washington was responsible for all British Army personnel stationed in America. He made it very clear that we were to take our leave entitlement and should there be any problems he would speak to our American chiefs.

I was due some leave and applied for ten days which was immediately granted. The family set off in our Chevrolet Biscayne carrying a large tent bought locally and headed west through Richmond towards the Blue Ridge Mountains and the Skyline Drive. We found families at the camp sites very friendly and delighted to strike up conversation.

Even on the Skyline Drive some few thousand feet above the surrounding countryside it was still very hot in the mid day sun. Looking down on the Shenandoah Valley one could not but help think of the extraordinary stamina and courage of Stonewall Jacksons' Army and marvel at the feats of endurance of his soldiers. In the war between the States they had marched tens of miles a day in the heat of the summer sun. We visited Harpers Ferry and drove on to pitch our tent near Gettysburg.

Our trip coincided with the centennial celebrations of the war between the states and all the main battlefields had been made ready for visitors. Large map boards depicting different phases of a battle were set up at viewing points to enable the visitor to envisage how the opposing forces had reacted. There were panoramic displays and videos depicting the whole battle. These displays gave full details of the background and progress of events and everything was beautifully laid out. Our drive round the whole battle area took the whole day and we finished by viewing the scene from a helicopter.

Perhaps the most vivid impression of Gettysburg was the vast number of small memorials set up a few yards apart at different positions where minor skirmishes resulting in casualties had taken place. These were in addition to the large memorials placed by the different States as a tribute to their fallen.

After Gettysburg we drove north and spent a night at Letchworth Park, known as the Grand Canyon of the North before travelling on to spend a night in a motel at Niagara on the American side of the falls. Next morning having seen the falls from the American side we crossed to the Canadian side where the view was far more spectacular. We took a trip in The 'Maid of the Mist' which cruised close below the Horseshoe Falls. The spray from the falls was like a tropical downpour which was why all passengers were provided with waterproof clothing. We took the swinging car over the whirlpool looking down on the swirling waters and stayed to enjoy the sight of the floodlit falls by night. Niagara Falls made a deep impression. The mass of water tumbling down over the falls and the thunder of the water crashing to join the river below was awe inspiring. It was the highlight of the holiday.

After two days we drove south spending a time in Amish country and seeing their way of farming without modern equipment. On again and home over the Chesapeake Bay bridge tunnel, a structure of twenty two miles of roadway above water with two tunnels beneath channels to allow shipping to move to and fro the ports.

The holidays drew to an end and with heavy hearts we saw the children off at Norfolk. The three thousand miles seemed a long, long way and it would be Christmas before we saw them again.

General Fyffe organised a staff gathering each year of all British Army officers in Washington with their wives. This gave a chance for the General to get to know everyone and for us to be brought up to date on things going on at home. We were required to give a presentation of the organisation we were attached to and an outline of our work. We joined our wives for visits round The White House and the FBI. This gathering coincided with an annual visit of a British Army Band to tour the USA. We all showed up at the performance in full mess kit and gave the band our support. Our visits to Washington were always enjoyable as we were put up by our old friends David and Margaret Owen.

Headquarters USCONARC was on the list of visits by senior British Army officers who visited the USA from the UK. The Director General of Military Training General Leng was one such visitor. He was known to Colonel Shettle of the Individual Training Division who had been the US Army liaison officer at the School of Infantry Warminster when General Leng was commanding there.

I sat in on the briefing during the morning and accompanied General Leng to show him round Colonial Williamsburg in the afternoon. He regaled the local guide with stories of one of the Colonial Governors who had served in his regiment. That evening Pat and I were invited by the Shettles to join them and help entertain the General on a boat trip up the James River.

There were two other Colonels who had served as liaison officers in the UK and they all spoke highly of their regard for the British Army.

We had visited the Yorktown battlefield shortly after we arrived at Fort Monroe. The victory over the British was celebrated each year with a big parade, with a march past a local general. Local militia dressed in period costume and re-enacted the bombardment and closing up to the British fortifications.

There was a custom to invite a representative from a country which had fought alongside the French and American force. Some eighteen renegade Canadians had fought on the American side and during our second year at Fort Monroe the Canadian Liaison Officer from Fort Monroe found himself on the saluting dais. On this occasion the salute was being taken by General Harvey. H. Fisher the Deputy Commanding General USCONARC. There were contingents of two hundred and fifty men from The Marines, the US Navy, the US Army, the US Air Force and the Coast Guard. The whole show was well worth watching and I went along in plain clothes with Pat and we found a good view point opposite the podium. I took some good pictures of the parade.

A few days later I met General Fisher at a drinks party. "I saw you at Yorktown the other day with your camera," he said, "What were you up to?" I replied "General I was collecting evidence to take home to show the way you are still revelling in the defeat of your staunchest ally after all these years. I feel this celebration is unfortunate". "You Brits always have an answer" he replied with a hearty chuckle.

As the sole British officer on post I used any visit by other British officers from the embassy or the UK to host evening drink parties or curry lunches. The latter became very popular as Pat produced a good curry dish and found herself being asked to show the padre, Colonel Campbell, how to prepare one himself.

I was allowed a reasonable ration of duty free liquor each month and the price was very fair. I drove over to Norfolk to the Naval Headquarters at SACLANT where our Royal Navy detachment held a liquor store for the Royal Navy personnel stationed there. The ration was twelve bottles a month and I built up a reserve of whisky and gin to meet contingencies. I also acquired some Mead as an alternative British drink.

We learnt the custom as host was to offer the first drink after which the men would help themselves and assist with recharging the glasses of the ladies. This system allowed the host and hostess more freedom for mingling with the guests. We felt it was one of the better American customs.

As the weeks and months passed we widened our guest list but made a point of inviting those with whom we had struck up a firm friendship.

216

There was a great deal of publicity about keeping the post tidy and looking after the yard - the term for the garden. There was little we could do at the back of the quarter as this was used to park cars so Pat set to and planted flowers in the front alongside the path and beside the house. We had always made the best of the garden whenever we moved so this activity was automatic. The response of our neighbours in our block was immediate and they too joined in planting shrubs and flowers. Impetus was given by the favourable comments passed by senior officers as they walked by. I cannot help but think that initially our neighbours blessed us for drawing attention to the frontage though once the end result was on show they took great pride in the result and were glad to share in the praise from above.

The Christmas holidays came and with them the children. We had a few days off between Christmas and the New Year and decided to explore to the South. Unfortunately our departure was delayed as I had a temperature. Once this cleared we took off and visited the exhibition at Kitty Hawk showing the short distance of the first powered flight. Driving on from there we visited the fortifications of 'The Lost Colony' at Roanoake Island.

We stayed in inns and spent the first night at South Bern. Passing through Wilmington we went aboard a second world war battleship moored there. The size of the armament and the vastness of the ship made an impression on us all. We pressed on along the coast passing through Charleston and eventually stopping for the night at Savannah.

It was now time to retrace our steps and we drove back inland through Fayetville spending another night in a motel before arriving in Williamsburg on the last leg of the journey in time for a spectacular fire work display.

The holidays ended all too quickly and the children departed for home once more. We were glad to know that Pat's father had travelled over to England from Ireland and visited both children during term time.

Chapter Thirty

USA - Further Visits

Colonel Murphy retired and Colonel Joy Valery took over The Training Division. Two new officers Lieutenant Colonel Aebischer and Major Sherwin had joined TA&E but we were still below strength. The tempo of visits increased as more units and formations were training prior to going to Vietnam. As more formations became embroiled in the fighting there were competing demands upon the Pentagon for men to build up the formations and units due to deploy overseas. Equally vital demands were made for individual reinforcements to replace battle casualties in the units and formations already in Vietnam.

Computers were being used to provide up to the minute information on all army units down to the equivalent of company level within Continental Army Command. Officers commanding these units filled in a proforma giving details of their strength, training status and readiness. It was unlikely that an officer would enter any derogatory item which might reflect on his ability so these reports were suspect in some instances. On receipt the reports were fed into a massive main frame computer, which all but filled a large room, and sent to the Pentagon for briefing the Secretary for War Mr McNamara. The print out ran to many, many pages. In many instances the information was outdated by the time it was used for planning purposes.

It was the custom that any staff officer on a visit to a station would be provided with an escort. The officer given this task would meet him at the airfield and then act as an aide throughout the stay. I always tried to get to know these young men and asked them questions as to their background. On a visit to Fort Jackson I found out that the young Lieutenant who was my aide had just been in the army with a commission for six months. He was now commanding a training company preparing recruits for deployment overseas.

My next trip with Colonel Horace Brown was to the West Coast. We were to visit Fort Lewis near Seattle to observe the 4th Infantry Division taking part in final exercises prior to deployment to Vietnam before going to Headquarters Sixth Army at 'The Preasidio' San Francisco and Fort Irwin in the Mojave Desert.

The 4th Division exercise was going well but the disturbing aspect was that a large number of the staff officers at Divisional Head-quarters who had done all the preparatory training to develop an efficient team were due to be posted away. The new staff officers would arrive days before the division set forth. This was a pattern we had seen before with the Air Cavalry Division and which would be repeated at Fort Irwin when we visited a Medium Artillery Battalion. In the latter case the battalion was due to set off overseas in a fortnight, short of three hundred of the soldiers whom they had trained. These soldiers had been ordered overseas as individual reinforcements by the Pentagon. These actions indicated a lack of communication between the Personnel and Operations staff at the Pentagon.

Visiting Headquarters Sixth Army we were given a half hour with the Chief of Staff and commented on this problem as well as recording our views on our return to Fort Monroe.

The Chief of Staff at San Francisco regaled us with a story about General Fyffe and General Jack Harman of the British Army, who had attended a senior officers course at Fort Huachuka. Apparently the Colonel, who was the Post Commander there, was regarded as being somewhat pompous and fond of himself. This obviously became very evident when these senior officers were there. The Colonel was pontificating at a formal dinner in the mess and the two British Generals excused themselves and went out. They quickly changed their dress and came in attired in the full dress of two American Army Military Police complete with highly polished steel helmets (chrome domes). They advanced on the Colonel and standing one on either side stated that he was under house arrest and would he accompany them outside. They then took him by the arms and marched him out of the room to the cheers of all present. This act so amused the others present the story spread around and gave our host the greatest delight in the telling.

We flew from San Francisco to Las Vegas where we were meant to be picked up for a short hop to Fort Irwin but the aircraft was not airworthy so we had a hot three hour drive across arid country to Barstow where we took a branch road to the camp. Fort Irwin was set in the midst of the Mojave desert in most inhospitable country near where the initial nuclear tests had taken place. We spent a day there and saw some tank training.

Next morning we drove down to Los Angeles to catch our return flight home. It was very hot and I took my jacket off in the car. Arriving at the airport we had not much time to book in. Grabbing my jacket and baggage I followed Colonel Horace to the desk. I withdrew my airline ticket from my pocket and discovered my wallet with cash and identity documents was missing. I rushed back to see if our driver was still there but he had driven off. Colonel Horace gave me $5 and I went off to report to an information desk to enquire whether the wallet had been handed in while the Colonel booked our baggage in.

My enquiries were fruitless and returning to the booking in counter could see no sign of Colonel Brown but was disturbed to hear a call over the loudspeaker system saying "Positively the last call for Flight No 432 to Washington National". This was our flight and seeing no sign of Colonel Brown I ran along the tunnel to the boarding area. Arriving at the terminal gate I presented my ticket to an attractive airline hostess to be told boarding was completed. I must have looked pretty abject as the air line hostess grabbed me by the hand and rushed with me to the boarding gang way. In spite of her efforts I was not allowed aboard. I could see faces at the windows of the plane but had no means of finding out whether Colonel Brown was on board.

The air line hostess now told me there was a flight boarding for Washington Dulles and she would get me a seat on that plane. I was anxious to try and find Colonel Brown and said I wished to return to the booking in desk to look for him. "If you go away from here I can not guarantee getting you out of here before tomorrow" she said. I requested her to call over the loudspeaker system for Colonel Brown telling him where I was and the flight I was going to take out. She kindly made this announcement. As it was possible Colonel Brown could have taken off on our scheduled flight I also asked her to send a message to Washington National addressed to Colonel Brown giving full details of my movements. Having satisfied myself that I could not do anything more I boarded the aircraft.

Arriving at Dulles I paid $3.50 for a taxi ride to National Airport. I was now down to $1.50!

At National I had a three hour wait before the short flight to Newport News. Checking in there was no sign of the Colonel. I went to the airline desk and saw his flight had arrived. I asked whether Colonel Brown had collected a message only to be handed the message I had originated from Los Angeles myself. The air hostess had done as she was asked but where was Colonel Brown?

Later on arriving at Newport News I was met by a driver who told me Colonel Brown had missed the flight. Once I was home I rang Chick Brown and enquired of the whereabouts of her husband. "He's in Chicago and flying in tomorrow morning, where are you?". Chick was somewhat amazed when I replied "I'm at 94 Ingalls Road".

I checked the time of arrival of the Colonels' flight and arranged for the driver to collect me the next morning to take me to the airport. Arriving at the airport in the morning our baggage was awaiting collection so I loaded it into the car. It was a dreary damp morning. The plane came in and off got Colonel Horace who spotting me said "Hi Rob, what did you do - press the panic button?" We had a good laugh. Things had turned out well but it was not funny being separated from baggage and means of identification three thousand miles from home with only $5 in my pocket.

This was not the end of this episode. Whenever an officer of Training Division was posted away it was customary for a farewell ceremony when the officer was thanked for his contribution and wished well. A few weeks after my trip to the West Coast a brother officer was being sent off and there was the usual gathering together to say farewell.

After this officer had been toasted I was called forward and my brother officers from TA&E presented me with a 'Survival Kit'. This comprised of a whistle to be blown in an emergency. A tag to be fastened round my wrist labelled H.B.M.P.C. - this was defined as Her Britannic Majestys' Problem Child. A set of jacks to prevent boredom when waiting for plane departure. A First Aid Kit in case of injury. Pills to relieve a headache after a heavy party and a wallet containing a wad of play dollars. We all had a good laugh. I still have this survival kit after all it may be handy one day !

I had now been in post for over a year and was given the task of setting up and making all the arrangements for the annual training conference. The programme had to be agreed, speakers nominated and formal entertainment fixed. Representatives attended from all the six Continental Armies so accommodation needed to be booked. Nell Gerringer helped with the issue of folders and booking in of representatives but some of them were taken aback to find an attached British Officer handling things. In any event the conference went well so I could relax a little.

The Summer holidays came round once more and air travel was complicated as there was a National Air Traffic Controllers strike. Oonagh flew out and movements managed to get her down from New York but she did not arrive until 11 pm. With the five hour time difference the poor child was almost a walking zombie when we met her.

A day or so later we received a telephone call from Conn Hackett in Belfast to say Colonel Peter, Pat's Father, was ill and had been admitted to hospital and so Pat decided she should fly to Ireland to see him. The movements staff again were splendid in getting Pat to New York for her flight to Dublin.

The local air travel ticket office let me have Pat's ticket even though I had no cash. Having seen Pat off I went to the bank in Newport News parking in a cash car park where I put money in the parking meter. On returning from the bank I found a parking ticket had been placed on my car with a cash penalty. Oonagh was with me and I drove to the local police station. The clerk demanded that I pay the fine but I explained that I had put the money in the machine on the left as I would do in England and not in the meter on the right of the car. I had made a genuine mistake and did not feel I should pay a fine. The ticket was torn up. Recounting this problem later General Gunn said "You Brits get away with anything".

Guy arrived the day after Pat left and our friends rallied round and made sure we lacked for nothing. In return I cooked up a curry lunch and though the temperature was hot they valiantly ate the offering.

Pat wrote to say she was visiting her father in hospital and he was a little better. She said a lovely 'Get Well' card had been received from Fort Monroe Headquarters wishing Grandad well from all Our American friends. This was a lovely gesture and much appreciated. Grandad died a few days later and again a lovely wreath was sent by the Headquarters. These thoughtful acts helped Pat cope with all the funeral arrangements which were complicated as the body had to be transported from Belfast to Tidworth Military cemetery for burial alongside his wife.

I was due leave and had planned a trip out to the West Coast and back by road. On her return we met Pat off the plane and set off the following day so she had no time to brood. We drove via Chicago to Wall South Dakota, Mount Rushmoor, and Yellowstone where we took a great picture of a grizzly bear immersed nose down raiding a rubbish bin just across the road from our tent. Our next stop was Seattle where we stayed four days with the Whittakers who had retired to Seattle from Fort Monroe. They had not met the children but made us all very welcome. They had a lovely house on Mercer Island and showed us the local sights.

On to Newport on the Pacific coast, back to Crater Lake and on to the Humbolt Forests and San Francisco before heading for Carson City via Reno where we stayed with the Neills. Sam had been a fellow student at Camberley in 1949 and as a Coast Artillery man had been stationed at Fort Monroe before the war. We had kept in touch and Sam and Marthalina had stayed with us at Fort Monroe on a trip to the East Coast a year earlier. They showed us round Lake Taho and Virginia City before we set forth once more.

This time to Las Vegas and Boulder Dam via Yosemite and Death Valley then on to Flagstaff and the Grand Canyon. There followed a long drive through Amarillo, Oklahoma City, Little Rock and Chattanooga, Ashville and back to Fort Monroe. A journey of over eight thousand miles in twenty three days.

The trip had been a wonderful experience for Guy and Oonagh and they were of an age to enjoy it all. We were lucky with the weather and the scenery offered such a variety of breathtaking views. We camped most of the time breaking this routine by staying in a motel every so often. The stay with the Whitakers and Neills made a very pleasant break and provided the icing on the cake.

Once again the holidays came to an end. We were becoming used to saying goodbye to the children and the wrench of parting was not so hard. However the separation was more difficult for the children as they no longer had the visits by Grandad during the term time. The authorised number of trips had been taken up so they would not see us again until we returned home six months later.

The United States of America (Holiday Trips)   **Map 11**

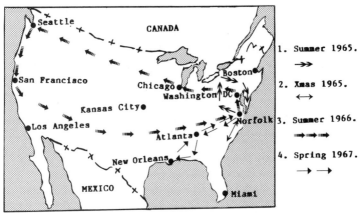

One of the pleasant sides of my liaison job was talking to civilian groups. I had been invited to lecture to the local Rotary Club who had asked me to talk about Rhodesia. I received a directive from the Embassy that I was not to talk on this subject. I spoke about Wales showing some coloured slides. The audience were polite but were not much interested in my alternative subject. I feel relationships with the locals lost a few points.

We used to receive pink sheets from the Embassy telling what we were not to talk about and Rhodesia was a hot potato at this time. These directives were not greeted with the respect which I am sure the originators expected. The senior Royal Navy Captain at SACLANT would telephone me whenever one of these slips arrived. "Have you received such and such a paper?". On receiving my acknowledgement the answer was invariably "Well I have binned mine what was your reaction?". Our main objection was the frame of mind of these civilians that we could not be trusted to be sensible about things.

Papers flew around when Smith declared UDI in Rhodesia. A day or so later I was at a drink party when General Duncan, the Chief of Staff, cornered me and asked my view on things. I smartly played the ball back and said "General, What is your view?". "Well those little guys are only doing what we did to you people one hundred and eighty years ago. I would like to take an army out there to help them". I replied - "General may I come on your staff?". This conversation shows the difference between straight forward thinking of soldiers compared with the convoluted approach of politicians.

Colonel Horace was posted to West Point Military Academy and we gave him a special branch bar-b-que on Dog beach. It was forbidden to swim at this beach but the party went well and took to the water. Colonel Joy Vallery assuming himself to be a walrus made a loud howling noise which we felt would be bound to attract the attention of the Military Police. Fortunately the sounds did not carry and the party dispersed without anyone being had up for breaking regulations.

Before we had set out from Wales we had sought information about climatic variations and had been told the temperatures were mild during the winter months. There was a national emergency in Virginia during our first winter. Fourteen inches of snow settled on post. Moreover it was so cold the sea froze locally in the bay!

We used to attend the Episcopalian Chapel on post and as Remembrance Sunday was coming up I mentioned this to Padre Campbell and asked if he would make mention of this special day for the British Forces. His response was to invite me and the Canadian Liaison Officer to attend in Number 1 Dress with swords and medals and to read the lessons.

Colonel Garrett had been posted in in place of Colonel Brown and two new officers joined the branch Majors Fieodorowich and Rudelhuber. Major Sherwin had departed to the Pentagon and Lieutenant Colonel Aebischer had moved to Individual Training.

Chapter Thirty One

USA - Further Visits and Farewell

There was an annual exchange system between the American and British Armies and British troops came to the States whilst an equivalent force of American soldiers went to the UK. These interchanges were timed to allow the participating troops to take part in major exercises using the equipment, tanks and vehicles of the host nation. Fort Carson, Colorado where the 5th US Infantry Division was stationed was chosen to host the British contingent. Close by, deep inside the local mountains was Headquarters NORAD, responsible for managing and controlling the US Air Defence System.

Hearing I was going on a visit to the British troops one of my colleagues enquired why Fort Carson had been selected. I replied - You remember I said a while ago that 'when we return to the USA we will not make the same mistake we made in 1776 at Yorktown. Next time we come we will stay. Fort Carson is close to Headquarters NORAD'. I had been around for long enough for my office companions to be aware of the British sense of humour though it was a moment before the implication sank in and raised a laugh.

Colonel Joy Vallery, the Head of the Training Division, joined me on the trip to watch the exercise at Fort Carson. The company from the Cheshire Regiment with a troop of tanks in support had quickly adapted to the American equipment and acquitted themselves well. On the second morning as we drove out to the battle area we could see a thick mist settled over the location held by the British contingent. It was tear gas simulating a gas attack. The area was affected for a few hours and prevented the soldiers having their breakfast and mid day snacks. The means of retaliation was a fighting patrol which unfortunately led to damage of some equipment and feelings began to run high. This is where our presence paid off and Colonel Vallery umpired the battle and everything was sorted out amicably.

Later that day as we were following an attacking force. The enemy counter attacked and threw tear gas which drove us away from the scene as the effect quickly hit our eyes and throats. We had not been issued gas masks so we beat a very hasty retreat. The exercise finished with a live fire demonstration including aircraft dropping napalm and an Honest John rocket launching a missile. It was possible to watch this missile from launch to impact as the demonstration took place overlooking a vast flat prairie.

After the exercise Colonel Vallery insisted on inviting all the British Officers to dine in the local officers mess as he wanted to meet them all and find out what they thought of the exchange and of the equipment in comparison to their own. This exchange showed the contrast between the two armies in the delegation of authority. The British Army company commander had fifteen or so years experience and even his junior subaltern had two years service. Such luxury was unheard of in the US Army where experience at the lower levels of command was in short supply. Comparison was not possible as the differences were not between two comparable organisations. The US Army comprised very large numbers of draftees whilst the British Army was very small and professional.

General Fyffe, the Military Attache, had come down from Washington to visit the British troops and observe part of the exercise. He spent time with the British contingent and was shown round the 5th Division Headquarters set up in the field and lunched in the Headquarters Mess.

I had been asked by General Freeman to invite General Fyffe down to Fort Monroe for a formal visit. He accepted and after persuasion agreed to be received with an Honour Guard as I advised him the Americans always had a Guard for all visiting dignitaries.

I had watched a number of these formal parades and noticed the dignitary being honoured walked rapidly round the ranks without ever speaking to any of the soldiers. General Fyffe inspected the Guard of Honour in the manner followed in the British Army stopping and speaking to about six of the soldiers. This formality was noticed and remarked upon in the next issue of USCONARC Orders. Inspecting officers were directed to talk to men and not walk past without any recognition!

On the day General Fyffe arrived with his wife he was invited by General Freeman to dinner together with Pat and me. This was a very cheerful party. After the Honour Guard next morning General Freeman saw General Fyffe in his office and gave a very frank appraisal of the problems facing his command. After this there were the routine briefing followed by a lunch for all the key Heads of Departments which I hosted as British Liaison Officer. After lunch General Fyffe gave a lucid account covering the commitments of the British Army supporting NATO in Europe and emphasising the burden of activities in the conflict in Indonesia. There were those who wondered why we had not sent troops to help fight in Vietnam especially as Australia had sent a contingent. The scale of involvement of British Forces in Borneo had not been fully appreciated. His discourse was well received.

The build up of forces in Vietnam continued and operational reports flowed into TA&E Branch. Production of 'Lessons Learned' became a routine activity. In spite of all the latest equipment the brunt of the action fell upon the infantry and the casualty rate at platoon leader and squad leader level was high. The enemy had been honing his skills against the French long before the Americans became involved. Ho Chi Min was adept in the art of guerilla tactics. Years before the French had had to accept defeat. I was told when I was attached to the French army in 1952 that a complete output from St Cyr, the officer training school, had been killed in Vietnam. No Army can withstand such loss and it was evident the Americans had taken on an unenviable task. Unless the local civilians could be protected from being intimidated the battle would be long and difficult. Jungle warfare needs infantry who can operate for days and weeks on end in isolated areas setting ambushes and living rough. Guns, tanks and aircraft alone will not win the battle. This type of warfare needs hard graft from the foot soldier.

Bob Sullivan was a third generation American whose roots were from Ireland. He had been stationed in Ireland and England in WWII before fighting in North West Europe. He had a deep respect of the British Army. He invited us to a party at his house on Saint Patrick's Day and we were amazed to find our American friends wearing green shamrocks and hats and really getting down to partying. The surprising thing was that after the third or fourth drink the American drawl was being replaced by a distinctive Irish brogue. This was all the more surprising as this 'Irish' effect only seemed to occur on Saint Patrick's Day.

Christmas came and it was strange not to have Guy and Oonagh with us. They went to Ireland to stay with Pats' cousin Conn and Kay Hackett who kindly agreed to have them.

Another Department party was coming up and I found myself with six others detailed as volunteers as part of the entertainment group. We were to strip to the waist and have jackets fastened below the waist with their arms stuffed and with white gloves. Eyes and eyebrows would be painted on our chests, a nose would be stuck just below the ribs and a small mouth added round the belly button. Our arms would hold up a tall top hat which would come just below the shoulder line. Our team consisted of six tall men and one of below average height.

The group was announced as a visiting party from another planet and trooped in in line to the music of 'The bridge over the River

Kwai'. Our instructions were to wiggle our bellies in time to the music as this we were told gave the appearance of whistling. We held a dress rehearsal, did what we were told and everything went well.

On the night to ensure decorum in case the weight of the bolstered jacket might cause underwear to slip we were directed to wear swimming trunks as extra protection. This was in effect our undoing. We were all somewhat nervous as we were now to exit by passing in front of the Generals' table where we were to perform an extra whistle.

The line entered led by our smallest member and I brought up the rear. As we processed I felt my jacket slowly beginning to slip. With each pace it slipped further and the swimming trunks were now very evident. There was only one answer and I lowered one arm from inside the top hat and grasped the jacket heaving it back into place. However this was a losing battle as with each forward move the slippage continued and the use of a grasping arm had to be resorted to again. The top hat restricted vision ahead to such a degree I could not see any of the other members of our group and so I pressed on regardless. With a final heave to adjust the jacket I did my act before the General and retired hurt.

The act had been so chaotic that it brought the audience to tears. Pat not realising things had not gone as intended recognised my swimming trunks and was creasing herself with laughter. She thought my activities were all part of the act.

Having escaped I quaffed a drink and whilst changing heard the rest of the gang had all had similar problems. Joining Pat at our table I was somewhat taken aback to be told all the others had fled very early on and I was the only chump to complete the full course. It was all good clean fun and as always each individual who took part received a thank you letter from General Gray.

This formal etiquette was part of the make up of the US Army at Fort Monroe. On the two birthdays I spent on General Grays' staff I received a personal letter from him wishing me well. Such thoughts were a nice touch in a very busy Headquarters.

I was due some more leave and I timed it to go down to New Orleans at the time of Mardi Gras. The aides in General Freeman's office could not have been more helpful and arranged for us to have billets on Army Posts en route. The drive south gave me a chance to pass by Fort Benning, The Infantry School, and show it to Pat. We drove on and spent the night at the Army Air Corps camp in Florida. Driving along the coast route next day we found ourselves caught up in a drenching downpour and did not see much of the countryside. The sun came out later in the afternoon and we sought accommodation. Arriving in New Orleans we found that flood water had entered the ground floors of many of the motels and the carpets were soaked.

Next morning was sunny and we had breakfast at 'Brennans' which we had been told was the thing to do. The meal was fun and worth the early rise. Next we explored the French Quarter which had a number of bars and I was glad Pat was with me as Transvestites were seeking drinking companions.

The streets were filled with people out to enjoy the celebrations many of them in fancy dress. We managed to find a good viewing point to watch the procession of splendidly decorated floats most imaginatively decorated with different themes. The colours of the costumes were a sight to behold. It was obvious that great effort had been put in by everyone concerned and we were told that preparation had in many cases started weeks earlier. The judging to decide the best entry could not have been easy.

After watching the procession which apart from the floats had numbers of gallantly dressed men wearing masks riding lovely steeds we repaired back to our motel. The time had passed by quickly and we felt tired so after a meal we decided against going out again for the evening procession and watched events on television instead.

We set off on our return journey next day and stopped at Fort MacPherson Atlanta where we dined with General George Duncan. He was Deputy Commanding General of the Third US Army having left Fort Monroe a few months earlier. He was a great character and his wife who came from Georgia encouraged me to speak with a 'Southern Accent'. It was particularly nice to know that they had stipulated we would stay at Fort MacPherson and dine with them on this trip.

Returning to Fort Monroe time was now shortening before Lieutenant Colonel Donald Heffill, Royal Tanks, came out to replace me. A note came from General Freeman to say he was going to Australia and then on to Vietnam and could I accompany him? This would have entailed a change of my posting date and was not authorised by The War Office. This was short sighted to say the least as at that time we had not had any entry into the Vietnam war zone. Moreover going there with a four star general would have been particularly informative and interesting. I was also sad to miss a chance to visit the Australian Forces in their homeland.

Donald Heffill arrived and we went into the hand over routine where apart from briefing him on his role in the office I took him round to meet people. We had met in 1948 when he was serving at

Fayid. There were farewell parties which over these two weeks built up to a crescendo. The Americans were determined to make sure we were properly seen off.

I had noticed Nell Gerringer drafting a letter which she shielded from me in a somewhat obvious manner. I questioned her about it and suspecting it was something to do with a recommendation for an award persuaded her to let me in on the secret. I then told her that I did not wish to be placed in the awkward position of having to refuse to accept an award as this was contrary to the agreement between out governments in peace time. A recommendation for the award of a 'Legion of Merit' was sent to the Pentagon and a copy passed to the British Army staff. I was given a copy of the acknowledgement by the Pentagon of this recommendation.

The United States Army was meticulous in recording thanks to officers on the completion of their tour of duty. Officers departing the Headquarters were formally thanked by the Head of Department and Senior Officers were given their citation with an Honour Guard. I received letters of Commendation from Colonel Vallery as Head of the Training Division and General Symroski on behalf of General Gray as Deputy Chief of Staff Unit Training and Readiness. In addition as British Liaison Officer there was a formal ceremony in the General's Office where General Gray, representing the Commanding General, presented me with a Certificate of Appreciation, a CONARC Plaque and Swagger Cane and a Certificate for Community Service.

Pat stood beside me throughout this part of the ceremony and was herself given a Certificate for Community Service for all she had done. This was richly deserved as she had taken an active part in many of the wives activities and hosted many friendly and also formal parties. She had helped me fly the flag and besides her Wives Club activities she joined with the Royal Navy wives at Norfolk as a host on their 'British Day'.

After the presentations and speeches senior officers and their ladies and a few special friends filed past and shook hands. Photographs of this event were taken and placed in an album which was signed by General Gray and presented as a memento.

I was able to hand the General an inscribed Regimental Plaque in return which Pat concealed in her hand bag until the appropriate moment. Perhaps the most moving part of this event was that the Senior Warrant Officer on post had requested to attend the ceremony. I felt very touched to say good bye to him and felt greatly honoured at the attendance of the senior officers and their wives.

Presenting a "Royal Anglian Regiment" badge to Major General David Gray on leaving HQ USCONARC.

The next morning we were hosted with a champagne breakfast and then driven to the airport where Don Heffill had arranged a surprise seeing off party in the VIP lounge. When we booked in for our flight we found it had been brought forward and we were rushed aboard the aircraft so we flew off and Don and our friends enjoyed a party without us!

We spent two days in Washington staying with Colonel Wheeler who was my link with the British Army Staff before flying to New York. We were picked up by a driver and taken to West Point to stay with Colonel Horace and Chick Brown. Colonel Brown was adamant that we should stay with him before we sailed for home.

Our short stay at West Point was memorable as we were shown round the establishment which is set in beautiful countryside beside the River Hudson. I was amazed at the size of the Dining Hall and the Chapel set on the side of a hill was very impressive. The knock out blow came at dinner when Colonel Brown asked me whether I would join his office as his assistant. Initially I found this proposal hard to accept. A retired British Redcoat in the office of the Association of Graduates of West Point surely he was joking. I commented on this aspect. Colonel Brown continued - "No Rob that is no problem at all. I know you and you could handle the job well". He continued by giving a proposed salary and accommodation provisions and asked if the sum was adequate. I was astonished this proposal was quite unexpected. Pat then asked what would happen when Colonel Brown retired and moved on? "That has all been taken care of".

We were due to sail on the Queen Mary the following day. Our heavy baggage was loaded and my Mother aged 87 who was very frail and the children were looking forward to seeing us again. I explained all this to Colonel Brown and thanked him for the offer saying that I could not have been more honoured. I did feel I had to return home and see how things were. My decision was accepted and it was left that an offer would be posted to me.

We had sufficient time in New York to go to the top of The Empire State building and look down on the Queen Mary at her berth. We left the USA with messages of good will from many of the friends we had made and headed East.

Vern and Elaine Reaugh at Pant-y-Goitre.

Chapter Thirty Two
The U.K. - Ashford 1967 to 1970

My next posting was to the Headquarters of the Intelligence Centre in the Planning Wing. There were no quarters available so we decided Pat would move back into our house in Camberley and I would live in the mess at Ashford during the week. This meant leaving home on Sunday evening and returning on Friday evening. The mess was a modern purpose built building designed to provide accommodation for students attending courses as well as the permanent staff. The barracks were in a green fields site in a lovely part of Kent.

The work was interesting as it was looking at future equipments for surveillance and target acquisition. This entailed not only close work with all the Army Schools and Research Establishments but also Industry. It also meant visits to Headquarters 1st British Corps in Germany and work on joint NATO panels in Brussels. The Branch worked under the auspices of a branch in the Military Intelligence Directorate which determined policy. Regular visits to the War Office ensured a close understanding existed between us. Once settled into the weekly routine I was able at times to arrange liaison work at the War Office on Mondays and Fridays which allowed a longer week end.

The Intelligence School was in the same barracks as our office and I went on a six weeks course to be brought up to date. I had attended a similar course in 1945 but there had been many changes. This course was helpful on two scores. First it gave me a broader understanding of what I would be dealing with and secondly I got to know other officers on the course whom I would be working with in the months ahead. One was John Hemsley of The Light Infantry whom I would see when I visited Headquarters 1st British Corps in Germany.

Colonel George Goulding who had transferred into The Intelligence Corps from the Royal Artillery ran the Planning Wing. He required all his staff officers to attend a Computer Programming Course at The Royal Corps of Signals Depot at Catterick.

The course which I went on was made up of a number of officers from the three Services mainly from the technical arms. There was one other infantry officer Geoff Strong from The Surreys and six Royal Signals officers who we learnt had arrived earlier to be given an introductory session.

The course was well run and we were taught how to programme on a very basic early Elliot machine. On completion I at least had acquired a rudimentary understanding of what 'Automatic Data Processing' was about.

Visits to Research Establishments and Industry fired my interest in the progress being made in the design and testing of new surveillance equipments. Meetings in Brussels and visits to other NATO Countries increased understanding of the use of data processing for command and control. It also assisted in helping provide material which would aid in determining policy decisions.

War Gaming was a means of testing out ideas and the office regularly observed the many exercise scenarios which were played. The Intelligence Planning Wing helped ensure that Intelligence information being fed into these exercises was as realistic as possible. This was important as new ideas, weapons and techniques were introduced into these games. The commanders taking part were brought in from their units and this gave them the chance of manoeuvre with a mixed force without the cost entailed in a live exercise. Again this research provided pointers to the practicability of possible weapons and future tactics. These war games were interesting to observe and visits were an important part of our work.

On the social side the mess were offered membership of the local golf club and with others like myself living away from home I took advantage of this offer. In the summer evenings we would set off sharp at 5 pm and were able to fit in eighteen holes before returning for dinner. That filled in time in the light evenings during the summer. In the winter I took part with the Thespian group which provided a few laughs.

I was acting the part of a forgetful priest in one of these performances - The Black Sheep of the Family - and allowed my hair to grow abnormally long. After the dress rehearsal I returned to the mess still wearing a dog collar and cassock. The WRVS lady who was responsible for props was with me. Students attending a new short course had arrived that evening and many of these officers were in the bar. We entered and I was about to offer my companion a drink when a student officer interrupted and said "No Padre this is on me" to which I replied "Bless you my son, thank you very much". Next morning at breakfast when I appeared in my correct dress the student was a little nonplussed. I returned him the compliment at lunch time.

The play itself went off well. I was amused to be told the wife of one of our staff had commented "That officer you work for seems very forgetful. He seemed to have difficulty with his lines".

Colonel Goulding had moved on and had been replaced by Murray Stephen who had formerly been an Infantryman. There is a suspicion within the combat arms of any specialist, and this suspicion applied to "Intelligence", which was looked upon as something

The absent minded vicar in 'The Black Sheep of the Family' Ashford 1969.

slightly peculiar. It was easier to establish relaxed links with other arms when those conversing on the subject had themselves had had first hand experience in a combat unit. Both George Goulding and Murray Stephen benefited from their early backgrounds.

A further part of our work was to visit Headquarters 1st British Corps in Germany on exercises as observers. Ideas were fermenting on the use of computers in the handling of combat intelligence. Initial studies and work had shown that this was a possibility but cash priorities had put these on hold.

A visit to the French Army in Paris a few months later showed that they had advanced much further ahead in this art.

They had a working automatic map display and it was interesting to see many of their methods were very similar to those we had adopted in our approach to the problem. It made us somewhat envious and proved the benefit of the exchange of ideas pursued by the NATO working panels.

A chance of a quarter at Ashford came up after twenty months but a move to Kent would have further complicated week end travelling. Guy was at Haileybury in Hertfordshire whilst Oonagh was at The Royal School Bath. We visited them once every month and took them out for a meal. My Mother was ill in a nursing home in Devon and visiting her took a full weekend once a month. After eighteen months

Mother died and it was only then I realised the strain this regime had imposed on us.

We had kept in touch with the friends we had made on our tour in the USA. George Sgalitzer came over and went to the Salzberg Festival each year staying in London en route. We met up with them on these visits and on one occasion they came down to Camberley. Another visitor was George Smith the Newspaper Manager at Newport News who came over with his wife and daughter. There was also an officer who had been in another part of the Operations department at Fort Monroe who was working at the American Embassy. I had not known him very well but he got in touch and we met up.

Guy was now a house prefect and in his final year. He hoped to read chemistry and visited a number of universities to decide where he would like to go. He passed his exams and qualified and was accepted for The University of Kent at Canterbury.

The three years at Ashford passed very quickly. The remit to the Planning Wing allowed a loose rein and this meant that it was possible to keep up with all the latest ideas in Industry and the Research Establishments. It brought me into contact with numbers of brilliant research engineers and extended my understanding of computers and the developing techniques of image intensification and infra red surveillance equipments.

My final project was to look into the use of microfilm with a view to reducing the amount of paper which mobile headquarters carried round on exercises. I went on a short course to learn about microfilm and microfiche techniques. After my research I put in a report and this resulted in putting on a demonstration to the Army Headquarters in Germany. Kodak Ltd helped considerably in preparing copy .

My relief had arrived and he was to come with me and assist in the demonstrations at Headquarters British Army of The Rhine and Headquarters 1st British Corps. This visit was made more exciting as the plane due to bring out the equipment was given another priority task. It was Saturday morning and the Corps Commander and all the Divisional Commanders and key officers and staff were coming in on Monday morning for the demonstration. Calls were made to the duty officer in the War Office and Movements Control to unravel this problem. Late in the afternoon I was told the kit would be sent to Frankfurt.

The next problem was to acquire a driver and vehicle to set off South from Bielefield that afternoon. Our hosts came up trumps and I left knowing that we would need to find an overnight stop. The next morning, Sunday, arriving at Frankfurt and enquiring about the flight

I was told there was no record. This needed a number of calls back to the Duty Officer at Bielefield who had to find out what was going on from England. Meantime the hours were ticking by and still no equipment for the demonstration. Eventually about 1400hrs I was told the aircraft had taken the kit to the USAF Airbase at Frankfurt.

Finding the driver, who by this time thought me quite mad, we drove to the USAF Base and eventually found where our kit had been off loaded. On stating what I was looking for the Top Sergeant said "I knew you were sure to come along sometime. We have had this kit here since early this morning". I thanked him, loaded all our kit into the vehicle and set off on our return journey. It was now almost 1500 hrs.

We arrived back at Bielefield after 2100hrs and having dug the rest of our team out of the mess set the equipment up ready for the next morning. Everything was working satisfactorily so I slept in a happier frame of mind. The next day went off without a hitch.

Following this demonstration we were now due to go to Headquarters British Army of The Rhine at Rheindalen and found that our driver was the lad who had driven all over Southern Germany with me over the week end. Driving on the autobahn he began to doze off and we relieved him from driving for safety reasons.

Having arrived at the Headquarters we set up the kit and repaired to the mess. Murray Stephen joined us from England and after dinner we went out to a local hostelry with some WRVS ladies. My relief had got to know two of them when he remained behind at Bielefield whilst I was collecting the kit from Frankfurt. He thought it would be fun to play a prank on Murray and asked the ladies to pretend to have a crush on him. They fell in with this scheme and danced closely cheek to cheek. Murray was taken aback a little and whispered to me had I found the ladies a little forward? I replied no and asked him why he thought this. We kept this up and Murray became very agitated.

The next morning we made our presentation to the hierarchy before driving back to Bielefield for our return flight to England. We let Murray off the hook on the way home and let him know the very affectionate ladies had been a set up.

I felt that it would be a nice follow on to this episode if I could play a joke on my relief who obviously enjoyed a prank. The branch had a nice custom of dining out members when they left. Arriving at the rendezvous with Pat, who knew what I had planned, we waited for my relief to arrive with his wife.

Immediately she entered the room I leapt forward and grasping her warmly to me said "Angela darling, how amazing, it is ages since we last met. How lovely to see you again after all these years. I had no idea you were married to John". The wife played up and initially John was taken in. Afterwards we all had a good laugh. The party had got off to a good start and we left the branch on a high note.

I had been particularly lucky in having Murray as my chief. He had a sound brain and we both got on well together and respected each other. I was very sad to hear that he had died very soon after he retired from the army three years later.

My next posting was to a Project team in Germany tasked with examining ways and means of introducing data handling for command and control. I was to be the Intelligence 'Expert'.

This meant sorting our kit out and finding tenants to live in our house at Camberley. We were lucky in this respect as there was always a demand for houses for foreign students attending The Staff College Course at Camberley. Our agent obtained a let with the Canadian Army and 'Crash' Adams moved in. Pat and I flew out from Gatwick to Hannover in an RAF 'Comet' and moved into a married quarter. The children came out a day later by train as this move coincided with their holidays.

Chapter Thirty Three

Germany - 1970 to 1973

We were met at the airport by David Warne a young officer in the Royal Tanks and driven to our quarter in an army patch, a semi detached house in a residential area on the outskirts of Hannover. He was part of the Operations study team in my new unit. The other part of the house was lived in by an American Intelligence Officer. Our other neighbour was Colonel Bruce McDiarmid, RAMC a surgeon in the local British Military Hospital. He became famous as the surgeon who looked after Guardsman Weston of the Welsh Guards burned in the Falklands. There was a NAAFI Shop close by as well as a Salvation Army coffee shop.

The full title of the set up I was to join was 'Joint Operational Project Team (Project Wavell)' or JOCPT for short. I was now holding a technical staff appointment.

Project Wavell was one of three study teams under direction from a Headquarters at Wilton under the command of Brigadier Peter Leuchars. The Brigadier visited us a few times and had quickly appreciated the potential of developing ideas for using computers in the command structure of the Army.

Project Wavell was housed in Barracks at Hildesheim. On entering the office although other officers and clerks were there I found there was hardly any furniture. We were awaiting filing cabinets, typewriters and stationery. A day or so later our spirits rose when a packing case arrived addressed to JOCPT. On opening this package imagine our surprise when instead of office equipment we unravelled a set of sports kit including a discus, hammer and shot, a starting pistol and time keeping watches. The PT part of our title had been interpreted by some person as 'Physical Training'. A full entitlement of office equipment did eventually arrive a few days later.

The JOCPT was made up of staff officers who came from all the different Arms and Services, Armour, Artillery, Engineers, Signals, Infantry, RAOC and REME, all of whom had completed courses in data processing. This spread across the different Arms and Services helped the team to integrate with the different Headquarters whose staff were inclined to be somewhat suspicious of any 'boffin'. Initially officers would wonder who and what we were and I overheard this query when we were taking part in a Corps Headquarters inter branch shooting competition. Perhaps their suspicions were allayed when our team won the falling plate competition.

Our offices were at Hildesheim sharing the barracks with Headquarters 7th Artillery Brigade and 32 Medium Regiment Royal Artillery. We were attached to 1st British Corps Headquarters and early work was with the staff branches. Initially I liaised with John Hemsley who had been on the same intelligence course at Ashford with me. We agreed a series of message formats.

There were numerous exercises throughout the year and we took part in all of them either as observers or as watchkeepers in the 'Operations' vehicle. This was interesting work as it helped us in our studies and at the same time we got to know members of the staff on a first name basis.

Our studies included visits to all of the Division Headquarters and most of the Brigades. After these visits we wrote up a report which defined the work activities of the different elements and sent a copy to the Headquarters involved.

I continued to go to NATO meetings in Brussels where we would hear how other NATO members were progressing in developing data processing for command and control. The working language was either French or English and translators covered all the sessions. These discussions helped improve my French. Much detailed work went into setting up these meetings and papers and agenda were issued. I must have attended this particular panel over a period of six years representing the British Army. It soon became apparent that it took an inordinate time to reach agreement, years as against weeks and months. The pace of progress was frustrating. This was the worst means of working if this was what resulted from trying to reach agreements between the different NATO Countries on integration.

Representatives from Industry would often appear at these times among them Freddie Prichard from Ferranti Computer Systems. I had first met Freddie when he paid a few visits to Ashford to tell us of the latest advance in map displays. As his firm's Army Sales Representative he liaised with us and other research organisations to find out what the Army was looking for.

We worked very closely with our opposites on the staff at Bielefield as it was important that any development would not only meet the operational requirement but that it would be user friendly. Unfortunately the hardware used to test new ideas was in the UK at Fort Halsted. We found there were times when the civilian experts there went off at a tangent on their own. This would have been less likely had we been sited nearer to each other.

There was one significant incident which took place during one of the major exercises. At the time I was observing the activities in the Intelligence office at Corps Headquarters squeezed into a minute space in the corner of the vehicle. The Director of RARDE was being led round by a civilian head of department. Arriving in the vehicle the questioning centred on the number of messages having to be dealt with in the office. No attention was drawn to the key fact that the content from all messages would be extracted and marked onto a map as part of the continually changing battle picture. The staff officer answered the questions but because transferring information onto the map was an automatic action he did not emphasise the importance of data on the map. In any case he was on duty in the middle of an exercise and the sooner he could satisfy direct questions and be left in peace to carry on so much the better. After a few more questions all related to message traffic the visitors departed. As they left the escorting boffin remarked "Well Sir you can see the main problem is in handling messages". Not a word was said about map displays and the key place the map played in interpreting what was happening!

It is such misdirection that not only delays the services receiving the correct equipment but also adds extra cost in the long term. I reported these observations to John Spackman who had arrived to run our team in the hope he might have the chance of talking about map displays. John was a ball of fire with a fund of knowledge in data processing. The studies were progressing well and helping considerably in determining the way ahead.

The War Office had decided that an initial system should be developed and advised Industry. We were directed to receive delegations from Marconi, Plessey and Ferranti and give their teams a full briefing on our work and our ideas. Our design work had divided neatly into two teams, one for operations and intelligence and the other for logistics. Members in the teams worked closely together and understanding grew of what would be feasible. The visit went off well and we formed our own ideas as to which company we felt best suited to take on the work.

I had held this appointment for two years and a replacement, Major Ferraby, was posted in. However it was felt there was further work on the handling of intelligence which I should progress and I was left with the Project Wavell team but attached to JOCPT Headquarters at Wilton.

Guy had completed his degree course at Canterbury and before taking up work came to stay with us. Pat was working during the day on flight bookings run by Welfare. Guy had been with us about a week when Pat received a call from the British Military Hospital Hannover to say Guy had been admitted and had been diagnosed as having TB. For the first few days he was isolated and we wore masks and protective clothing during visits. He responded to the treatment and

241

was able to return to the UK a few weeks later and take up a job with Lionel Hitchen Essential Oils Ltd in Reigate. Lionel was an old friend and we had kept in touch through the years. He had visited us in Hannover with Louie.

While this was happening Oonagh had taken a holiday in Greece and news came through offering her a place at Liverpool University. It took time to contact her and request an urgent return home. She found the quickest route took her through East Germany and we hoped she would not be held up at the border. As luck would have it she passed through the border controls without being questioned and we breathed again.

At the same time our good friends Bob and Nicki Sullivan from America arrived to stay with us. This was the first of many reunions and we were able to take them to Goslar and the Harz mountains.

Bob and Nicki Sullivan, Goslar 1972.

Later during that summer we drove down to Salzburg with Oonagh and met up with George and Hanna Sgalitzer. They had come over from The States for the festival. George had been brought up in the city and spent a whole morning as guide round this picturesque city with its old castle.

We got to know Brigadier Tim Morony who commanded the Artillery Brigade well and were invited to formal parties at his house. The Divisional Commander General Jack Harman who had been a fellow student at Staff College was also a guest at one of these parties. I was older than the Brigadier and as we left Tim said "Robin you may call me Tim". I replied "Thank you Sir but I must decline. Other younger officers would not understand and I would be setting a bad example. I will call you by your first name as soon as I am retired". He replied, "You are quite right and we respect you for it".

A few evenings later in Hannover I had been gardening and was returning to my quarter in scruff order. Brigadier Tim immaculately dressed in a dinner jacket and black tie leapt out of a car parked by the road and standing to attention saluted and said "Good evening Sir". He was a lovely character and our paths would cross in later years.

There was a Church Service in the British Military Hospital Chapel every Sunday. The Padre was anxious to start a choir and called for volunteers. I thought I might as well offer to join as once my singing voice was heard I was sure I would be discharged. However I was accepted and found this pastime very enjoyable.

There were visits to the UK to liaise with RARDE and our UK Headquarters at Wilton as well as keeping in touch with Ashford. On one visit I was contacted by Freddy Prichard and invited to go to his home for a drink. There were three suitcases for the daughter of a friend in Germany and would I be able to take them back with me? It so happened this young lady had just arrived in Hannover as a School teacher. I had checked on his behalf that she had settled in happily. I had come over with my car so the answer was yes. There were a number of guests and the drink flowed freely. I was about to leave when Freddy said "Have you ever considered retiring and seeking a job in industry. As number of firms are looking for people like you with knowledge of army organisation?" This question came out of the blue and I said I was not in the frame of mind to discuss things there and then but would get in touch after I had returned to Germany.

On my return I talked over the situation with John Spackman and decided to say I was interested and asked Freddy to put me in touch with the relevant firm. I received an application form from Ferranti plc by return mail.

Filling in the form I felt somewhat deflated as apart from my staff college training I had no formal technical qualification. The initial response from the firm was negative but a few weeks later I was invited to attend for an interview. I was given permission and linked the visit to a duty visit to Wilton and Fort Halsted.

Arriving at Bracknell Freddy Prichard took me out to lunch and advised me to speak out and hold my corner. He seemed to be even more nervous than I was. I was unaware that I was the third army man he had introduced to the firm and the two previous men had failed their interviews. He was anxious that I should not follow in their wake.

After a delicious lunch with wine I was taken to an office and introduced to John Harper a retired RAF Officer, who ran a branch of retired officers responsible for assisting in the design of military systems. I was shown some design documentation which he explained to me. I was able to understand the logic and find my way round the document which gave me encouragement. The other individual who took part in the interview was a bright civilian engineer with a double first named Walford and he took up the questions. I had brought one of the design papers with me which I had produced and gave it to him so he would have an idea of the type of work I was involved in. This paper had my name and regiment on the frontispiece.

Walford now produced a drawing of a warship with guns, radar and sonar equipment marked on the design paper. "Here is a warship. You have three Ferranti Computers I would like you to design a system linking the computers to the different equipments". I was a little taken aback and replied "If there is one thing I have learnt in the short time I have been working in the design of data processing systems it is 'Never to embark on instant analysis'. I know nothing about these radars whether they are Surveillance or Target Acquisition nor do I have any idea of the capability of the weapons". Walford replied "Fair comment, but see what you can do. I will come back in thirty minutes". With that he took my design paper with him and left me to ponder on the challenge of this naval problem.

I settled down and linked the computers to the equipments ensuring that should any one computer go down its tasks would be covered by the other two as 'Fail Safe' was something which I knew was not to be forgotten. Walford returned with my papers and commented that the detail was minimal. I agreed and explained that the paper was the first top level design document and we foresaw at least three or four more lower levels to expand the design. He accepted this comment and then asked who the other person 'Royal Anglian' was who had produced the paper with me. I was somewhat embarrassed to have to explain it was my paper and Royal Anglian was my Regiment. After a few more questions and pleasantries the interview came to a close and Freddy Prichard saw me off.

I left to head for Wilton feeling the interview had been interesting but I was not hopeful that I had passed muster. Three weeks later back at my desk in Germany I received an offer of a job as a Senior Systems Engineer with Ferranti at Bracknell only a few miles from our home at Camberley. The job specification might have been written by me. The tasks listed were all well within my capability. I went in to John Spackman and he agreed. In response to his query I told him I was interested. He asked to be left with the papers and told me he would call for me later. Subsequently I heard that John had rung through to Freddy at Ferranti and checked that the job offer was secure and that I would not be discarded after my immediate service knowledge had been used up. He was only prepared to let me go on such an undertaking.

John called me back and gave the green light which was the start of the evolved process of getting out of the Services before my final retirement date. Papers came to confirm I had no outstanding debts, defining my retired pay and gratuity, confirming any leave entitlement and stating my date of discharge. Instead of taking any leave I opted for a three week indoctrination course at Ferranti. All this took some five months and Ferranti were good enough to accept this time delay.

The last three years had not only been interesting from the work angle it had also allowed us to take holidays in North Italy on the Lakes and in Spain with friends. We had driven down the 'Romantica Strasser' with the fascinating old towns and churches and had visited Blenheim (Blindheim) where my Regiment had fought under Marlborough.

We were dined out in style and Pat said goodbye after seventeen years as an army wife and I on completion of thirty four years active service.

Chapter Thirty Four

Industry - 1973 to 1984

Freddy and Gem Prichard had helped us find temporary accommodation at Waltham St Lawrence with friends of theirs. A Canadian Staff college student was in our house and his course did not finish until mid December so we needed a pied a terre. The flat was a convenient distance from the offices at Bracknell and covered the three months nicely before we could take up residence at 'The Firs' in Camberley.

Whilst we were at Waltham St Lawrence I invited Brigadier Tim Morony, who was now Deputy Commandant at the Army Staff College, to dine. We renewed our friendship and I took up his invitation to use his first name. As I had sung in our small church choir in Hannover he suggested I approach the Royal Military Academy at Sandhurst with a view to singing in their choir. I followed this suggestion up and the result was six years joy of being a member of a first rate choir. At Evensong there was a different version of 'The Magnificat' and 'Nunc Dimittus' each Sunday as well as a new Anthem.

The Chapel at Sandhurst has a number of stained glass windows dedicated to the memory of Field Marshals. On one memorable Sunday there was a service to dedicate a window to The Duke of Gloucester. We sat in our choir stalls on one side with members of the Royal Family facing us across the Nave.

The services were always well attended and there was no restraint in the singing. We also enjoyed high dignitaries of both the Anglican and Roman Church as guest preachers. All in all an uplifting experience.

I arrived for my first day at the office and was introduced by John Harper who was my group head. He ran the Operational Requirements group. He had been a test pilot in the RAF. The other members of the 'Operational Requirements Group' were all retired officers three ex Royal Navy, two ex RAF John Harper and Charles Ridgeway and myself. I was put under the wing of Mike Champney who had been a Submariner.

On the first Monday I went off to join my course which consisted of some ten young graduates in computer sciences, a retired RAF chap and myself. As I walked in the Instructor seemed in a worried state and addressed me as 'Major'. I quickly told him I was no longer in the service and I wished to be called Robin. At this response he straightened up as though a heavy load had been on his shoulders." When I heard you were on the course I was very concerned, thank you for your response". National Service had ended nearly fifteen years previously and it was obvious that impressions of the Army officer among a generation with no contact with the Services was based on such TV series as 'It Ain't Half Hot Mum'.

I chose to be addressed by my first name at work and only used military rank when I was visiting military establishments.

I found the first week of the course very hard going. On the Friday afternoon we were given an exam paper. Having read the questions I could see that I knew the answers but time was not on my side in setting my answers down in writing. I drew flow charts to identify my approach in answering the problems before going back to set down the answers in detail. The instructor saw what I was doing and told me to bring my answers in on Monday.

When the course gathered on the Monday my spirits rose considerably when it transpired two of the university graduates had fallen out as they had found things too difficult. It was very good for my morale and I completed the course in a much happier frame of mind and with a better understanding.

Returning to my desk I was now given the task of writing the design documentation for System Start Up and Shut Down for a Maritime Headquarters System for a foreign navy. Mike Champney was writing all the operational tasks. I visited a Naval Headquarters at Plymouth to see how they were organised and the layout of their operations room. This helped considerably when I sat down and set about defining the actions of the different key figures who would be operating the system we were developing.

The interesting time came when the system was coming together and we could load up and test it to see how it performed. Later we had the added pleasure in training sailors on the system before it was delivered.

I had been with Ferranti about six months and one morning I bumped into one of the senior engineers in our department. "I met a friend of yours at a meeting in Reading last night - a Major Ferraby. He was asking about you. I had no idea you had been in the Army". This again helps to illustrate the inbuilt concept at that time of the Army Officer as a person apart from the rest of the human race. Those with any experience of National Service were senior management, the young engineers and programmers had had no links to the Services.

After about a year I took some leave and went off with Pat to tour round Scotland. On the first evening we booked into a hotel at

Carlisle. Sorting ourselves out in our room I switched on the TV to hear an announcement about Ferranti going bankrupt and wondered whether I would have a job when I returned after leave. It did not seem a very auspicious start to a holiday. We visited Edinburgh and visited Brigadier Ian Buchanan Dunlop. We then toured round through Inverness to the West coast and back through Oban and Inverary. On return to the office I found things were being sorted out and I still had a job which was a relief.

Once the work on the Maritime Headquarters System was completed I found myself attached to the Advanced System Studies Group. They were engaged on a study for the Royal Aircraft Establishment Ranges at Aberporth in Wales. The Ranges had a problem affecting the number of weapon trials which could be carried out safely in Cardigan Bay. The existing range area was affected by scallop fishing fleets and there was the added possibility of oil exploration in the Bay.

Our studies entailed visits to the establishment to find out their organisation and working methods so as to determine a solution to their problems. The Establishment already had a computer system to manage aircraft trials. After a number of visits and many discussions with the staff over a period of months we came up with a proposal for a new range safety system.

One of my study papers drew very favourable comment. I was amused when the Team manager commented "Well it was no problem for you with your background as a retired Royal Artillery man". He was taken aback when I told him I was retired "Infantry". It was even more amusing to learn that I had been asked for as a member of the study team on his false assumption.

The visits to Aberporth were a break from the office and the drive down from Bracknell took us through some lovely country. There was a comfortable hotel at Newcastle Emlyn which we stayed at. We varied our route to and from Aberporth from the A40 which we picked up at Raglan having cut over the hill from the Severn Bridge. This took us past Crickhowell and I often called by to say hello to Jimmy Rice Evans and his wife Elizabeth. Jimmy had handled staff officer postings at Headquarters Wales when I was serving there in the early 60s. He was as usual the perfect host and said he expected me to call by anytime I was passing. This was an offer I was only too happy to take up.

Following our studies the Royal Aircraft Establishment came up with a requirement for a range safety system. Ferranti decided to bid for the contract and we set to to put a proposal together for a system to meet their need. We gained the contract against other interested competitors and I joined the design team.

This was the second of a number of different systems I became involved with over the next few years. They all involved working with the Ministry Departments responsible and the linked Research Establishments. There were numerous projects which the Sales Staff brought to us. Each of these projects required a detailed proposal paper setting down our proposed solution with costs. This work involved coordination between the different departments each of whom would set down a forecast estimate of time, labour and materials. Such was the nature of the work that the links with the Services remained close and I hardly noticed any change in my work ethic.

Now we were settled in our own house in Camberley we were visited by the Sgalitzers and other friends from Fort Monroe days. We received invites to visit the States and decided we would make the effort. We stayed first of all with the Sgalitzers in Washington D.C. and then went to Concord to visit the Smiths whom we had met in Hannover. He was second master at St Pauls School. It was of great interest to be shown around this private school with splendid buildings and set in beautiful surroundings. Nancy Smith was a great traditionalist and daily afternoon tea was a gracious formality. We were delighted to renew our friendship.

We then flew to Norfolk, Virginia and stayed with our friends the Sullivans in Hampton. Attending a drink party the first evening we met up with any number of officers whom we had known fifteen odd years earlier tallying nearly forty. The hospitality was quite overcoming. Bob Sullivan loaned us his car and we drove down to Ashville in North Carolina to stay with Horace and Chick Brown.

On our return to Hampton we stayed with the Reaughs. Again they had gathered many old friends to meet us and our holiday was a wonderfully relaxing escape from the detailed work in the office.

The pressure of work in the office broadened my understanding of the engineering aspects of system design. There were team meetings when the engineers explained how the data would be handled. The logic of the design documentation became more meaningful as I could see how it tied the different disciplines of hardware, software and ergonomics and operator interface together. From time to time we would be given a teach in session on new developments.

I found that I needed to have other things to do in the evenings to clear the mind. Pat had become involved in helping the local

Conservatives and she roped me in to collect subscriptions when they were due to be renewed. I found this contact with people interesting and a complete change from the technical and detailed chores of the day. As a result I returned to the fray next morning with a fresh relaxed mind. The local branch of the Conservatives benefited as over the next fifteen months the number of members grew from under one hundred to just short of nine hundred.

We also tackled the garden and were repaid for our efforts as the vegetable plot produced in abundance. We changed the layout of the flower beds and dug a place for a fish pond.

Our trip to the USA had spurred our American friends to visit the UK and we happily entertained those who had looked after us on our trip. Besides the Sgalitzers and Sullivans we had the whole Dix family. This was great as Oonagh had attended her first slumber party with their two daughters when we were at Fort Monroe. We always showed our visitors round the Royal Military Academy at Sandhurst. Another favourite location was Stonehenge.

The Pomeroys came and visited us as he had a posting to SHAPE. Angus Robertson, who first introduced us was also at SHAPE following a tour as the British Liaison Officer at the US Infantry School at Fort Benning in Georgia. Our posting to the USA in 1965 had widened our circle of friends considerably.

Pat was anxious to take a holiday in Ireland to visit Limerick, where her maternal grandfather had been the Dean, and to return to her family roots. We set off with a tent and camped in the deep South West and toured round the beautiful shore line. We had only been there a couple of days when the present troubles erupted. The many Northerners holidaying nearby upped sticks and fled North saying "They'll be murdering us in our beds". We continued our tour visiting a small village where the Dean had been the priest and on to Limerick where he was buried. Members of the Cathedral staff spoke highly of him. He had been greatly respected by men of both faiths.

Travelling on to Burr Pat went into the Tourist Office to enquire the way to the old family home. The Tourist Office was crowded with visitors queueing in front of five desks. Eventually Pat asked the girl behind one of the desks if she could help her in her quest to trace her forbears. "Oh when did they come over here, was it after the war?". Pat replied "No it was some time before that". She did not wish to refer to William in case this was taken as William of Orange and caused an upset. The questioning continued - "Was it before the First World War?" Again "No" until Pat told the girl the family came over with William the Conqueror. There was a hushed silence for a moment and then bedlam broke loose. The tourist clerk shouted "For sure you're one of us, listen here girls", she then proceeded to gather all the other office staff round her and relate Pat's family history. Meanwhile everyone else was left standing. The saga continued and we were given detailed directions to find the old family home. Unfortunately after all the excitement in the office the directions were wrong and we never found the place!

We continued with our holiday revelling in the scenery and being fortunate with the weather. We visited the wild countryside where Alcock and Brown had landed after the first transatlantic flight. The next day we crossed the border into Northern Ireland and were amazed that we were not challenged. Entering Belfast from the motor way we missed our route and found ourselves in the Falls Road. The change of scenery and outlook was incredible. Ahead of us was a barricade with three armed civilians manning it. The street itself was empty with doors and windows shut and no sign of life. There were some armed soldiers sitting leaning against the front wall of one of the houses. I pulled up and asked them the way to be told they had not a clue as they had only arrived an hour or so before. One of the civilians at the barricade came over and when I asked for directions he kindly gave a detailed response. We reversed and following his route got back into the hubbub of the city traffic and found our way to the Hacketts' home.

We stayed with them a few days and then drove to Rosslare via Dublin. We met up with Steve Bloomer in Dublin. Steve had served with The Buffs and shared an office with me at Fayed in 1947. He was now working with the British Legion in Dublin looking after the interests of all the old British regular soldiers who lived in Eire.

Our trip had been full of interest and Pat had been able to show us why she had such happy memories of times spent in Ireland in her youth.

The Staff College sought civilians to assist as sponsors for their foreign students and have them in their homes. We decided this would be a worthwhile thing to do and attended a meeting to find out more about it all. There was a list of foreign students and we were invited to say whom we were prepared to look after. I asked to have a student from Malawi a Colonel MacPeter Simoko as I could still remember my Cinyanja. In the end I found myself also sponsoring an officer from Kenya and another from the USA.

On the first Sunday after the course started I went to the Officers Mess and introduced myself to Peter Simoko. We chatted over a beer

251

and I found out that he had had to leave his family behind in Malawi. As I stood up to leave I said in Cinyanja "Kalani Bwino" which roughly translated means 'Fare thee well'. Peter's face lit up and he wanted to know how I knew his language. We had another drink before I left and checked the calendar to find when he could come and spend time with us.

The Kenyan was an Indian in the Kenya Army who spoke very good English. The American had arrived with a large mobile home so all Camberley knew where he was.

We had a party for these officers and introduced them to a number of our friends. Peter Simoko visited our cottage at Letcombe Regis and we got to know him well. I wrote a letter to his wife in Cinyanja letting her know we were doing our best to look after him. We received a lovely letter in reply. Peter became one of the family and we felt very privileged to be given the title of 'Baba' and 'Mai' - Father and Mother.

I had been fortunate enough to serve alongside African soldiers in Africa and Burma and was delighted to be able to repay their friendship and trust in a very small way. At the end of the year the American was posted to Fort Monroe so we showed him our slides of the area.

This system of sponsorship allowed the students to get away from the pressure of the staff college programme, relax in a different environment and see our way of life. Peter went back home on completing the course. We were very sad to hear a few months later that he had died after a tragic road accident. He was on his way back home after a rehearsal for HM The Queens' visit to Malawi where he was to act as Aide de Camp to Her Majesty.

Pat had retained the cottage her parents had owned in Berkshire and we spent time just before one Christmas doing it up before letting it to tenants. Returning to Camberley on Christmas Eve so I could join the RMAS choir for a carol service we found the front door of our house open. On entering it was evident the house had been burgled as drawers had been emptied all over the floors and china and silver was missing. We phoned the police who told us to leave everything in place. This was trying as they could not come down that evening. Looking around we found some of our china jumbled into our suitcases which were to be used by the thieves to abscond with their haul. They had obviously been disturbed by a neighbour delivering a Christmas card. There were jemmy marks on all the down stairs windows and having had no success there the thieves eventually had forced a back bedroom window. Subsequently we heard that the same jemmy marks were found on six other houses in a half square mile radius. The gang were not caught and we never recovered any of our property.

I felt particularly upset as Pat had wanted a figurine of the Shepherd and Shepherdess and I had bought this in Hannover as a retirement gift when I knew I was leaving the army. I felt grieved that my wartime medals were also taken not for any value but because of the sentimentality. It was annoying also to have a cigarette box engraved with the crest of The Hertfordshire Regiment which had been presented to me by that Regiment. I was also sad to loose four small Victorian Memorabilia broaches which held cuttings of hair belonging to my Mother and her sisters. Small trinkets of little value but of great importance to me.

I had at that time a large model railway layout in an attic bedroom and although the thieves had ransacked every other room this had been left untouched. This was probably due to the fact they had more than enough to carry away already.

This was not the end of our misfortunes. Returning to the cottage in Berkshire there was a sound of running water as the front door was opened. Entering through the front door the sound increased and we found the water pouring through the ceiling of the sitting room which had just been repainted. The ceiling had fallen down and all the furnishings were soaked. A radiator which had been removed for painting in a bedroom had not been put back properly so when the heating system came on the full flow of water escaped. That was probably the worst Christmas the family ever had!

Ferranti had decided to set up a factory in Wales at Cwmbran which would break away from the Factory at Bracknell which was primarily interested in developing systems for the Royal Navy. Cwmbran would devote more time to systems to support the Army and RAF. Volunteers were invited to apply to move to Wales.

We thought about things as this would mean I would be responsible for setting up and running my own department. The thought of moving back to Wales appealed as the Usk Valley was a lovely part of the country. We had also kept in touch with some of the friends we had made when we lived at Crickhowell in the early sixties. The firm encouraged me to take on the job and offered generous moving expenses.

We set about finding somewhere to live driving down at weekends and looking at many different properties. This search took some time and once we had made our choice we put our Camberley house on the market. As luck would have it this coincided with a major slump in the

General Sir Timothy Morony visits Ferranti plc - Cwmbran 1982.

housing market. We found ourselves caught up in the maddening chain of people wanting to buy and placing a deposit only to withdraw as they were unable to sell their own houses. Our hopes were raised a number of times but this process dragged on for nearly two years.

Meanwhile we had bought the Georgian wing of an old property in the Usk Valley at Pant-y-Goitre near Abergavenny and I moved to take up my new job. We now lived a nomadic life as I would remain in Wales for a weekend so I could maintain the garden and keep the grass cut and Pat would travel down to be with me. The next weekend I would set off for Camberley to visit Pat and help keep the garden there under control.

I was not the only person working with the firm who found myself in these straits. I interviewed a number of individuals ex army and RAF to work in my department and they also needed accommodation during the week. It seemed sensible to let them make use of the spare bedrooms at Pant-y-Goitre while they searched for a new home. As many as four members of the department stayed in the house. This worked out well for all concerned and it was almost like a small Army Mess.

One evening we decided to have a dinner and invite a new civilian member of staff and a retired Royal Signals officer Maurice Pack-Davison as guests. Between us we had cooked up a five course meal and Bob Grattan, a retired RAF Group Captain, decided to provide Gregorian Chants as a musical background. The music needed an added supporting touch so it was decided as hosts we would wrap old khaki army blankets around ourselves with a belt at the waist and be a group of monks! Ron Bradbeer a retired RAF Squadron Leader, one of our number, refused to come into line with a khaki blanket and opted for a pink one instead. Ron was shorter in stature than most of us so we named him Brother 'Gloria' after the character in 'It ain't Half Hot Mum'.

The scene was now set to receive our guests. All lights were turned off and a number of candles were placed around the rooms. Bob switched on his recorder and the Gregorian chants sounded from a darkened kitchen. Our guests arrived and Pack Davidson took it all in his stride but the civilian engineer was somewhat taken aback. He needed a strong drink to settle down and accept we were not all insane. The party went well and our guests departed having enjoyed a hearty meal and good company. Our conviviality made such an impression that news of the evening got round and my home was named 'The Monastery'.

We were very lucky with our neighbours all of whom took pity on me when I was on my own over week ends. Sir William Crawshay lived across the road. I had met him when I was working in Brecon in the early sixties. Vivienne Glasspool another old friend of Pat's lived at Llanarth close by and we had kept in touch with a number of friends from the Brecon days. There was Chris and Anne Hill at Brynderi and Jimmy Rice Evans at Crickhowell.

Murray Kerr had moved into the other wing of the house and Nick Simpson was in the old stables. They could not have been more neighbourly. These links made the prospect of leaving the house in Camberley after eighteen years less of a wrench. It took some eighteen months before we eventually sold 'The Firs' in Camberley and were able to set up house in Wales.

Oonagh left Ferranti where she had worked as a programmer and after taking a secretarial course joined Conoco in London.

Guy left Lionel Hitchen Essential Oils and joined Bush, Boake and Allen seeking to gain broader experience in a larger firm. He qualified in a Course of Business Management. He had found 'digs' in Reigate and enjoyed taking part in amateur theatricals with the Reigate Amateur Theatrical Society (RATS).

Lionel and Louise Hitchen at Pant-y-Goitre.

The 'Dix' family at Pant-y-Goitre 1982.

Chapter Thirty Five

Wales 1979 onwards

The task of setting up a department from scratch was a very worthwhile challenge. The success depended on my finding the right people to take on the anticipated work. Applicants would come down for interview and I could then assess whether they were suitable and would fit in.

The interview took most of the day. The candidate was asked to arrive by 10.30 am and I would then go through the application form and seek to determine whether moving to Wales might cause any family problems. There was the question of ageing parents to consider especially if they needed to be visited in the event of serious illness. Service experience was explored. Candidates aspirations and answering questions about the job specification took up the rest of the morning. We would go down to the canteen for lunch and meet up with other members of the branch with whom the applicant would be working. After lunch the candidate was encouraged to ask questions about the way the firm worked, pay, pension, holidays and the like. It was a case of each of us interviewing the other. Once we were both satisfied all queries had been answered I took the applicant to have a half hour session with John Adams who was the Senior Manager of the Engineering Department. This interview completed the assessment and the applicant was sent on his way knowing he would have a definite answer within 48 hours whether a job offer would be made.

I would tell John Adams whether I wished to take the man on giving my reasons. He would always support my recommendation and together we would agree a starting salary. The rest of the day was spent in my drawing up a written report and recommendation of employment for John Adams to endorse before sending the papers to Personnel. This was all completed very quickly so I could telephone the individual within twenty four hours and confirm whether an offer was to be made or not.

I must have interviewed about eighteen individuals and only turned down four. Two because the applicants were asking for a much higher starting rate of pay than they were worth, taking their background into account. The other two because they were both very negative in their response to questions.

The firm had a staff consultative committee and Cwmbran was told to nominate two representatives. Representatives were required to have been with the firm for at least a year which reduced the number of those eligible to apply. I put my name forward and was elected. The committee met about four times a year and discussed with senior management items of major interest. Pat pulled my leg and called me 'The Shop Steward'. I tried to keep a balanced view and made sure all staff were advised of what was going on.

Not long after this I was elected to represent Cwmbran on the Firm's Pension Committee. This committee met about twice a year in Manchester with the Managing Director and again was very worthwhile as I could talk sensibly to staff about pension options.

Daily work was perhaps even more interesting as I was now involved in the many different projects on which my staff were working. There were also numerous proposals to be drafted and costed.

We had started in offices in Newport and moved to other offices in Cwmbran town centre whilst purpose built offices were being built. After two years we moved into the new premises at Ty Coch, Cwmbran which meant all the disciplines were now under the same roof. This made liaison between departments much easier. There was also a good canteen and the whole building smacked of technical efficiency.

It had taken a long time to sell our house in Camberley. We found ourselves at the end of a chain on a number of occasions the prospective buyers being dependent on selling their own property. On one occasion we had all but signed the contract and as a result decided to adopt a lovely stray English Setter which had walked into our garden. The poor dog was now even more confused as having to accept a new name he spent hours on the road travelling between our two houses. Eventually after some eighteen frustrating months a sale went through and Pat moved down. During this time we had spent alternate weekends in one of the two houses in our efforts to keep on top of the gardens. Every other week end Pat came to Wales to 'muck me out'. We were now able to pick up a normal life style once more.

Guy had decided that he would seek work overseas as he felt Bush Boake and Allen were restricting his interests. In 1981 he accepted a job on the Mazoe Citrus Estates in Zimbabwe a few miles outside Harare as an Industrial Chemist. The contrast between organising an overseas move as a civilian to our service moves was vast. Perhaps Guy's best decision was to ship out his VW Polo as this stood him in good stead. We helped him sort his heavy baggage and saw him off at Gatwick. We received photos and letters from him and were amused to hear of his efforts in beautification around his bungalow. It was good to hear he had acquired the service of a cook boy.

The Range Safety System for the Ranges at Aberporth, which I had been working on, was completed and we set off to train their staff and hand the system over to them. As luck would have it the evening after we had arrived it snowed so heavily that no vehicles could move as the roads were blocked. We found ourselves snowed up in a hotel near Cardigan for two days before life returned to a more normal routine. Even then we had to negotiate driving through deep snow drifts to get to the camp. For the rest of the week we demonstrated how to use the system to the RAE staff.

Meanwhile Pat was trying to cope on her own. Our neighbour Murray Kerr had been snowed in at his factory near Cardiff and Charles Fisher upstairs was away overseas on holiday. Luckily Joanna Kerrs' father brought milk on a tractor as all the local roads were blocked. I did not return before the end of the week by which time traffic was beginning to move once more.

In 1982 we were delighted to have the whole Dix family from Virginia come and stay. The drive up the valley to Llanthony Abbey and on over the top at Hay Bluff was but one of the local views that took their breath away. 'Dixie' did not seem to be on his usual form and we put it down to the fact that he was chauffeur and general handyman to four ladies. They had hired a house near Winchester and we joined them there for a farewell party. It was the last time we saw 'Dixie' as he died the next Spring. Dixie was a great character who had a lovely personality. He and Frannie had helped make our stay at Fort Monroe that much more enjoyable. We now appreciated we were of an age when friends would be departing this life.

Socially we were beginning to meet our neighbours and one day we received an invitation to have dinner with the Lord Lieutenant, Richard Hanbury Tenison. A week later Sir William Crawshay the Vice Lord Lieutenant invited me to drop round for a drink as he said the Lord Lieutenant had a proposition for me. Having been given a charged glass I sat down. "Would I be prepared to become the Chairman of the Council of the Most Venerable Sovereign Order of St John of Jerusalem for the County of Gwent?". My first reaction as I was approaching my sixty fourth year was that I was too old. Lady Crawshay, who was herself a member of the Council, suggested I at least attended a meeting before I arrived at a decision. I agreed to her proposal.

I was somewhat taken aback when I went along to the next meeting of the St John Council to find a greater proportion of the members were approaching their eighties. I felt I should accept the challenge and received a letter from Lord Aberdare, the Prior of The Order for Wales formally appointing me as Chairman.

The first task was to liven things up and look to bring in new blood and people with influence in their spheres of work. In two months I had enrolled the new Chief Constable, John Over; the Chief Executive Officer of the County Council, Mike Perry and the Bishop of Monmouth, The Very Rev Clifford Wright. The St John Council now set about publicising the work of the St John Ambulance Brigade and raising funds to help them in their work.

I had much to learn about the organisation of the St John Ambulance and was greatly assisted in this by Dr John Lloyd the Commissioner for Gwent and all his officers.

Guy, who was now fully settled in on the Mazoe Citrus Estates, suggested we visit him for Christmas and this seemed a good idea. The warmth of Zimbabwe was a delight after the English Winter. One of the Managers on the Mazoe Estates was Billy Conn who had served with the 1st Battalion The Northern Rhodesia Regiment after the war. We met in the Estate Club and I was greeted with the cry 'Ole Ole'. This was amazing as this cry had originated in Austria when six of us from the 1st Bedfords had joined a Royal Navy ski party in 1957. Our instructor used to shout out 'Ole Ole' each time before we set forth down a run. We had taken this call back to the battalion in Goslar where it had been adopted on the ski slopes. John Salazar, who had taken up the call whilst skiing with the battalion in the Harz Mountains, went out to serve with the 1st Battalion of The Northern Rhodesia Regiment and initiated this cry there. This was how Billy Conn knew this form of greeting. It is a small world.

Guy arranged tours to Victoria Falls and Wankie Safari Park as well as the Eastern Highlands so we enjoyed seeing some of the fabulous scenery and wild life. He had settled down well and was enjoying an active social life. His cook boy was a treasure and we were happy he was well looked after. I found many of his staff understood Cinyanja and was able to enter into conversation with them. The fact that 'the Boss's Father knew their tongue was a bonus for Guy.

I returned to work from leave refreshed. The work coming in required forecasts of effort for the different projects and forward planning in conjunction with the sales staff to ensure I would have the staff with the necessary experience to take on projected tasks. These forecasts were updated quarterly. Not only did I have to nominate individuals to work alongside the hardware and software experts on existing projects there was also the need to nominate individuals to assist in writing and preparing proposal documents in a bid for new work.

I found myself flying out to Delhi with a sales representative to respond to an idea which had been floated for an air defence system. This is but one example of the many different and varied projects we were working on.

I had been very lucky in the Service Officers who had wished to join the firm. Ron Bradbeer, John Prentice, Robbie Burns, Bob Grattan, Ron Mahendron and Brian Robinson from the RAF. Maurice Pack Davison, Brian Leggett, John Harris, Sam Jones and Keith Riddell from the Army. They all apart from Keith settled in very quickly and set about taking a full part in the design of new systems.

Keith had problems with remembering things and found the work was stretching him beyond his capability. He had been interviewed for the job by Mike Champney so I had little to go on and this problem needed to be resolved. The firms doctor was consulted but Keith could hold his own for periods of up to an hour. We found a less demanding job in another department but even this proved to be too much. Eventually Keith was given a small pension and made redundant. He died only months later. It was all very sad as he had earlier enjoyed a broad breadth of experience as a Royal Artillery Air Observation Pilot and also as a Naval Gunnery Liaison Officer receiving splendid confidential reports. It transpired he was suffering from a disease which affected the brain and that an elder sister had also suffered a similar complaint and died at an early age. It was all very, very sad.

The firm was expanding rapidly at Cwmbran and with so many new staff joining I felt it important to try and establish a branch team spirit. I arranged a series of dining nights when we all met together with our wives, many of whom had also newly arrived in the area. These parties were well received and I believe helped get the branch off to a good start.

We had moved into our purpose built factory with all disciplines under the same roof. My days before reaching retirement were drawing to a close. The days and weeks seemed to be rushing past. I could not have wished for a more challenging and interesting way in which to end my working life.

Oonagh, who had been working in the Head Offices of CONOCO in London had met a charming young American geophysicist Bob Bastille and a date was set for the wedding. Bob's parents came over from Boston and stayed at the Three Salmons in Usk. They came to dinner and we found them a delightful couple. There was a registry wedding attended by family and the Richardsons as they could not make the church ceremony two days later. Jack had been my best man. This start to the proceedings went off well.

Bob's youngest brother Ned flew in and the Bastilles arranged a dinner party to welcome Oonagh into their family. The next day The Rev Roy Fenton Cale took a Service of Blessing which he conducted with great feeling and many friends travelled many miles to support this function. The celebrations went off well. Tony Ward Booth in his speech commented - "When I first saw this house I thought Robin mad to buy it. I now realise he chose it especially for the lovely setting it provides for this wedding of his daughter".

Again the day was beautifully sunny and hot. A number of ancient swimming suits were unearthed for guests to swim in the River Usk near the house before they departed. Guy was able to take leave and join us for the wedding. This was a time when both Bob and Guy had decided to enhance their image by growing beards. Luckily this proved to be a passing fancy as neither I nor Pat felt this hirsute growth enhanced their image.

A month later we welcomed Bob and Nicki Sullivan on their first visit to Wales. They were always perfect guests and so easy to look after. Their visit established a firmer bond and mutual visits would continue in the years ahead. It also made us realise how little the Americans knew about the attractions of Wales from a visitors viewpoint. The scenery and ancient monuments and castles were overshadowed by Stratford, Oxford and Scotland.

On my last day in the office I was presented with a beautiful crystal decanter and glasses by John Adams in the Staff Dining Room. Afterwards we repaired to a local pub for a quick drink with colleagues before returning to clear my desk.

The branch were kind enough to dine me out accompanied by Pat. Maurice Pack Davison was a qualified pilot. He had flown over the house with Sam Jones tasked to take photos which were then passed to an artist. The result was a beautifully painted picture of Pant-y-Goitre House and grounds from the air which they had commissioned. I was most touched to receive this retiring present. It hangs prominently where I may look at it as I enter and leave the house.

On the day after I finished work Pat organised a lunch time drinks party and encouraged those invited to bring along an appropriate silly gift. Peter Lutter and Gill arrived with a wheel chair. Mike Leatham had painted a walking stick white to ensure I was able to cross roads safely. There was a bogus set of pension documents to mention but a few of the trophies of the day. The walking stick is still in constant use.

I was now a Senior Citizen!! I no longer had to go to an office each morning. I was looking forward to walking my English Setter and enjoying his company. Tragically he was taken ill and died within three weeks of my retirement and I lost a good companion. He had been with us for six years since he had arrived on the doorstep as a stray

I wondered how I would occupy my time. I need not have worried it was not long before I found plenty to do to keep myself busy.

Chapter Thirty Six

A Life of Leisure

It seemed strange on reaching retirement to accept a new form of self discipline was necessary. Life in the Army and Industry had imposed a set of regulations which became normal routine. One had become used to a set pattern. Now this imposed discipline had vanished overnight time was mine to use as I pleased.

There were pamphlets on 'Preparing for Retirement' almost as if life without full employment was something to dread as opposed to being another step forward. Retirement was a new challenge and things seemed to fall into place. There were no worries indeed the transition to full time leisure from the discipline of office routine seemed another natural progression.

There was plenty to do in the garden. We had about two and a half acres of ground mainly grass and this took a lot of mowing. The flower beds had been created by Pat and were beginning to repay her for all the hard work she had put in. Working in the garden was a happy chore but it did demand time. We soon discovered that the soil favoured azaleas and rhododendrons and were blessed with some well established bushes. A bed was created for miniature azaleas interspersed with roses set on the flanks of the lawn which offset the new border which had been made when the property was divided. As chairman of The St John Council for Gwent I had already become involved in an activity which became more demanding on time. There was a Joint Emergency Executive Committee (JEEC) of the Red Cross and St John with the WRVS in support which was being resuscitated under the leadership of the Red Cross President Margaret Herbert. I found myself on this committee with Dr John Lloyd the St John Ambulance Brigade County Commissioner. Pat had become the WRVS Emergency Organiser for the County so we sat in on the meetings together. George Goulding and John Fitzgerald were the two officers of the Emergency Planning Staff at Gwent County Council offices. They gave unstinted support to all the activities of the JEEC Committee. Importantly representatives of the Emergency services, Police, Fire and Ambulance were members of the JEEC Committee and sat in on the meetings giving their advice and support.

Initially the exercises were set by Headquarters of the Red Cross in London. These were a series of seminars defining how to manage in an emergency such as helping in the event of a major incident.

Joan Smeeden was part of the WRVS team and it was not long before we discovered that her husband Ted had been commanding the

Royal Monmouthshire Royal Engineers Militia during our time at Headquarters Wales. We discovered that our paths had crossed on a number of times and through them joined the Monmouthshire Reel Club. This dancing was to give us much pleasure during the Winter months and extend our circle of friends.

Oonagh came home from Morocco heavy with child to enjoy the facilities of Nevill Hall Hospital. The Reaugh's came over from Hampton, Virginia and we were able to show them round many of the local beauty spots. Vern could not get over seeing so many sheep grazing whenever we went off on a sight seeing trip. Dining one evening we all placed bets on the likely weight of the baby due a few days ahead. Not unnaturally Oonagh, with inside knowledge, won the bet. She presented us with our first grandson, James, a week later. Bob managed to get home for a few days and Oonagh followed him back to Morocco a few weeks later.

As Bob had been married before, the option of the use of 'Grannie' by Pat was no longer available. She disliked the idea of being addressed as 'Grandma'. Quite fortuitously another option presented itself. Boo Ward Booth was called 'Gerry' by her grandchildren. Enquiring as to why this was so Boo explained "Oh my dear it's very simple it's short for geriatric". Pat decided from then on she would be 'Gerry' to the grand-children. It was only natural that as her partner I should be called 'Tom'. These titles were adopted and Bob presented us both with sweat shirts which had these names on them. Thus I became Grandad 'Tom'.

The opportunity to visit Bob and Oonagh in Morocco for Christmas in 1985 was too good to miss and as Guy was able to join us it was a happy family event. We were able to visit Marrakesh and enjoy seeing some of the country.

Cooperation between the Red Cross and St John became well established and it was important to have a continuing series of exercises to ensure the volunteers of both organisations became adept at responding to a challenge and more importantly working closely together. Exercise scenario were all but my bread and butter so I was charged with coming up with plans for these joint exercises. Robin Jones, the Red Cross training Officer was a great enthusiast and with Pat responsible for arranging WRVS participation my task was made much easier. A number of exercises were set up over the years with the Scouts and Service Cadet units providing bodies to be made up as casualties.

It became obvious early on that it would be useful to have an agreed set of Standing Operating Procedures defining the role of an Emergency First Aid Station and the tasks of the individuals making up the team. One aspect which had become apparent from the earlier exercises was the importance of concise documentation for each casualty showing identification, next of kin, location and destination when discharged. I drafted these rules helped by Robin Jones. The rules were then circulated to all concerned for their approval before being issued.

A copy was sent to Major General Leuchars the St John representative at Headquarters of The British Red Cross who complimented us on this effort.

At the time of the GULF War the JEEC, which had now been retitled the Voluntary Aid Societies Emergency Committee (VASEC) put its plans into operation and were ready to provide the services with nursing staff and ambulances had they been called upon. Rehearsals of call out of ambulance crews and individuals took place. It was evident our volunteers were ready to meet the demands expected of them. The response of the volunteers in The Red Cross and St John to the emergency was exemplary. Fortunately our services were not needed.

The St John Council was responsible for supporting the uniformed members of the St John Ambulance Brigade and for fund raising. A 'Gala Day' was organised with the 'Red Devil' free fall parachute team as the main attraction. There were 'Open Gardens' and Concerts and further 'Gala Days' all of which took time to set up. I also found myself as a representative on the Chapter of the Priory for Wales which usually met in Cardiff but did at times meet at other locations.

There were first aid competitions where teams from the different Divisions from all over Wales competed for trophies. It was well worth attending these as a spectator as the casualties were made up very realistically and played their roles well. I felt I should at least learn the rudiments of First Aid and took a First Aid at Work Course. Quite apart from learning how to cope in an emergency it meant I could follow the actions of the competitors with a deeper understanding.

It was important to seek new blood to join the St John Council as regrettably we lost some members through death. Others moved away whilst there were those who lost interest. Thus maintaining an active team was a continuing effort. I was fortunate in having the support of a hard working and loyal team. It was gratifying to be able to recommend some of them for St John awards which were all well merited.

Perhaps also when more time is to hand one is inclined to think back to earlier times. In 1941 I had set down notes on the early days of the war in France and I felt the urge to edit these and produce a small booklet to coincide with the Fiftieth Anniversary of the evacuation from Dunkirk. Thus "Five Days to Live - France 1939/1940" was printed expressing the feelings of a young man pitch forked into action at the start of the conflict. It was a tribute to the solid worth of the infantry soldier I was privileged to serve with.

Before moving to Wales I had been a member of the Woking Branch of the Dunkirk Veterans Association. Now that I had more time available I sought out and joined the Gwent Branch which at that time met in The Royal British Legion Club in Usk.

The fiftieth anniversary of the evacuation from Dunkirk was coming up and I accepted the task of coordinating the arrangements for a party from the branch to travel to Belgium for these celebrations. In the event we managed to take a party of about thirty and our branch standard. We joined up with the Swansea Branch and all stayed in the same hotel in Ostend.

Our contingent was a small part of some two thousand veterans who paraded at Dunkirk and De Panne to remember and pay respects to those who did not return. The elder brother of a member of the Swansea Branch had been killed and buried in a shallow grave in the grounds of a chateau at Peute near Vilvorde during the retreat. The Germans moved in and dug up the two British dead and buried them with full military honours in the local cemetery. Two young Belgian teenage girls took it upon themselves to tend these graves. After the war the family went over to Belgium and met up with Lucy the Belgian lady who was continuing with her task of love by regularly tending the grave. A deep friendship developed and whenever the Swansea Branch travelled to the battle fields a visit to Peute was part of the programme.

The veterans formed up on the village square and marched to the cemetery for a short service. The Mayor and other civic dignitaries together with many locals joined in this simple act of remembrance. Afterwards everyone repaired to the local estaminet for refreshments.

Five years later on a similar visit the Lord Mayor of Vilvorde honoured the Belgian Lady who had tended the grave through all the years and the British Veterans who returned to pay their respects to fallen comrades. The Lord Mayor, Monsieur Cortois, met our party at Peute with a number of Civic Dignitaries, the Police and Fire Service Chiefs and Belgian Army Officers. Also present at his invitation were British expatriates living locally with their wives. At his insistence our detachment of veterans headed the procession to the cemetery - a signal honour.

After the simple service we repaired to the town hall in Vilvorde for a formal presentation to Madame in recognition of her dedication in tending the graves and to each of our party for returning regularly to pay respect to our fallen comrades. We all signed the Gold Book of Vilvorde and it fell to me to respond in French to the Lord Mayor. In response to the Lord Mayor I was able to make reference that the last time I had been in the city of Vilvorde was in May 1940 and to say how glad and privileged we were to be present celebrating fifty years of freedom with them.

After this formal ceremony we all went for lunch in a local hospital restaurant before being warmly sent off by the Lord Mayor and his Councillors.

The rebuilding at De Panne made it difficult to remember the scenes of yesteryear. Oost Dunkerque had changed a great deal. There was a new church with open surrounds replacing the wooded area alongside the church, where under shell fire, we had sheltered from view before moving to take up positions at Wulpen astride the Nieuport Furnes Canal in 1940. Wulpen however had hardly changed from the day I had dug in astride the road. The only change being a high level footbridge replacing the old road bridge which had been blown up as part of our defences. Many of the houses were there and memories flooded back. It was fascinating to cross over the footbridge and look at the location from the other side of the canal and see everything as the Germans had seen things.

Moving back to another position I found many more houses where the platoon had dug in. Looking forward there was now a long view across open flat fields. The hedgerows which had divided these fields and restricted our view had all been removed.

Another nostalgic trip passed by the company defensive position on Messines Ridge with World War I cemeteries set in the midst of our 1940 battle line.

A visit to the British Cemetery at Dunkirk perhaps was even more incredible. A number of Bedfords were listed on the Memorial. Searching to see whether I could find the grave of any Bedford I came across but one in the whole of that cemetery. It belonged to Corporal McCaffery who had been a Corporal in my platoon when I first joined the battalion. He had been wounded on Messines Ridge, evacuated and subsequently captured. He died later of his wounds. It was uncanny that his grave should have been the only one from the Regiment in that Cemetery.

These visits remind one of the great good fortune of still enjoying life. The memory of Cpl McCaffery as a vibrant living person remains very vivid. It is refreshing for the soul to remember and pay respect to those who did not return home.

Welfare is a key aspect of the function of any 'Old Comrades' organisation and for this reason I asked the Rev John Stacey if he would become the Padre to the Gwent Branch of The Dunkirk

Veterans Association. John was kind enough to accept this role and we could not have wished for better support. He not only visited the sick, took the burial services and comforted the bereaved but always attended our monthly meetings. All this on top of his commitments to the Gwent Army Cadet Force as Senior Chaplain, to the four churches in his parish as well as other interests.

John had spent time as an Army Chaplain and had been wounded in Aden serving as Chaplain to the Royal Northumberland Fusiliers. He tackled all his tasks with energy and charming enthusiasm and as a result had many friends. He would walk the lanes round his four parishes with his dog and drop in for a chat. It was a dreadful sadness when he became ill and died inside four months in his early sixties. The church at Usk was not large enough to seat all who had come to bid him farewell and the Dunkirk Veterans Branch Standard took part in the procession. I had known John for but twelve years and in that time we had become dear friends. He is often in my thoughts.

We had got to know members of the Cardiff and Swansea Branches and were granted permission to group together for management purposes with a representative on the National Executive Council. I was honoured by being nominated for this role and was able to help in sorting any problems affecting membership.

I was rung up one day by our Regimental Secretary, David Thorogood, asking me to become a member of the Executive Committee of the Regimental Association. Although I have sat in on a number of committees I dislike them intensely as very often they are time wasting, tedious and non productive. I replied I would not consider joining unless there was a job for me. "You can be responsible for writing the Obituaries for the Regimental Journal". I accepted but as things would prove this was but the beginning.

A few years earlier a Story of the Regiment had been published. A short history had been produced by Brigadier Bill Peters but there was a mass of material which had been gathered and which needed to be dealt with. John Barrow, who had been the last Commanding Officer of the 1st Battalion and who had also commanded the battalion in Burma in 1944 leading a 'Chindit' column, took on this task even though he was not at all well. His work was published in two volumes covering the story of the Regiment from 1688 to the present day. It had been a mammoth task. A special effort was made to see this dedicated effort in print so that John could take pleasure from his efforts. This was as well as not many months later John died.

Inevitably there were those who felt this story had not told the actions of some of the battalions in as much detail as they deserved. The Association Executive Committee made me Chairman of the

History Sub Committee and I was tasked with determining whether a further volume was necessary. After consideration it was agreed that if possible more detail should be sought about the actions of the 2nd Battalion in North Africa and Italy. There were still a number of individuals alive who had fought in the war and it was important to gather whatever memories they held and commit them to paper. The work was not just restricted to the 2nd Battalion but was to take other battalions into account.

I was given the go ahead. Luck was with me as Bill Whittaker who had commanded the 2nd Battalion in North Africa and Italy was living in London. Some thirty or so wartime officers from the battalion met annually and I had other contacts for the Hertfords. Dougie Douglass accepted responsibility for gathering material covering North Africa whilst Frank Snape tackled Italy. I took on France and Greece. Bill Peters and John Evans in Australia helped with the story of 1st Hertfords in Italy. Jack Leech provided a mass of information on 'Bedfords' who had fought with the Commandos and Tom McMillen told the story of a Glider Pilot.

Together the team produced the material which they had gathered from many individuals. It was now my task to sort, sift, and set it all down in a readable manner. I had acquired a word processor so this at least simplified things. The end product was "Cap Badge" published by 'Pen and Sword'. This work covered the activities of four battalions during the period 1939-1947. The task of editing had been fascinating. I learnt much about the North African and Italian Campaigns. This made me marvel at the endurance of all the soldiers involved. It was all so well worth the time and effort to have Bill Whitaker and Bill Peters, for both of whom I have the greatest respect, comment favourably on the end result.

Not long after I retired I was rung up by the Secretary of the local Territorial Army and Auxiliary Forces Association. "Would I consider joining the local committee as a member". As there would not be more than three meeting a year I expressed my thanks for the honour and accepted. I was then asked my age. "I'm sixty five I replied". "Oh dear you are too old!". I replied that the whole offer had been a great honour and after saying goodbye thought no more of it. However a few weeks later I received notification of a meeting and discovered I was a non voting member invited to sit with the committee in an advisory capacity.

This extra activity broadened my contacts and I got to know Colonel Peter Meade the County Commandant of the Army Cadets in Gwent. Whenever I was looking for casualties for our First Aid Exercises I asked Peter for help and was never turned down.

In Zimbabwe Guy was now the Senior Chemist on the Estate and Production Manager. He told us that he had proposed to Elizabeth Peck and we were invited to the wedding which was to be in Harare in February 1986. Oonagh came home from Morocco with James and flew out with us from Gatwick.

The wedding completed Guy and Elizabeth set forth on their honeymoon leaving us to enjoy ourselves in Guy's bungalow. We were due to fly down to Durban as soon as they returned to stay with Tony and Pooh Fawssett. We had not seen them since 1959 when I was working at the War Office and Tony was at Rhodesia House.

Two days before the happy couple returned I was taken ill and rushed into hospital where I was operated on with Gall Bladder problems. The operation could not be completed due to infection and a drain was put in. Pat was told I was seriously ill and might be returned to the UK in a box. Sanctions had created a drug problem as there was nothing between a simple aspirin and morphine. I was pumped full of toxic drugs and suffered hallucinations. The treatment was first class. I pulled through and was discharged three weeks later to recuperate sufficiently for the gall bladder to be removed at a later date.

We had missed our trip to South Africa and meeting up with Tony and Pooh. Tony had organised a trip to the Drakensburg Mountain Range and the old battle fields. We never made it and Tony died before we were able to meet again.

Seven weeks later the offending gall bladder was removed with well over one hundred stones and we at long last returned home after thirteen weeks absence having overstayed our welcome with Guy and Elizabeth.

The contacts made with the TA, St John, VASEC resulted in my being invited to join the County Scout Executive Committee where I was asked to look at the management organisation. Over the years a series of committees had come into being and as a result those at the top of their area were so occupied in attending meetings that they were becoming overwhelmed by paper and not having time to direct and assist younger leaders.

I had never been involved with 'Scouting' before and was much impressed by the dedication of those involved. I set to with a small committee made up of representatives from the different areas. Initially I listened to their views of the problems facing them at grass roots level. It was then possible for an analysis of what appeared to be wrong and to look at possible ways of resolving things. Constructive ideas would be set down and copies of decisions were circulated to all concerned. The committee came up with a paper setting out the possibility of discarding some of the top level committees. After some five years the purpose for which we had been set up had been resolved and the committee was disbanded. It had been an interesting insight into the working of another voluntary organisation.

Another facet of life was to be appointed a 'Governor' of Llanellen Church of England Primary School. It was important to give the teachers full support and attend concerts, fund raising events and speech days. I suppose because of my height I was coerced into taking the role of 'Father Christmas' each year. I did my best to ensure no child saw me arrive and change before entering the room and also hid away from sight afterwards until I could slip away casually.

The expression on the faces of the very young was something to be seen to wonder at and enjoy. I well remember one young boy who sidled close and whispered in my ear "You are the real Father Christmas aren't you?"

I suppose as a grandparent one perhaps has a closer affinity to young children. I have the greatest respect for all the voluntary organisations which provide an outlet for young people and help them to become useful citizens. The Scouts and Guides, the St John Ambulance Badgers and Cadets, the Army, Air and Sea Cadets as an example. Then there are the youth orchestras encouraging young people in the joys of making music. All these organisations owe so much to the youth leaders. They are helping the youngsters to become aware of their responsibilities in life. Regrettably their numbers are few and far too many of the general public are inclined to take their voluntary work for granted.

I think as a soldier one probably has a deep suspicion of politicians. After all it is the actions of politicians which gets us into wars and the soldier is then left to sort things out. As a professional soldier there were three subjects taboo in the mess - politics, religion and women. It is understandable why these topics were barred as each topic in its own right could lead to heated discussion and possibly lead to animosity. A serviceman has his vote but he serves God, Queen and Country. Thus it was only after leaving the forces that I became interested in the views of a political party. Again this educated me in the whole system of the selection of a candidate and party organisation. I did perhaps become somewhat cynical of those who jumped on the band wagon from self interest. It did provide the opportunity to meet and talk to a number of very interesting personalities when they visited the Constituency. I am convinced it is important that individuals take an interest in politics and ensure that their views are made known. If we stay silent we are neglecting our duty as a citizen.

Chapter Thirty Seven
Family and Friends

As the years rolled on the family grew in numbers. Bob and Oonagh managed a pigeon pair and Ann Patricia was born in December 1986. We enjoyed a visit that year from David Bastille who came over from Boston on his honeymoon with Annie. This was the first time we had met each other and their first visit to the UK. They were a delightful young couple and easy to entertain. We had now met all Bob's family. The weather was kind and we all swam in the river.

General Paul and Mrs Mary Anne Freeman visiting Wales.

I was fascinated to receive a letter one day from the World Wild Life Trust signed by a George Medley. I decided to write to see whether we were related as Grandfather had been named George and this name occurred in earlier generations. Grandmother had left a family tree which went back to a Guy Medley circa 1602 so I sent a copy of this listing along with my enquiry.

A few days later a phone call from George Medley thanked me for my letter. "You belong to the Pontefract branch of the family. I have sent on your papers to my Uncle who has been working on the family history for a number of years. He will be getting in touch with you".

So began another fascinating activity learning with the help of the research of Captain Ralph Medley (the same naval Captain I had met in 1952 at the dinner at Latimer) much more detailed information about family history. Ralph at that time was living at Aynho. This was on my route to Bedford to attend Regimental Association Council meetings. We called in and met Ralph and his wife Letty and got to know one another and became good friends. His research had proved common ancestry back to 1180 and my Grandmothers' efforts had helped fill in some gaps.

Guy was with his family now living with us whilst looking for work as he had decided to return to the UK from Africa. Marcus had been adopted and taken into the family. In 1986 Elizabeth produced Adam so we now had two sons to continue the family line. Eventually Guy went back to work with his Godfather, Lionel Hitchen, who owned Lionel Hitchen Essential Oils Ltd. He found a house in Andover not far from where Tony and Boo Ward Booth had bought a house. Lionel was an old friend whom I had first met as a boy and we had kept in touch through all the years.

In 1990 we made a trip over to the USA and Canada visiting Conn and Kay Hackett near Vancouver. As the only son of an only son I had no close relatives. Pat's brother, having survived the war had been killed on the Artillery Ranges at Larkhill in 1948 so apart from Conn her first cousin we had no other close family links. Pat's Mother had been the sister of Conn's Father.

Conn and Kay Hackett - Pat's cousin.

273

Conn drove us on a trip to see the 'Rockies' passing through Kamloops, Jasper, Revelstoke, Vernon and Osoyous in a grand circular tour which took us four days. The scenery was so different from what we had seen years before when touring to the West coast of America. The Hacketts lived at Whonnock overlooking the Fraser River with rugged mountain peaks in the background. The nearest township was Maple Ridge which was about thirty miles from Vancouver. There was so much to see and enjoy. It was nice to be able to spend time with the Hackett family, who had emigrated from Wales some six years earlier, and catch up with their expanding family.

We flew on from them to visit our old friends in the USA, the Sullivans, Browns, Reaughs and Pomeroys ending the trip staying in Boston with Bob's parents. Our hosts could not have been more hospitable and it was lovely to see them all again and enjoy a relaxing holiday.

Bob Pomeroy owned a splendid motor cruiser and we enjoyed a day sailing across The Chesapeake Bay to visit St Michaels. This was where in the War of 1812 the locals bluffed the British Naval Commander into thinking there was a large defensive force on hand thereby deterring an armed landing. Whenever we stayed with Bob we would send a combined greeting to Angus and Gillian Robertson, similarly we would receive such a greeting when the Robertsons were visiting the 'Poms'.

The aim of these visits was to maintain the links and encourage our American friends to visit us in Wales. A year later Jeanne Treacy came over with her niece. Jeanne was an Army nurse who had been tasked with assisting me in writing the medical aspects of a training pamphlet at Headquarters US Continental Army Command in 1965. She found the countryside and castles in Wales quite something.

Pant-y-Goitre House was the Georgian wing built in 1776 which had been added onto a Queen Anne house which had been built around earlier structures. There had been a mill house on the site since the 12th Century. The architect responsible for building the Georgian part had had his initials and 1776 inscribed on the timber ceiling support in the cellars. This inscription always caught the imagination of our American guests. I would explain we were so occupied building the house we had little time to be concerned about Yorktown!

1991 was a vintage year as Her Majesty was gracious enough to approve my appointment as a Deputy Lieutenant for the County of Gwent. Promotion within the Order of St John to Commander (Brother) also received Her Majesty's blessing. These honours were in recognition of voluntary work, something which I found very worthwhile and which gave me great pleasure. I had a great respect for the volunteer members of the St John Ambulance Brigade. They gave of their time willingly and bought their own uniforms and first aid equipment. I was particularly impressed with the dedicated leadership given to the youth element, the Badgers and Cadets and the enthusiasm shown by these young people.

Tribute is owed to the wholehearted support in all these activities in which I was involved by Pat who was always there providing encouragement.

Our two years with the Bedfords at Goslar in 1956/1958 were historic as it was the end of an era. The Bedfords, who had been raised in 1688 had amalgamated with the Essex Regiment in 1958 and been retitled the East Anglians. At Goslar the Bedfords had lived on their own many miles away from other units and a happy relationship had developed throughout 'the mess'. It was not unnatural for old friendships to develope further and new friendships to be born. These ties were bound closer when families became linked through becoming Godparents. As a result although individuals were posted away for duties elsewhere the ties were maintained and indeed became stronger through the years.

John Kitto decided after twenty years the friendships formed at Goslar were too good to lose and with support from Gillian Robertson he organised a 'Goslar Reunion' at Old High House, Kettlebaston. Well over forty members of the officers mess turned up and this gathering was counted a great success. A few years later we hosted a week end at Pant-y-Goitre and again the numbers attending showed this gathering was welcomed. The Rev John Stacey was a little taken aback when our contingent, arriving at the church for the morning service as the first hymn was just starting, all walked to their pews singing lustily. It so happened the first hymn happened to be known to all as it was 'He who would Valiant Be' - the regimental Hymn.

These reunions now took place more regularly. Not only did the original members come along they brought their sons and daughters who in turn brought their own children. The gatherings are always a joyful and happy family occasion not only for the seniors but friendships grew between the children and the regimental family expanded. An example of this was when Alex Robertson who was Goddaughter to Pat asked our daughter Oonagh to be Godmother to her first child and Alex became Godmother to James Bastille.

It was with sadness we heard from Jeanne Treacy that Elaine Reaugh had died. Elaine had been a wonderful neighbour at Fort Monroe. She had suffered from rheumatroid arthritis through her life but had courageously lived life fully. We were so pleased she and Vern had been able to stay with us in Wales when it was possible to show them the Elan Valley, The Gower, Llantony Abbey and Hay on Wye as a very small thank you for their friendship over the years.

In May, Guy and Elizabeth had another son whom they named Paul. They now had a string of three sons and looked to find another house with a larger garden. They eventually found what they wanted at Upper Clatford in the country near Andover. It was closer to their church and more convenient for schools.

Oonagh had made contact with a John Medley living in New Zealand, who was listed in Ralph Medley's 'Medley Omnibus'. One evening we were due to have a Hog Roast to raise money for the St John Ambulance Brigade and had been rushing around preparing things. Just as we were about to sit down and relax for a while before people started to arrive the door bell rang. There was an unknown man on the doorstep who greeted me by saying 'You are Robin' and seeing Pat in the background added 'and that is Pat over there'. Taken aback somewhat I asked him who he was. It turned out it was John from New Zealand, who was touring the UK with his wife Maureen. As they had not any fixed accommodation they were persuaded to spend the night with us and join in the party. Fortunately we were able to talk about family links over breakfast the next day before they set forth on their journey.

Later in the summer of 1993 we visited our friends in the USA again. On this visit we started the trip in Boston with the Bastilles. There was an outdoor performance depicting local history and we went along. Unfortunately the weather was not kind and the heavens opened. The performance went on and we sat beneath umbrellas with the rain dripping down onto our seats. In spite of this we enjoyed the valiant effort of the performers and soon dried out on our return home.

We flew to Richmond where we were met by Bob and Nicky Sullivan. Nicky was not too well and did not feel she could have us to stay. Beth Bray, whose first husband Eddie, had worked alongside me in the Training Division at Headquarters US CONARC in 1965 had kindly agreed to look after us. Bob Sullivan was recovering from a traffic accident after another car had run into the side of his vehicle and he was not in too good shape either. Beth lived in a lovely house at Elizabeth Lakes over looking water and Jeanne Treacy's house was on the opposite bank. The night we arrived with Beth, Vern Reaugh dropped by and invited us all to dinner later that week. Vern invited the Belts round to his dinner party. He had been staff officer to General Gray.

We hired a car and drove down to Asheville to stay with Horace and Chick Brown who were their usual cheerful selves. The drive down took us through the Piedmont region of North Carolina whilst Ashville was located among the mountains. We returned to spend time with Jeanne Treacy at Elizabeth Lakes and enjoyed the opportunity to worship at The Chapel of the Centurian in Fort Monroe where we met General Gunn who had been George Sgalitzers' boss. Jeanne arranged a party and her niece, who had visited us in Wales came with her husband.

Bob Pomeroy picked us up from Jeanne Treacy and drove us over to Portsmouth to spend the night with his daughter Dianne whom we had not seen since 1966. Their house was on a creek with a landing pier where Bob had moored his boat. We were due to sail back to his mooring near Annapolis the next day. The course took us past Norfolk Naval base and we had a splendid view of at least three of the massive nuclear powered aircraft carriers. Then on past Fort Monroe with a splendid view from the water as we sailed by. The weather was extremely hot and there was a sultry following wind so we all felt the heat. That evening we moored at Crisfield on the East shore and ate out in a hotel before retiring to our bunks. We mananged to be back at the home mooring by early evening next day and repaired to a bed in the Pomeroy home in Alexandria.

Whilst staying with the Pomeroy's we made contact with Bill Sprigg who was living in Washington DC. Bill had been staff officer to General Gray and we had been good friends. On one occasion we had all joined up in a party at Virginia Beach with the Reaugh's when they had brought their young son along. This young man was now a Captain in the US Navy in command of an aircraft carrier! Bill and Cornelia had not changed at all and we saw some of her talented paintings and sculptures.

These reunions were very special. Our American hosts were very, very kind and we much enjoyed building on the friendships we had made. It was always a pleasure to meet again after a gap of years and pick up the threads. Christmas cards and messages kept the links strong but physical contact helped bind the friendships closer.

Our final port of call was to Peter and Gill Lutter our neighbours at Pant-y-Goitre. Peter had been posted to Washington as the Royal Army Medical Corps Liaison Officer and the opportunity to meet up was too good to miss. Peter had found a lovely house and was obviously enjoying his work with the Americans as much as I had. One day we all went off for a day with the Pomeroys on their boat sailing around Chesapeake Bay and looking at Annapolis Naval Academy from the water. The Lutter's saw us off for our return home. The whole holiday had been a time of renewing friendships and enjoying wonderful hospitality.

The next year we received the sad new that Vern Reaugh had died and not long after Jeanne Treacy phoned to tell us of Nicky Sullivans' death. I phoned Bob Sullivan at once and suggested he came over to stay with us for a while. Bob accepted the offer and it transpired he would be with us in Wales at the time when the Annual Dinner of The Abergavenny and Border Counties Show would take place.

I had been invited to become a Patron of The Show soon after moving to Wales. The Show took place in late July each year in a lovely setting just outside Abergavenny. One evening I was rung up and asked if I would be prepared to be the President the following year which was to celebrate one hundred and fifty years. I felt very honoured and agreed to accept the offer.

The President had the responsibility of determining the theme for the year. I chose to place the emphasis on youth and invited all the local youth organisations to parade in the arena. Any awards would be presented to the recipients before the public by the VIP. The young people turned out led by the Abergavenny Air Training Corps Band and marched to the centre of the main arena. General Sir Peter de la Billiere had kindly accepted the invitation to come and support the show. He inspected the youngsters and presented their awards. The whole event went off splendidly and the General spoke to many of the youngsters and inspired them with a short address. One young cadet was so thrilled that when he got back home he telephoned every relative in the family and all his friends. He has been given a commission in the Territorial Army.

President Abergavenny & Border Counties Show with VIP guests General Sir Peter and Lady de la Billiere.

Bob Sullivan arrived with us from Scotland carrying his tuxedo to join us for the annual dinner dance of the Abergavenny and Border Counties Show. It fell to me to propose the toast to the guests so I was able to pay tribute to the way Bob had looked after us when we were foreigners at Fort Monroe and his continuing friendship through the years.

Pooh Fawssett was visiting the UK from South Africa following the death of Tony. We invited her to come and stay and her visit coincided with Bob's stay. Bob was feeling the loss of Nicky and Pooh was able to help him with his grieving. We were pleased Bob had felt able to take up our offer to come and stay and hoped the change of scenery helped him in his time of grief and stress.

Mike Leatham, who had lost his wife Freda a few months earlier, had proposed and been accepted by Sally Allsop. I was asked to be best man and probably set a record by taking on this role for the first time when in my mid seventies! We had got to know Mike and Freda not long after we moved down to Wales. Mike had fought in Burma and had a dry sense of humour. When Pat had arranged a drink party for my sixty fifth birthday she suggested those invited bring along an appropriate gift. Mike brought along a walking stick which he had painted white. I still have it and it has been most useful. Sally was another friend and we were delighted to encourage them to get together. The wedding went off well on the day and it was good to see two very good friends who had lost their first spouses picking up the pieces and starting anew.

Bob Sullivan had remarried and came over on a visit to London with Emily his new wife. Some time earlier Mike Leatham had been looked after by Bob and shown around Williamsburg when touring round the 'States'. So as Bob could not fit in a trip to Wales we all decided to drive up to London where we met Emily, his second wife, and all enjoyed a happy lunch together.

In October the Pomeroys' came to stay during a whistle stop rush round the UK. As always the 'Poms' were in great form and had managed to visit friends in almost every County!

The Regimental Association Executive Committee met every six months and these trips gave us the opportunity to call by on Ralph and Letty at Aynho. We also made a point of attending the Regimental Remembrance Parade and Service at Bedford which took place a week after the National Remembrance Day in November.

Ralph was always delighted to see us and we felt very privileged to be invited to attend his ninetieth birthday party. Ralph had been the Flag Lieutenant to Admiral Harwood during the battle of the River Plate and the sinking of the Graf Spee in 1939.

His continued research into family history had shown a John Medley had emigrated to America in 1635. An American cousin sent over a mammoth book on the descendants of John Medley researched and written by a nun Mary Louise Donnelly. It was a massive work and contained over seven thousand listings. On reading this book I found out that John Medley had landed in Maryland not too far from where we had been stationed at Fort Monroe. I determined I would visit this spot on my next visit to the USA.

It was a happy coincidence that Bob Pomeroy, whose forebears had emigrated to America with the early settlers, also had an interest in tracing his family lineage. He had succeeded in proving links with the Pomeroy family in Somerset and was more than happy to help in my research and set time aside for us to visit Leonardtown in Maryland when next we stayed with them.

St Clement's Bay Area of St Mary's County, Maryland

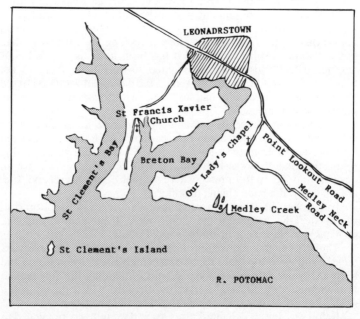

This sketch shows the location where John Medley settled after he arrived in America in 1653. Leonardstown is shown as it is today.

Map 12

1997 started auspiciously as I was advised Her Majesty had approved my elevation in the Order of St John to the dignity of 'Knight of Grace'. I was formally greeted by Norman Lloyd Edwards, the Prior for Wales, at the Annual Investiture in Cardiff before being summoned to attend the Ceremony at Kensington Palace. Pat and Oonagh came down to Cardiff to support me for this occasion.

Our next visit to the USA and Canada was in August and after visiting the Bastilles' in Boston we flew down to Washington. Bob Pomeroy had motored down to Leonardtown and visited the local historical society and gathered information about John Medley. There were detailed records of his life as one of the early settlers of the group which had arrived in Maryland in 1634/35.

We set out with Bob and were received most hospitably at the Council offices in St Mary's County. Prior to this visit I had researched the family of John Medley and set out a listing of the 'Medley' line from Adam de Methley in Yorkshire in c1200 showing my relationship to the present descendants of John Medley. This homework was much appreciated. A distant cousin worked in the offices and would be returning in the afternoon so we repaired to a local hostelry for lunch.

Returning to the Civic Offices after lunch we met my distant cousin and it was apparent our visit had been broadcast around as became evident later that day. Leaving the offices we headed off down 'Medley Neck Road' to locate the original 'Medley property'. We called in on a farm and the owner promptly dropped what he was about to talk and drive us to 'Medley Creek'. Somehow we took the wrong route and were in a dead end when a vehicle drove up behind. The driver identified us and took over the task of showing us around. I joined him in his truck and Bob and Pat followed. He described the features and boundaries of the original property, showed us where the early homestead had rested and stood with us on the shores of 'Medley Creek'.

We thanked him for his courtesy and set off to the local church to see whether we could find any evidence of any of the family. The Church was closed but there was one grave of a Louis Medley. The whole visit had been of particular interest and one was mindfull of the remarkable fortitude and courage of those individuals who had accepted the challenges and rigours leaving England to start life anew in a far distant land. This group of settlers were all Roman Catholics escaping from persecution for their faith. It is due to their perseverance that The Roman Catholic Church continues in strength in St Mary's County to this day.

Visiting 'Medley Creek', Maryland USA.

We drove back to Alexandria feeling that this exploration of early family history had been a highlight of our visit particularly as Bob Pomeroy was obviously enjoying it as much as us. That evening Carol had arranged a party. Casually she had mentioned a name, Gwen Kelley. Pat enquired about this lady and realised she had been in the same office with her in Egypt in 1947 and that she had last met her in 1966. Carol promptly got on the phone and Gwen came to the party. Gwen had married an RAF Officer who had retired to the USA and gone into the Realty Business. Their family grew up in the States and Gwen stayed on after Philip died. It was good to see her again and the years just rolled away.

Whilst with the Pomeroys' we had managed to renew contact with General Paul Freemans' widow Mary Anne and joined her for lunch. It was some seven years since we had last seen each other in Wales.

Bob and Carol drove us down to Hampton to stay with Jeanne Treacy. I had rashly agreed to give a talk to the Fort Monroe Historical

Society and had chosen the battle of Cassino as the subject. Some ninety people turned up for my talk including General Symroski, who had been the Deputy to General Gray at HQ US Continental Army Command and had presented me with a letter of commendation on my departure. Others from that time were the Belts, Beth Bray and Bob Sullivan. I was also very honoured to have the serving British Liaison Officer give moral support.

We next went to Williamsburg and were hosted by Bob and Emily Sullivan. General 'Chuck' Symroski came to a drink party and was delighted when I showed him a photo shaking hands with me prior to my leaving Fort Monroe in 1966. The General had ridden in the Olympics against Sir Harry Llewellyn and had fond memories of those days. He was now having problems at times with his memory and the photo helped him remember things.

Horace and Chick Brown had invited us to visit them in Asheville and we were loaned a car by Bob so we could travel by road. The visit was as always a great pleasure and I took the opportunity to ask 'Brownie' how it came about that I had been assigned to his branch. "Well Rob" he replied "when I was on a joint staff in Turkey there were three British Officers on the staff and all of them were efficient and worked their stint. The same could not be said of many of the other national representatives. When General Gray asked for a volunteer to take on a British Officer I had no hesitation in saying I would be happy to do so and that is how you joined my branch". It is nice to know that our staunchest allies have this opinion of the British Army.

We returned to Williamsburg to hand over the car and then flew on to Vancouver to stay with the Hacketts. It so happened our 'Golden Wedding Anniversary' would fall whilst we were there and we had hoped to have a quiet celebration with them. It was not to be as news had filtered through to them and a splendid party was set up with a beautifully iced cake to round things off. So we celebrated in fine style with Conn and his family and friends. A week later we set off to Vancouver to fly home early one morning in pouring rain and feeling distinctly cool. In sharp contrast we were met at Heathrow by Bob Bastille in blazing sunshine having to discard all the sweaters we had doffed earlier in Canada.

Guy and Oonagh were determined that our fiftieth should be properly celebrated in their presence and a week end was arranged when old friends and family gathered for dinner which included the grandchildren. Marcus was away on a camp and Paul was not old enough for a late evening do. Adam and Paul sat at the foot of the table and behaved impeccably. The men changed their place between courses and James joined in this activity.

Elizabeth had baked a cake for the party in the shape of an Army File with classification and marking to indicate the King David Hotel where Pat had helped sort out my files when we first met in 1946. It was beautifully done and a clever idea and the cake was delicious.

The next day there was a drink party and lunch with many local friends. It rounded off 1997 nicely.

The grandchildren are all a great source of pleasure. We see more of James and Anne as they live close by but Guy brings his boys down on regular visits to stay. Marcus was showing a keen interest in the cornet and played in the junior Hampshire Youth Orchestra. Adam decided he would learn to play the clarinet and also showed an interest in riding. Anne joined a local youth group and started to play the violin and also took up riding. James succeeded in equalling the long jump record for his age group at the annual school sports day at Christ College, Brecon .

It is lovely to see them grow in stature and blossom into young people with an energetic approach to life.

Colonel Jeanne Treacy (centre) at Llanthony Abbey with Pat and Linda Kelly, June 1991.

Chapter Thirty Eight

Old Soldiers and the Regiment

All 'Service' organisations have their own 'Comrades' branches which have the aim of keeping in touch with men who have served in their units and helping those in need. The links between the regular units and those returned to civilian life are maintained by these groups. This is the regimental family.

The Royal British Legion, founded after the First World War, has branches across the world and acts as an important link for any serviceman returning to civilian life especially those who live away from their regimental recruiting area. This is useful as very often regimental branches are tied to a county.

There are further groupings resulting from different actions and battles as individuals taking part in these events share a common interest. It is natural that Royal Naval members who sailed in the 'Arctic Convoys', Army personnel who fought at Dunkirk, Cassino, El Alamein, Normandy and Burma, and Royal Air Force 'Aircrew' should belong to their "Special" Association.

Soon after I started working with Ferranti at Bracknell I was invited to join the Dunkirk Veterans Association by a Bombardier, whose house I passed when taking a short cut to the local shops. I joined the Woking Branch and transferred to the Gwent Branch after I moved to Wales.

The Dunkirk Veterans had celebrated their fiftieth anniversary in 1990 with some two thousand veterans making the pilgrimage to Dunkirk and De Panne. There was a special parade before Her Majesty the Queen at Aldershot with coaches travelling from all over the country. The weather was glorious and Padre John Stacey came with us and took some good pictures on my camcorder.

Five years later when the Dunkirk Veterans were remembering their fifty fifth anniversary the country was celebrating Victory in Europe and Victory over Japan and fifty years peace.

"VE Day" did not have the same meaning to those of us who had fought in Burma with 'The Forgotten Army'. Although Germany had ceased to fight, the war in the Far East was still to be won. I was in Norfolk on "VE Day" helping train soldiers earmarked to invade Japan. There was still a long way to go. The final end of the war "VJ Day" would be the time for celebration and thanksgiving.

I am a member of the Newport Branch of the 'Burma Star Association' and on the fiftieth anniversary of "VJ Day" with some eight thousand veterans of the Burma Campaign proudly marched down 'The Mall' led by The Duke of Edinburgh and Viscount Slim. The following day we marched past the Prince of Wales in Cardiff.

The ethos of these two Associations was very special but very different. Dunkirk could not but remain a vivid memory never to be forgotten. As the years roll on I am amazed I was spared and thankful for the gift of long life. Those who were there were all Regular and Territorial volunteers, many with pre war service, there were but a few who had been called up. The citizen armies were yet to be formed. To be a 'Dunkirk Veteran' was special, akin to those entitled to the Mons star in World War I.

Burma is summed up by Lord Louis Mountbattens' expression of 'The Forgotten Army'. The Japanese were a very different foe from the Germans and Italians. The climate, terrain and diseases were peculiar to the tropics. Once committed to the line, a unit could expect to be continuously engaged for at least five months before relief. Initially mail from home took days and weeks to arrive and there was a feeling of being a long way from home. General Bill Slim had built up morale and any member of the Fourteenth Army felt very proud. This bond was evident even before the war ended. In London anyone seeing another soldier wearing the 14th Army Flash immediately crossed the road and found a place to share a drink. Although the man was a complete stranger having been in the same theatre of operations was enough to merit an exchange of news over a beer.

It is natural that having shared danger and experienced these different conditions old soldiers should meet up in their branches and take an interest in the welfare of their members.

"VJ Day" brought me into contact with a group of Ex Servicemen at Torfaen. Determined to have a Church Service and Parade they asked the Lord Lieutenant if he would attend and take the salute. I was asked to take on this duty and found the whole affair had been well organised. These men then set to and set up an ex servicemens and ex servicewomens branch and asked me to be their President. I accepted after I was assured there was no other organisation close by and felt very honoured. I was even more delighted when a year or so later this small group set up a Charity Concert raising over £900.

These different groups provide a meeting place when members listen to visiting speakers and trips are arranged to visit such places as the RNAS Museum at Yeovilton. All the groups together with the Far East Prisoners of War join on day trips which makes it easier to fill a coach. This combined working is sensible especially as with the passing of the years and declining membership an amalgamation may well be appropriate ere too long.

The Regimental Association of The Bedfordshire and Hertfordshire Regiment holds a gathering every year at Bedford on the Sunday after the National Remembrance Service. On this Sunday a short parade and service takes place opposite Kempston Barracks where two obelisks stand in remembrance of those killed in both World Wars. A book listing the dead is housed in a small memorial behind the obelisks whilst behind these memorials there is a garden of remembrance. Wreaths are laid during the service and afterwards detachments from the Territorial battalions parade with the Old Comrades and march past the Colonel of the Regiment before falling out to meet together and socialise.

An Association Dinner Dance is organised annually by Stan Mansfield of the Hertford Branch which is always well attended. These two functions are focal points in the year and Pat and I always make the effort to attend.

In 1958 Dereck Tewkesbury, who was commanding The Depot, told me that Officers and men who had fought with the 2nd Bedfords during the war met in London every year. I went along to a dinner and found I knew some of those attending, in particular Bill Whittaker who had been in the same company in France in 1939/40. I continued to attend these functions whilst I was still serving whenever I was in the UK and every year after I had retired from the Army. The majority of those attending were war time officers who far out numbered the surviving regulars. For well over forty five years more than thirty members attended, travelling to London from as far afield as Northumberland and Devon. Such was the esprit that individuals made a point of attending the funeral services of their friends. Bill Whittaker who had commanded the battalion in North Africa and at Cassino attended until the forty eighth gathering just before he died.

Much of the credit for organising the dinner and keeping in touch was due initially to Jack Douglas who had joined the battalion in 1940 and fought with it throughout the war. Glyn Lloyd took over this task in 1957. The gathering was deliberately timed for early November as an act of remembrance of fallen comrades. A decision was taken to close down after fifty years in 1997 when there were fourteen members. This is an example of the ties of comradeship forged in battle.

There was a major reorganisation of the infantry after the war and in 1958 the 1st Bedfords amalgamated with the 1st Essex to become the 3rd Battalion of The East Anglian Regiment 16/44th. The title was later changed to The Royal Anglian Regiment.

The Bedfords were raised in 1688 so 'Tercentenary' celebrations took place in 1988 with massed bands beating the retreat on Horseguards in London. Further reductions in the infantry saw the disbandment of the 3rd Battalion Royal Anglians in 1992 and the Bedfords Comrades Association became affiliated to the 2nd Battalion Royal Anglians. The Commanding Officer Lieutenant Colonel Clements was anxious to maintain the close links between the regular battalion and the Old Comrades. He made a point of attending the Annual Dinner and Dance and invited parties of 'Comrades' to visit the battalion.

The battalion at this time was at Warminster carrying out the duties of demonstration battalion for the School of Infantry. In 1996 I was fortunate to visit the battalion with some eighteen members from our comrades branches. The Colonel gave of his time and briefed us on the role of the battalion for forty minutes. We were then taken out onto the ranges and shown all the latest equipment, given a meal in the field and shown the 'Warrior' armoured Personnel Carrier. Some of our number were given the chance to drive these vehicles and I was one of them. It was an exhilarating experience and I returned home that evening on a high.

The soldiers were wearing the old 'Black and Amber' flash on their combat kit. I had worn this flash in 1940 and remarked to a soldier how nice it was to see it being worn again as I had worn it during my service. He enquired when that was and was a little surprised to be told it was fifty six years earlier in France.

In 1996 I was honoured by my Regiment by being appointed Vice President of The Regimental Association. This was particularly pleasing as the Regiment had been very much a part of my life for fifty eight years and for Pat for forty nine years. We had both made many good and true friends and these friendships had extended to our children. The Regiment was family and this honour was particularly special.

Our interests were not solely confined to the Ex service groups. Soon after settling in Monmouthshire we were invited to join the Monmouthshire Hunt Club which supported the local hunt and met socially once a year.

Not long after, we had invited friends to a dinner party, one of whom was Ted Smeeden who hearing we had an interest in Scottish Country Dancing invited us to join the Monmouthshire Reel Club and this not only widened our group of friends but the dancing helped keep us fit.

There was a large hall at Pant-y-Goitre which was eminently suitable for parties and fund raising events for charity. We were happy to have the Hunt Club and Reel Club use the house for functions. The Church, St John Ambulance and others took advantage of the offer when raising funds.

After I had retired from Ferranti I was invited to become a member of the local Probus Club. The club met every other week and enjoyed talks covering a wide variety of subjects.

There had been a major restructuring of the management of St John and Gwent broke down into five new separate units. I joined Blaenau Gwent at the Commissioner's invitation. These changes caused much hard work at grass root level. In spite of all the upheaval the volunteers carried on. The Order of St John was another organisation which increased our circle of friends to include John Over and Terry Glossop the Chief Constable and Chief Fire Officer respectively and our Bishop, quite apart from the hierarchy of The Priory for Wales.

There was plenty to keep me occupied and Pat as usual encouraged and supported me in all my undertakings. She had taken an active part in the WRVS Emergency Services in the County and had supported the European Union of Women becoming Chairman for Wales. Unfortunately she had to resign for health reasons. Pat is a good organiser with plenty of energy and drive belying her years. It was through her activities as a membership secretary that I became involved with politics. We both enjoyed supporting parliamentary candidates and knocking on doors.

In between all these interests we both enjoyed gardening and had much pleasure in developing the garden at Pant-y-Goitre from scratch.

Visiting Bob and Carole Pomeroy in Alexandria 1997.

Chapter Thirty Nine

Reflections

It is now sixty years on since I arrived at The Royal Military College, Sandhurst as a Gentleman Cadet. The changes which took place between the wars when I was at school seemed at the time to be wonderful to a young mind. These pages have told a story of the life of a soldier and citizen. I am thankful I was spared to enjoy this lovely part of God's creation looking out towards the River Usk with the 'Black Mountains' in the background.

There are so many times when things might have been different. The course in France in December 1939 when I was asked by Peter Millward if I would change squads with him. I did and those in my squad were all killed in an accident on December the 16th. The battles in France and Dunkirk in 1940. Arriving back with the battalion at Yeovil, Brigadier Bubbles Barker greeted me saying, "Welcome back there were at least eleven times when I thought you had been killed". In Abyssinia in 1941 when the Italians put a bullet through my bush hat and Burma in 1944. Being out of my office when it was blown up when the King David Hotel was attacked in 1946 and the incident on the ranges at Sennelager in 1957. The protracted gall bladder illness in Zimbabwe in 1986.

I firmly believe in prayer and many times in battle pleaded for protection for myself and my men. These prayers were answered when I was in charge of a platoon during the seventy two hours before we got off the beaches at Dunkirk. While the two other platoons suffered casualties my platoon came through unscathed. Perhaps the cynical would think it could have been due to my having insisted on making sure each soldier was well dug in. I do not share that view. Another example was in Burma when although my company was heavily shelled and actively engaged we did not have any soldier hurt. These are but two examples which support my belief.

I had volunteered to become a soldier optimistically believing that by contributing to the strength of our forces with others of like mind and helping show our resolve we might maintain the peace. This was not to be and for six years with my generation spent the best years of our youth wondering how long the war would last. Never at any time did I think we would be beaten.

I came through the war without being wounded, instead I was laid low frequently with malaria and also felt the discomfort of dysentery and the rigours of tick typhus. Curiously once the battalion was committed in Burma I remained fit throughout the campaign when others, who had been fit in the months of the preceding years, succumbed and were evacuated to base hospitals. Once back home in England malaria caught up with me and I volunteered for service in the Middle East to escape the medical teams who were glad to use me as a guinea pig for new drugs. Unfortunately these drugs did not help and a nurse advised me to seek a warmer climate to avoid being downgraded medically.

It is a privilege to enjoy the support from good friends and I count myself lucky in the friends I have made in life's journey. Lionel Hitchen I count as my oldest friend as we met seventy years ago and have kept in touch through weddings of our generation and of our children. He took responsibility for Guy as a Godfather and fulfilled these important duties with deep sincerity.

After the war the pattern of life was beginning to evolve and friendships which would effect the years ahead took root. It was in Egypt where I met Pat who consented to be my wife. Jack Richardson had been with the Bedfords in Greece and he was kind enough to be my 'Best Man'. We would serve together as company commanders in Goslar in 1956/58. Tony Ward Booth from the Regiment came from Tripoli to Fayed to attend a Regular Commissions Board in 1947 and our paths would cross many times through the years. Pat becoming Godmother to Tony and Boo's first born daughter Susan.

The 1st Bedfords at Goslar were a happy and efficient unit. It is of interest that of the Captains one, Tony Ward Booth became a Major General, two, David Carter and Angus Robertson became Brigadiers, while Fergus McKain Bremner became a Colonel. Of the subalterns Bob Pike was promoted Brigadier and Stuart Green Colonel.

In 1949 whilst attending the Staff College as a student we met John and Averill Barrow. John was serving with the Parachute Brigade at Aldershot and was to be the commanding officer of the battalion at Goslar. Averill became Godmother to Oonagh. Later at Goslar also we met up with Angus and Gillian Robertson and Pat became Godmother to Alex their first daughter who in later years became Godmother to Oonagh's son James - all in the Regimental family. The Robertsons introduced us to their American friends Bob and Carol Pomeroy.

Qualifying at the staff college resulted in a variety of interesting staff appointments. This brought us into contact with an even wider circle and we made new friends. This was particularly true when I was posted to America on attachment to the US Army at Fort Monroe in 1965 resulting in a number of lasting friendships.

Then there were the times when I was posted as a regular officer to Territorial battalions where the other officers had civilian jobs. Ivor Grey commanding 'The Hertfords' worked in Lincoln's Inn Fields and Robert Humbert the second in command was a key member of Humbert and Flint the Estate Agents. Don Garrard of the 4/5th Essex was an administrator in the London Hospital.

One of the tasks with a TA Battalion was to take Certificate 'A' examinations at the local schools. This gave me the opportunity not only to get the feel of the atmosphere of the school but also to get to know the masters . This helped considerably in selecting Haileybury as the school for Guy. We visited it with him and he decided he liked the idea of going there and passed the entrance exam.

The insistence of George Goulding at the Intelligence Planning Wing in 1967 that all his staff officers would attend a computer programming course at the Royal Signals School provided sufficient understanding for me to retire from the Army to join Ferranti International plc a few years later.

My first job with Ferranti was at Bracknell which could not have been more convenient to our home in Camberley. Freddie Prichard in sales who had introduced me to the firm became a good friend and we visited the War Office and other Establishments together to discuss possible projects. Over the next few years we became very good friends. Freddie died of a massive heart attack at his desk and I missed his companionship.

The firm had decided to build a purpose built factory at Cwmbran in South Wales and were looking for staff to volunteer to move down there. I was offered the chance of running my own department and accepted the challenge. This led to our return to the Usk Valley. We had lived at Crickhowell in 1962/65 and still had friends there whom we had kept in touch with. It is a most beautiful part of the country and we enjoy lovely views from the house.

We had owned the house in Camberley but because of Army postings we had only lived in it for some seven years ourselves. Our move to Pant-y-Goitre was the seventeenth change of living accommodation since we married in 1947.

Once again arriving in Wales new horizons opened up with The Order of St John, VASEC, the Scouts, the TA & VFA and the Church locally.

Socially we were invited to join The Monmouth Hunt Dinner Club and The Monmouthshire Reel Club. The chairman of the last named club was Ted Smeeden. It was not long before we discovered our paths had crossed many times through the years. Our views on life were similar and we became close friends. Ted gave me tremendous support in St John fund raising activities.

Added to this was the fascination of learning about family roots through getting to know Ralph Medley. I knew that a Great-great-great Uncle had been consecrated the first Bishop Metropolitan of Canada at Frederickton in 1879. He was a prominent member of the Tractarians and corresponded with John Henry Newman, Edward Pusey, John Keeble and William Gladstone, the future Prime Minister. The last named is credited with the remark that John Medley had 'the wisest head that ever wore a mitre'. There were others who enjoyed a fascinating life style in different careers. In America descendants of John Medley moved West to Kentucky and brewed 'Medley' Kentucky Bourbon.

Another forbear was a Madras Engineer officer who laid the charges at the Delhi Gate during the Indian Mutiny.

Life has been deeply enriched by Pat Robinson who consented to marry me in 1947. The daughter of an Army Colonel she was happy to put up with the continual moves which were the norm of Army life. She had the ability and charm to always be a very gracious hostess and was a wonderful mother to Guy and Oonagh. They grew up and both gained degrees at University, married and gave us the pleasure of grandchildren.

Pat through her mother, who was a Hackett, could also trace her family roots back to the time William the Conqueror's Knights went to Ireland. Thus we both were lucky enough to have detailed knowledge of previous generations.

Life over the years had woven a tapestry full of varied and interesting patterns. We had been granted fifty years of marriage and been given the gift of children and grandchildren. Besides all this we had travelled together around the world and enjoyed lasting friendships which enriched our lives.

The preceding pages have set down a journey along life's way. At the start the World Map was largely coloured red depicting the British Empire. Over the last few decades it has been fashionable for some to decry its achievements and imply the British Raj exploited the native populace for selfish commercial gains. It was my good fortune to travel widely through Africa, India, Sri Lanka, Malaya, Hong Kong and Egypt. I spent many months living and working in these different countries and saw the evidence of the benefits brought to these territories by British jurisdiction. Inter tribal warfare was eradicated in Africa. The bitter religious battles between Hindu and Muslim held in check in India. In the Indian Army members of these different faiths served and fought alongside one another under British and Indian officers.

Industry not only provided employment and housing for their employees but on the estates in Africa, India and Sri Lanka housing and medical care for the families and schooling for the children. Individuals lived in peace under the benign but firm jurisdiction of the local District Commissioner.

It was compulsory for all British officials, civilian and military to learn to speak the local tongue. British justice was the way of life. The success of this approach was evidenced by the attention to local traditions and the support of local customs. The tribal elders in Africa were incorporated into the chain of local government whilst in India the Maharajahs retained a deal of self independence.

The British Empire is no more but had it not been benign and worked in cooperation with the local peoples there would not now be a Commonwealth of Nations. On being given their independence these nations asked to join the Commonwealth under Her Majesty the Queen.

I travelled to India in 1993 to discuss a project with the Indian Army, meeting not only staff officers but also a number of senior generals. All were extremely friendly and had nothing but good to say of us as a race. They also were keen to build on the history and traditions in their units and were proud of the battle honours of the past.

I could cite other instances but I feel these examples are sufficient to disprove the statements of those who unwittingly believe and spread false propaganda against The Empire. An Englishman may be justly proud of those many young men, District Officers, Police Officers, teachers, engineers, soldiers and many others who contributed to the rise and government of 'The Empire'.

The pattern of life in the Army not only provided this opportunity to travel the world but also taught me the rudiments of data processing. This led to employment with Ferranti which was a lead company in advanced technology.

School and training at the RMC Sandhurst set the foundations which were sharpened and tested during the war. The desire to do things well to the best of one's ability. To deal fairly in the handling of all problems involving decision. To be honest and just and to stand by one's convictions. To work hard and play hard. To show compassion and kindness to those less fortunate. To fear God and admit one's errors.

These were the same challenges of life faced by generations in the past, to be faced also in the future. Life is a gift from God. We may not know his purpose for us but we can acknowledge his great kindness in the blessing on this earth of family and friends.

I acknowledge this great kindness and give thanks for a wonderful wife and Mother to our children, for Guy and Oonagh and their families, for good health and for so many true friends.

50th Wedding Anniversary Party, Canada. 20th September 1997.

Appreciation

I wish to record my thanks to Gwilym for his cheerful help, to Leighton for his cover design, to Alison and all the staff of 'Old Bakehouse Publications' for their encouragement and help in producing this book.